THE ARCHITECTURE OF WALES

SERIES

General Editor

– Mary Wrenn
  Royal Society of Architects in Wales –
  Cymdeithas Frenhinol Penseiri yng Nghymru

Series Editors

– Bella Kerr

– David Thomas

– Jonathan Vining

Advisory Panel

– Irena Bauman, *Director, Bauman Lyons Architects, Leeds*

– Richard Parnaby, *formerly Professor of Architecture, UWE Bristol*
  and University of Wales Trinity Saint David

– Alan Powers, *author and architectural historian*

– Ian Pritchard, *Secretary General, Architects Council of Europe*
  (ACE)

– Damian Walford Davies, *Head of School, Cardiff School of*
  English, Communication and Philosophy, Cardiff University

THE
ARCHITECTURE
OF WALES
SERIES

Published in cooperation with
The Royal Society of Architects in Wales –
Cymdeithas Frenhinol Penseiri yng Nghymru

The Architecture of Wales

from the first to the twenty-first century

John B. Hilling

with a contribution from Simon Unwin

www.uwp.co.uk

British Library CIP Data

A catalogue record for this book is available from the British Library

ISBN   978-1-78683-284-9

eISBN   978-1-78683-285-6

The right of John B. Hilling to be identified as author of this work has been asserted in accordance with sections 77 and 79 of the Copyright, Designs and Patents Act 1988.

Design: www.theundercard.co.uk
Printed in Wales by Gomer Press

With thanks to the Royal Commission on the Ancient and Historical Monuments of Wales for supporting the publication of this book. The Royal Commission on the Ancient and Historical Monuments of Wales is the investigation body and national archive for the historic environment of Wales. It has the lead role in ensuring that Wales's archaeological, built and maritime heritage is authoritatively recorded and seeks to promote the understanding and appreciation of this heritage nationally and internationally.

Contents

General Editor's Preface

Given the conventional image of Wales as a land of song and poetry, architecture and the visual arts can be easily overlooked, a neglected poor relation to the country's seductive musical and literary traditions. Relatively little has been published about the architectural heritage of our nation, despite the fact that buildings and places have been created in Wales that bear comparison with contemporaneous examples elsewhere, produced by architects engaged in the same wider cultural currents and discourse. There are many reasons for this: Wales has so often been judged as being too small, too homely, or simply not distinctive or fashionable enough to attract the sustained attention of architectural critics and historians. Add to this a lack of consistent patronage and a deeply ingrained Nonconformist tradition that discourages any form of showing off, and it is not surprising perhaps that we lack a more complete record of the architectural achievements of past generations.

Of course, the truth is that Wales has a rich built heritage, from the medieval to the modern. Its architectural character is very different from that of the other nations of the British Isles, and it is this very distinctiveness that deserves to be celebrated. The Royal Society of Architects in Wales is delighted to present, with the University of Wales Press, a series of books exploring the architecture of Wales, adding new chapters to the evolving story of the buildings, places and spaces of our 'damp, demanding and obsessively interesting country'.[1]

Mary Wrenn, Director RSAW
The Royal Society of Architects in Wales (RSAW) represents and supports Chartered Members of the Royal Institute of British Architects (RIBA) in Wales

[1]   Jan Morris, *Wales: Epic Views of a Small Country*.

Letting the Light In
Gillian Clarke

Well building hath three Conditions:
Commodity, Firmness and Delight.
(Sir Henry Wotton, 1624)

A cwtsh of a country,
houses hunkered to the hill
in heartless, one-street towns.
The et cetera of terraces
like paragraphs of longhand
in an old language.

In our town by the sea, we children
were construction workers,
clearing glades in the woods for dens,
tree-houses, bird-hides, lookouts.
We'd ease into hollow trees
and whisper in the mushroomy dark.

Till suddenly called by the distant drum of a train
we'd race breathless to the viaduct,
to take the measure of it, to shout,
to touch the train's thunder in the stones,
sound and curve diminishing arch by arch
in lapsing loops and ellipses.

It prepared us for the lofty gravity
of museum, warehouse, galleried arcades,
Victorian covered market, old library
whispering its multilingual stories,
tea and talk under trees in the open air
at the Hayes Island Snack Bar.

In the re-imagined nation, let's dream
a waterfront where once the coal ships docked,
leafy squares where sunlight turns, touching
stalls, strollers, street musicians, a woman
at a pavement table, steam from a white cup,
coins in the fiddler's opened case.

Let's make fine buildings, go sandalfoot
into spaces of shadows and reflections,
see what stone, steel, slate and glass,
can make out of air and water and sunlight.
Let's open the city to the light,
to commodity, firmness, delight.

Reproduced courtesy of Gillian Clarke
and Carcanet Press Ltd. This poem was
commissioned by RSAW in 2003 to
mark the tenth anniversary of the RSAW
Annual Conference.

List of Illustrations
1–71

List of Illustrations
72–212

List of Illustrations
213–268

Illustrative Acknowledgements

A special debt is owed to the Royal Commission on the Ancient and Historical Monuments of Wales for providing 98 of the illustrations for this book, and for Cadw, Welsh Assembly Government for providing 39 of the illustrations for this book.

All images are Crown Copyright © Royal Commission on the Ancient and Historical Monuments of Wales, with the exception of the following:

Alamy Stock: 163

Author: 2, 7, 44, 56, 74, 77, 90, 106, 107, 125, 129, 136, 147, 148, 157, 159, 161, 165, 172, 176, 177, 185, 189, 190, 192, 199, 200, 202, 204, 205, 211, 212, 221, 224, 229, 243

© Crown Copyright (2017) Cadw, Welsh Assembly Government: 5, 7, 14, 15, 18, 21, 23, 29, 32, 34, 36, 38, 40, 41, 42, 45, 51, 55, 58, 61, 65, 69, 78, 79, 80, 87, 88, 92, 96, 100, 105, 113, 114, 151, 156, 158, 187

© Crown Copyright (2017) Visit Wales, via Cadw: 25

Architectural Press Archives / RIBA Collections: 239, 242

Pat Borer and David Lea: 261

Brecon Beacons National Park Authority: 252

Bridgend County Borough Council: 246

Cardiff University School of Music: 248

Paul Davis, via RCAHMW: 68, 103

Christopher Day: 262

Col Ford and Natasha de Vere (used under a Creative Commons Attribution 2.0 Generic Licence – https://creativecommons.org/licenses/by/2.0/; original source https://www.flickr.com/photos/24413864@N05/5083185557): 259

© Foster + Partners: 268

David Hilling: 1, 2, 3, 4, 6, 8, 9, 10,13, 16, 19, 20, 22, 24, 26, 28, 30, 31, 33, 35, 37, 39, 43, 46, 47, 49, 50, 53, 57, 64, 70, 73, 76, 82, 85, 86, 91, 93, 95, 99, 110, 115, 117, 119, 120, 121, 122, 124, 125, 137, 139, 144, 155, 169, 171, 173, 174, 184, 186, 191, 193, 214, 250, 251, 255, 256

Charles Hosea: 266

Ken Kirkwood, Courtesy of Rogers Stirk Harbour + Partners: 240

Flanagan Lawrence: 257

James Morris: 263

National Library of Wales: 134, 135, 152, 160

Neil Perry: 258

RIBA Collections: 245, 247

Sport Wales National Outdoor Centre, Plas Menai: 253

© Edmund Sumner / VIEW: 260

Simon Unwin: 254, 265

Andrew Wall Photography: 267

Yonda Aerial Systems: 249

Preface

At the end of 2016 I was asked to update my book *The Historic Architecture of Wales*, published by the University of Wales Press in 1976, more than forty years ago. After due consideration I agreed to take up the challenge, for not only had the original book been out of print for many years, but it was also out of date in many respects and excluded everything that had been built since 1939. Since the earlier book was published an incredible amount of information has become available: research based on the archaeological excavation of ancient sites, books and papers published in journals regarding individual buildings and scholarly articles about architects, some of which are listed in the Select Bibliography. I owe a debt to all of these sources of information, particularly to the remarkable Pevsner series, Buildings of Wales, which has long been my constant companion.

This book has been written with the intention of providing general readers (including architects) with a succinct overview of Wales's built environment over roughly twenty centuries, as viewed from the twenty-first century. It has been greatly expanded and rewritten, and contains many more illustrations, mostly in colour, than the original edition. In order to make the book as complete as possible, Simon Unwin, Emeritus Professor of Architecture at the University of Dundee and part-time lecturer at the Welsh School of Architecture, has kindly written the final chapter dealing with the most recent developments in Welsh architecture. For this I am most grateful. With regard to place-names, I have generally kept to the most commonly used versions, e.g. Aberaeron, not Aberayron. In a few instances, where there is only a single letter difference between the Welsh and Anglicised versions, I have used the Welsh spelling, e.g. Llandaf and Blaenafon.

Since the publication of my earlier book there has been a great increase in the charges made by many institutions and copyright holders for the right to reproduce photographs and drawings. In this respect I am especially grateful to the Royal Commission on the Ancient and Historic Monuments of Wales (RCAHMW) and Cadw: Welsh Historic Monuments for being generous in granting permissions without charge for the majority of images in this edition.

It is impossible to write a work of this nature without considerable input and help from many people, and I would like to take this opportunity to thank each and every one of the following for their invaluable contributions. David McLees read most of the manuscript, while Sian Rees read the Roman, Celtic and Early Medieval chapters and Mark Lewis read the Roman section; each made many perceptive comments and suggestions, and gave helpful advice. Penny Icke and Lynne Moore of the RCAHMW, Verity Hadfield of Cadw, Iwan ap Dafydd of the National Library of Wales and David Rossington of the Royal Society of Architects in Wales, all made my life easier by their help in choosing and obtaining photographic illustrations. David Hilling prepared fourteen maps based on my sketches, more than thirty plans of buildings, took a number of photographs and helped with computer problems. My warm thanks also to Mary Wrenn for inviting me to write the book as well as for her continued enthusiastic help and support; to Jonathan Vining who, together with Mary, prepared the list of architectural awards (at Appendix 2); to Dafydd William for insights on the reconstruction of buildings at the National History Museum, St Fagans; to Gillian Clarke for permission to use her poem 'Letting the Light In'; to Sarah Lewis, Siân Chapman, Henry Maas, Bethan Phillips, Dafydd Jones and staff at the University of Wales Press for their continuing commitment to bringing the book to fruition; and to Marc Jennings for designing the book with subtlety and skill. Lastly, but by no means least, I would like to thank my wife Liisa for her long-lasting patience and continued support.

1

Land, History and Architecture

Architecture, traditionally 'mother of the arts', has been likened to 'frozen music'. More to the point, it is 'frozen history', for though the people that make history inevitably pass away and their written records may be irretrievably lost, the buildings in which generations of men and women live, labour and worship, often remain, reminding us of their history, for many centuries. The walls of our buildings ring with voices from the past: the shout of triumph at Raglan, the cry of despair at Castell y Bere, the poetry of love at Ystrad Fflur, the hymn of hope at some Salem and the babble of children at some *tŷ clom*.

Physical Background

Until recently, the architecture of any country was conditioned by the physical environment in which it is set. Buildings were also conditioned by the religious, social, economic and political environments of the country, although these were, in one way or another, a reflection of the country's topography and situation. The physical environment includes the country's position, as well as its relief, climate and structure. Each of these affected buildings and the way in which they were constructed. Position dictates accessibility to outside influences. Relief, together with drainage, generally controlled the siting of individual buildings, as well as that of villages and towns. As Sir Cyril Fox pointed out in his ground-breaking book *The Personality of Britain*, Wales in general belongs to the Highland zone of Britain, and has been subject to different influences and histories from those of the Lowland zone. Much of Wales is above 305 m (1000 ft) above sea level and is indeed hilly or mountainous; consequently, settlements were, and still are, mostly restricted to the valleys and coastal plains. **(1)** The Welsh climate, wet though it is in parts, varies from place to place and affected the type of agriculture and associated farm buildings, as well as the growth of forests and availability of timber for construction. It also affected the design of external walls and roofs. While the buildings of Wales were largely built of stone, the colour and texture of the stone used varied considerably from one area to another. These variations were closely related to the pattern of rocks underlying the soil, just as were the presence of slate quarries and the location of brickworks and ironworks.

In earlier times, when transport was troublesome and problematic, it was natural to use the most convenient material to hand; and thus the rocks themselves contribute in no small way to the character of local buildings. Many of the geologically older rocks, for example, are so hard that 'dressing' and carving decoration is difficult, if not impossible, and the absence of any surface treatment of the stones gives the buildings of some areas an austere but immensely powerful character. The younger rocks on the other hand are usually softer and have well-developed planes of weakness so that they can be easily cut and shaped to give a more finished quality. In other places a different appearance may be given by the use of stones that are worn smooth by the action of running water such as the river-washed pebbles used in the cathedral at Llandaf. In marked contrast are certain mountainous districts of Eryri (Snowdonia) where the readily available building materials were the very large boulders which had been transported across country during the Ice Age.

The influence of masonry techniques on architectural character was well brought out in 1908 by Harold Hughes and H. L. North in their description of some farm buildings near Beddgelert, in *The Old Cottages of Snowdonia*:

'we note the enormous size of the stones ... at the base of the walls ... gradually smaller as the wall rises till, at the top, they are such as one man can easily lift. This is not only a practical arrangement, but gives great scale and dignity to the building. It is quite usual to see the lower courses of a cow-house, about 30 feet long, composed of five or six stones ranging from 5 to 7 feet in length. This, in contrast with the small slates of the roof, give a wonderful effect of scale, almost Cyclopean ...'

The colour of buildings also varies with the type of stone used. Thus in the Brecon area the dark red-brown hue of the Old Red Sandstone gives a distinctive warm effect to the buildings there. The commonest types of rock that have been used for buildings are the grits and sandstones that are found in most of the geological formations. Formerly, there were many hundreds of small quarries in Wales from which these materials were extracted, for the stones were more easily worked and could be conveniently trimmed to the required shape and size. They were used both in the isolated farms of rural areas and in the straggling terraces of the mining valleys. Today, however, there are only a few sandstone quarries working outside the coalfield areas, but stone buildings are still widely distributed throughout most of the country.

Timber buildings, though once quite widespread in

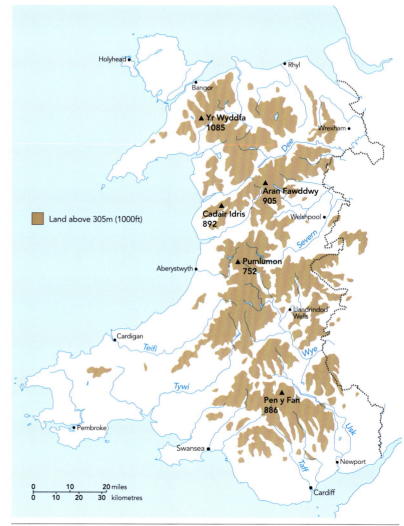

1 Welsh topography – Mountains and Rivers.

distribution, are now all confined to the eastern valleys and borderland regions. Up until medieval times most buildings over large parts of Wales – most of Europe, in fact – were constructed of wood. Even the earliest castles of the Welsh princes, as well as the local churches, were of timber; consequently, most have perished without trace save for the occasional 'footprint' discovered by archaeologists. In the eastern regions timber buildings developed from simple cruck-truss construction into more complicated box-frame structures with walls panelled in wattle-and-daub, resulting the 'black-and-white' houses of the north-east and the eastern borderland. In much of the south-west and parts of the north-west the scarcity of available timber suitable for building led to the development of dwellings constructed of pressed earth or clay – a kind of everyman's concrete. Some of these *tai clom* (earth houses) still stand in localized areas of Ceredigion, rare survivals of a type that must have once been much more widespread.

Paradoxically, thatched roofs were likewise once widespread in Wales. By the end of the nineteenth century, however, thatch had been largely superseded in the more populous districts by the ubiquitous slate which now, in turn, is being replaced by concrete tiles and roofing felt. But even as late as 1903, A. G. Bradley could still write, in *Highways and Byways in South Wales*:

> *dropping down into Carmarthenshire and the Towy valley*
> *we have passed from a land of slate into a land of thatch ...*
> *[this country], and still more Cardigan [Ceredigion], boasts*
> *of the quaintest and most picturesque thatched cottages in*
> *the world ... works of art that throw the thatched cottages*
> *of Devon and Northamptonshire, the best of their kind*
> *known to me in England, hopelessly into the shade. It is the*
> *artistic concealment of the chimneys in their braided sheaf*
> *of thatch, the billowing nature of the roof comb, and the*
> *neat coping of the fringes of gable, eave and comb, which*
> *gives the southern Welsh type a distinction unapproached*
> *elsewhere ... today there are thousands scattered*
> *[throughout the south-west] ... whole villages ... fifty years*
> *hence there will probably be none left*

– a melancholy prophecy which had almost been fulfilled by 1953. Walls, however, have greater permanence than roofs and occasionally dwellings – even mud-walled cottages – still stand intact except for their thatched roofs which are now covered with slate, asbestos or, more often, corrugated iron.

Brick, first used by the Romans, appears to have been reintroduced here – probably from the Netherlands – by Sir Richard Clough in 1567 at Bachegraig, Denbighshire. Its use in building construction spread very slowly, and for a long time brick buildings were virtually confined to comparatively small areas in the north-east and the south-east. Today, brick is the commonest walling material in all parts of Wales, although even this is now often replaced by other man-made materials such as concrete, aluminium and plastic.

The Impact of History
A further important influence on the buildings that we see around us has been the impact of man-made history, whether in the form of wars and revolutions, political changes or beneficial innovations. During the last two millennia the builders of Wales have responded to the repercussions of such ideological collisions by restoring, rebuilding and reshaping with the materials at hand. At least five far-reaching and transforming historical events can be identified. Each in some way has affected the architecture and buildings of Wales.

The first of these events is the Roman invasion in the first century AD and its aftermath. The Romans brought with them new materials, new tools and new ideas. During three and a half centuries they constructed numerous forts, two towns and many villas, each of which must have appeared at the time to be an extraordinary concept to the native people living in the localities where they were erected. Although Roman ideas seem to have quickly died away once the Romans had left at the end of the fourth century, it is difficult to believe that their influence was completely forgotten; perhaps it was more a difference in attitude and the difficulty of organizing sufficient people that prevented the native people from continuing the Mediterranean tradition.

The next transforming event was the patchy arrival

of the Normans in the late eleventh and twelfth centuries. Soon after the battle of Hastings in 1066 and the English collapse, the Anglo-Normans were probing the frontiers of Wales with their armies. Lowland Gwent in the south-east and Flintshire in the north-east had previously been raided, wasted and weakened by Anglo-Saxon incursions and these areas succumbed fairly quickly to the freebooters, while the remaining Welsh, refusing to capitulate, withdrew to the safety of the hills. As the invaders penetrated further along the country's perimeter, they erected castles to defend their newly won territories from the repeated incursions of the former owners, and churches to pray for forgiveness. The Welsh princes, learning from their adversaries, built their own castles and churches, often in the image of their antagonists' own buildings.

Two centuries later, in 1283, the Welsh were finally overwhelmed by King Edward I of England. Edward, in order 'to savour his great victory in Wales ... invited English and foreign knights to a lavish "round table" and other festivities at Nefyn' and, no doubt to humiliate the Welsh, 'set up his court in two of Llywelyn's favourite residences'.[1] In the Edwardian settlement which followed, he formally divided Wales into the king's Principality and the March, where descendants of the Anglo-Norman lords still held sway. **(2)** At the same time, to ensure that his occupation was militarily secure, he embarked on a massive programme of encirclement, with a chain of mighty castles and walled boroughs in the former lands of the Gwynedd princes. The Marcher lords completed his work with new and awesome castles of their own.

Passing by Glyndŵr's nationwide revolt in favour of independence, a century or so later the next transformative event was the passing of two important Acts in 1536: the Act of Union and the Act for the Dissolution of the Smaller Monasteries. The former united Wales with England, allowing Welshmen the same rights as Englishmen, and completed the shire system; the latter (together with the Act for the Dissolution of the Greater Monasteries in 1559) led to the abandonment of all the monasteries in Wales. Together, the acts led to a new wave of building as the Welsh gentry took advantage of their newly acquired rights and improved

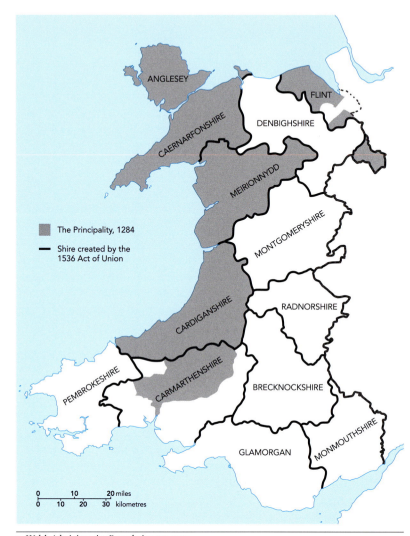

2 Welsh Administrative Boundaries, pre-1974.

ANGLESEY

FLINT

CAERNARFONSHIRE

DENBIGHSHIRE

MEIRIONNYDD

MONTGOMERYSHIRE

The Principality, 1284

Shire created by the 1536 Act of Union

CARDIGANSHIRE

RADNORSHIRE

PEMBROKESHIRE

CARMARTHENSHIRE

BRECKNOCKSHIRE

GLAMORGAN

MONMOUTHSHIRE

0   10   20 miles
0   10   20   30 kilometres

their properties, often buying or leasing the abandoned monasteries and using the masonry to rebuild.

Finally, there was the 'Industrial Revolution' of the late eighteenth and early nineteenth centuries, during which the Welsh iron, coal and slate industries began to flourish, culminating in enormous growth and development. The consequences were greater concentration of the industries themselves, rapid expansion of urban areas and attendant building, and an immense growth in Nonconformism that resulted in thousands of new chapels across Wales.

Architectural Character

Sir Cyril Fox noted, in *The Personality of Britain*, that there was a tendency for 'greater unity of culture in the Lowland Zone, but greater continuity of culture in the Highland Zone'. Wales forms part of the Highland Zone, where continuity of culture over two millennia is evident in the survival of her language, aptly called by J. R. R. Tolkien the 'senior British language'. Wales has in fact been one of the residual areas of Britain, where changes occurred less quickly, and traditions and customs tended to be long-lasting.

During the early medieval period and later, the mountainous nature of the country hindered Anglo-Saxon penetration and at the same time helped preserve the independent freedom of the Celtic Church. Consequently, what there was of church design was still nourished by Celtic tradition and custom until the medieval period. Continuity of culture meant that alien concepts were not easily accommodated, and the infiltration of non-Welsh ideas into Welsh society from the outside was, therefore, only a gradual process. Thus it was not until the end of the twelfth century that the last major Romanesque church to be built in Britain was erected at St David's, in the far western corner of Wales. The Nonconformist chapel architecture of the nineteenth century in Wales likewise continued with a classical repertoire of design details associated with eighteenth-century churches and chapels in England. By the mid-nineteenth century most places of worship in the latter country were conceived in 'Revival Gothic' styles, but in Wales this happened much later, and even then only

infrequently within the Welsh-speaking denominations.

One of the features of Welsh architecture is a difference in kind; that is to say that, broadly speaking, Welsh buildings often fall into types and groupings, not exactly paralleled by those in the English lowlands. Furthermore, though Wales is a small country it is also a land of regions, each with its own character. This regionalism can be detected in the varied character of the buildings, as the maps included in this book confirm. Usually, there is no hard and fast boundary to the regions or to the distribution of building types as they merge one with another or across the national boundary; it is more an emphasis of one type rather than another within a given region. Thus, during the Iron Age, great swathes of large hill forts (those over 1.2 ha) were raised along the broad marchland area that divided the east from the west on either side of the future English–Welsh boundary. Further west the country was densely filled with minor hill forts (under 1.2 ha); in contrast to this, there were hardly any minor hill forts to the east of the marchland. On the other hand, while there was in later centuries a fairly even distribution of Roman villas and Anglo-Saxon settlements over most parts of southern and Midland England, there was only a sparse representation of villas in Wales, while Anglo-Saxon towns and buildings are conspicuous by their absence. It was not until the end of the eighth century, however, that the boundary between the Celtic west and the Anglo-Saxon east was finally marked out by the great linear earth bank known as Offa's Dyke. Remains of medieval castles are widespread throughout Wales, except among the most inhospitable uplands; they are far less frequent in England and Scotland except in the marchlands. In England and Scotland, again, the parish church is usually the most important feature in the nucleated village. In Wales the church is often small and situated outside the village; its place within the community may be taken instead by a nineteenth-century Nonconformist chapel.

Another feature of Welsh buildings is one of size, particularly when compared with buildings found in England. Generally, the buildings of Wales appear smaller in size and more straightforward in construction than those in its neighbour. This is not of necessity because the Welsh builder always preferred simplicity, but because Wales has always been, for historical and geographical reasons, a country under severe pressures, and was in the past a relatively poor country with a sparsely distributed population. So the farms and churches of the upland areas are smaller than those in the rich lowlands east of the English border. Even when considering the castles of Wales, it is immediately apparent that those built by the native Welsh princes were usually smaller than those erected by the Anglo-Norman invaders. The native castles were mainly built for defensive purposes, whereas the invaders' castles were built as bases for armies of occupation and fortresses for the military garrisons required to control the conquered territories. The cathedrals in Wales are again diminutive when compared to some of the great soaring cathedrals of England. This is so despite the extremely long, continuous and venerable histories of some of the Welsh cathedrals; histories that stemmed from early conversion to Christianity in Roman and post-Roman times and remained unbroken to this day, while in England the succession was continually interrupted by pagan Anglo-Saxon and Viking invasions. Thus at both St David's and Llandaf there has been a longer, more continuous Christian presence than at either Canterbury or York ∎

01

Land, History and Architecture
References

1   Davies, *The Age of Conquest*, p. 355.

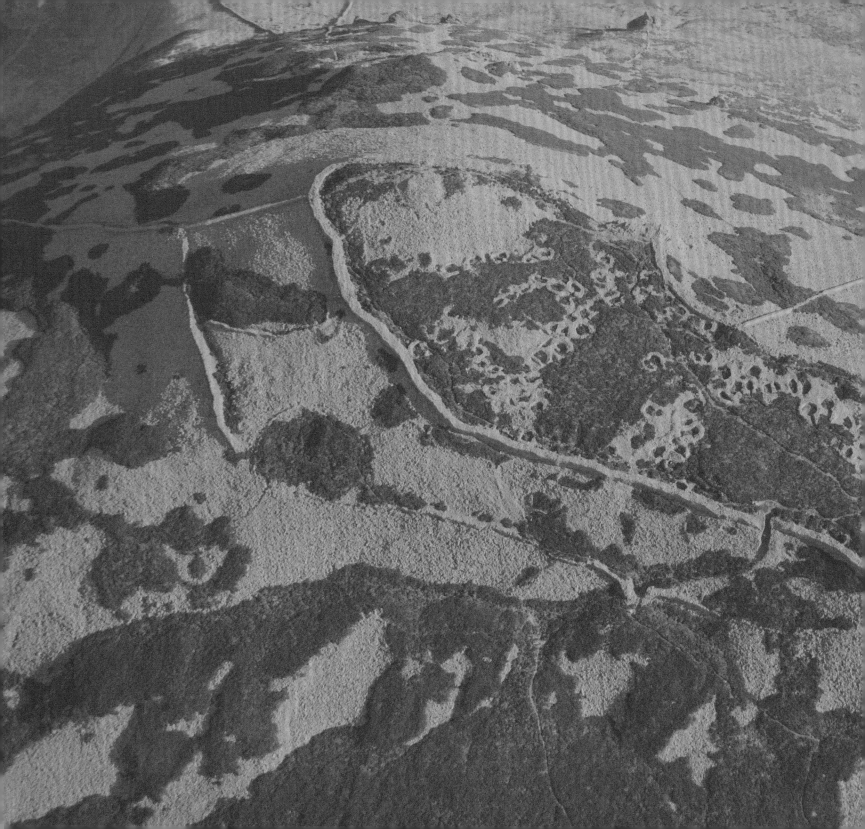

2

Roman Occupation and Celtic Survival, 47 to c.1080

Roman Occupation

The invasion of Britain by the Romans began in AD 43 at the south-eastern corner of what was to become England, and within a few short years, they had secured control of virtually all the territory to the east of the river Severn. The struggle to control the tribes in the west of Britain began in about AD 47 when the Roman governor Ostorius Scapula attacked the Deceangli in the north-east, and was later drawn into a long war against the Ordovices and the Silures. According to legend it was Caradog (Caractacus) who organized the Silures and

Ordovices and led them against the Roman legions. Caradog was defeated in AD 51, after which the Romans themselves suffered a number of reverses. Even so, the Romans had secured control of Silurian territory as far west as Cardiff. It was probably not until the late seventies, however, that the Romans were able, after a number of attempts, to reduce the remaining Celtic tribes – Demetae in the south-west and Ordovices in the north – fully into submission.

The Romans brought with them standardized building techniques, totally different from anything that had existed in Britain hitherto, which were partly derived from the Greek post-and-beam tradition and partly from the Etruscan system of arches and vaults. The Greeks' development of post-and-beam construction had culminated in the perfected types known as the 'orders'. The Romans introduced not only the Doric, Ionic and Corinthian orders to Britain, but also added two of their own invention, the Tuscan and the Composite. Their methods of building were also different, particularly in the use of concrete. This had originally consisted of small stones bedded in a mix of lime and volcanic sand, and was normally laid in horizontal courses, rather than poured as in modern concrete. It could be used in creating structures with curved surfaces, especially when vaulting across wide spaces.

The types of buildings used by the Romans were also different. Instead of organically irregular hill forts and circular dwellings, the Romans laid out forts and towns based on geometric grids, and over time built forums, baths, aqueducts, temples and amphitheatres, town houses and shops as well as, in rural areas, large farmhouses or villas. The invaders' buildings were constructed mainly of timber in the early days; later on, dressed stone, brick-faced concrete or brick with stucco was used, while their low-pitched roofs were covered with clay tiles, and their concrete floors might be finished with mosaic tiles. The extent to which they succeeded in adapting their Mediterranean-type buildings with their low roofs to Welsh conditions is a matter of conjecture; for though their solid walls were durable, the high rainfall and winds must have presented very different challenges.

The Roman occupation of what was to become known as Wales was, initially at least, essentially military in character. Thirty-five (possibly thirty-eight) auxiliary forts, varying in size from 1.25 ha to 2.5 ha, were erected across the country at regular intervals of a day's march. (3) As security improved, the number of forts was gradually reduced until, by the fourth century AD, only five remained occupied by the army. The forts were linked to each other and the legionary forts by a complete network of all-weather roads that allowed troops to move quickly to any trouble spot. The roads appear to have been the first planned communication system in Wales, although in fact many probably followed existing routes. Because of the topography of the land, the engineered roads of the Romans were not always as straight as those constructed by them in the lowlands of eastern Britain, though they usually had hard paved surfaces and avoided, where possible, very steep gradients.

The partially excavated remains of two auxiliary forts can be seen at Brecon (Y Gaer) and Caernarfon (Segontium). Outside Segontium was a small temple dedicated to Mithras. Sections of original Roman masonry from the late third-century rebuild of the Cardiff fort can be seen *in situ* at the base of the nineteenth-century walls of Cardiff Castle, while at the rear there is a realistic reconstruction of the fort's north gateway on its original foundations.

The occupation was controlled from two large legionary fortresses, with Deva (Chester) near the north-eastern corner and Isca (Caerleon), from AD 75, at the south-eastern corner of the country. Over the years, much of Roman Isca has been excavated by archaeologists. As the permanent base for the Second Augusta Legion for over two centuries, the rectangular fortress – 20.5 ha in extent, with rounded corners – was first defended by an earthen rampart and timber palisade, with timber gateways at the centre of each wall and timber towers at regular intervals. A quarter of a century later, the ramparts were refaced in stone, and the gateways and fortified towers rebuilt in stone. The enclosure was divided into two unequal parts by the principal street (*via principalis*), 7.6 m wide, along which were placed the main buildings such as the headquarters, gymnasium (part of the Fortress Baths) and officers' houses. (4) Behind these were the warehouses, granaries and workshops. The rest of

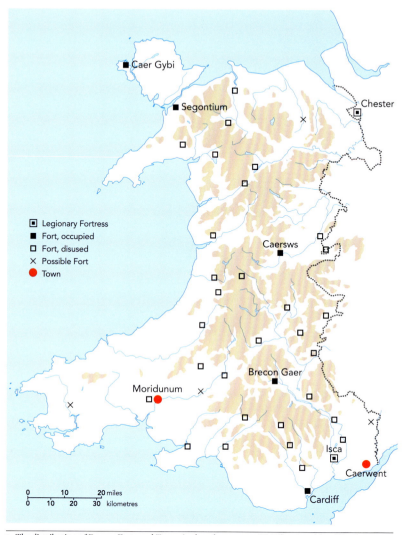

3 The distribution of Roman Forts and Towns in the 4th-centurty AD (After Arnold and Davies, *Roman & Early Medieval Wales*, Figs. 2.13F & G).

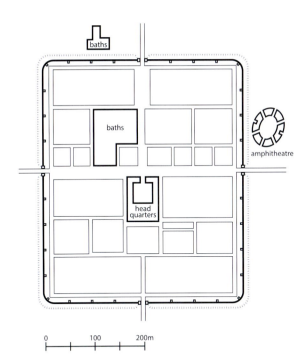

5 Caerleon Roman Fortress, the amphitheatre.

4 Caerleon
Legionary Fort.

the area within the walls was packed with barrack blocks arranged in pairs, each of which accommodated a company of 100 soldiers commanded by a centurion. Parts of the Fortress Baths – one of the largest buildings in the fortress – have been excavated and displayed; they illustrate the enormous scale of the complex. Built about AD 80, they were constructed in concrete, making it possible to vault the large spans above the swimming pool (*natatio*) and the cold water suite (*frigidarium*). Gerald of Wales was much impressed when he visited Caerleon in AD 1188, and it is worth quoting him to get a sense of what remained of Isca:

*There are immense palaces, which ... were embellished
with every architectural conceit. There is a lofty tower, and
beside it remarkable hot baths, the remains of temples and
an amphitheatre. All this is enclosed within impressive walls
... Wherever you look, both within and without the circuit
of these walls, you can see constructions dug deep into*

*the earth. Conduits for water, underground passages and
air-vents. Most remarkable of all to my mind are the stoves,
which once transmitted heat through narrow pipes inserted
in the side-walls and which are built with extraordinary skill.* [1]

Outside the fortress are the remains of a large elliptically shaped amphitheatre which had been built for games and the ceremonies of the legionary calendar as well as entertainments. It is the only completely excavated and displayed legionary amphitheatre in Britain, and forms one of our most impressive Roman monuments. **(5)** The arena, open to the sky, is encircled by an earthen bank that was originally buttressed with stone walls on the outside and acted as the base for the timber-framed superstructure of the auditorium (*cavea*), with tiered seating for some 6,000 spectators. An enormous courtyard building, one hectare in extent, has been discovered by geophysical survey between

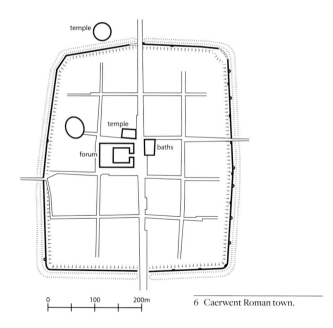

6 Caerwent Roman town.

7 Caerwent Roman town, the town walls.

the amphitheatre and the Usk river. It has not been possible to determine its function, however, despite trial excavations.

The only civil towns built by the Romans in Wales were at Venta Silurum (Caerwent) in the south-east and at Moridunum (Carmarthen) in the south-west. The former began to develop informally without civil status during the late first century AD, possibly as an urban focus for the Silures who had begun abandoning their nearby hill forts. It became recognized as the tribal capital (*civitas*) when the Silures were granted self-government, probably during the first half of the second century. By the close of the second century earth-and-timber defences had been raised around the settlement and streets had been laid out to a regular plan, similar to that adopted in the Roman forts. Roughly rectangular in plan, the town covered an area of 18 ha and was divided into twenty approximately square blocks (*insulae*), with the principal street (*via principalis*) running through the centre from east to west. (6) Later the town was enclosed by a defensive stone wall, much of which still survives in places up to 5 m high, and peripheral towers. (7)

On the north side of the *via principalis* was the *forum-basilica*, occupying the whole of the central building block or *insula*. The *forum* was a paved market place, probably entered through an archway. Roughly square, it was surrounded on three sides by open colonnades behind which were shops and offices. At the rear of the *forum* was the *basilica*, a large civic hall 40 m long by 20 m wide, with a high nave and aisles, as in a church. The clerestory, or upper part of the nave, was supported by giant Corinthian columns estimated to have been 9 m high, and the roof was covered by ceramic tiles. The plastered wall of the Council Chamber behind the *basilica* was painted with an architectural scene. Excavation of the *forum-basilica* in the 1990s revealed that the structure had been built in the early second century AD. As well as evidence for some of the building techniques used, such as the lifting devices, the excavations gave proof that the columns and Corinthian capitals had been carved on site with local sandstone.

To the east side of the *forum* are remains of a Romano-Celtic temple complex that was built about AD 330. Inside the sacred enclosure was the temple proper, with a covered ambulatory surrounding a square, tower-like shrine (*cella*) that had a semicircular sanctuary at the rear. An important feature of the town was the large public bath-house that lay on the opposite side of the *via principalis* to the *forum*, and was fed with water brought by aqueduct from the hills. The remaining *insulae* or building blocks were mostly occupied by courtyard houses, which would have been decorated with mosaic floors and wall-paintings. Some of the larger houses would have had their own baths.

The Roman town at Carmarthen may well have developed like Caerwent, as an urban focus for the Demetae tribe of south-west Wales. Possibly begun later than Venta Silurum, Moridunum is somewhat smaller in size at 13 ha, and was built to quadrilateral plan. Apart from the *via principalis* which underlies Priory Street, the street layout appears to have been more irregular than at Caerwent, and the properties – which were mainly of wood – less imposing. It was in a number of ways a less Romanized town than Caerwent, although it did possess a small amphitheatre on the outskirts.

Romanized settlements and farms are comparatively few in rural Wales outside the more fertile coastal areas such as the Vale of Glamorgan and Pembrokeshire, together with a few scattered in Anglesey and along the northern coast. High-status farmsteads, known as villas, were even scarcer in Wales, with perhaps a dozen so far discovered along the coast between the Gower peninsula and Caerwent, a few in Pembrokeshire, one each in the upper Usk and Tywi valleys and a further isolated example at Abermagwr, in the Ystwyth valley, Ceredigion. Of these the best known and largest was at Llantwit Major in the Vale of Glamorgan, where the stone-built farmhouse formed part of two angular groups of buildings surrounding a large L-shaped yard. **(8)** The farmhouse had decorated and plastered walls, floors covered with mosaic tiles, a bath-house and central heating supplied by a hypocaust system under the floors. The extensive outbuildings included workshops, stables and barns, suggesting that this was once the centre of a rich estate. In many cases, the villa complexes appear to have evolved from pre-Roman farmsteads. The villa at Whitton, near Cardiff, is one example. Apparently, this farmstead had begun life in the late Iron Age as a group of four round-houses within a roughly square enclosure bounded by a bank and ditch; by the mid-first century AD the round-

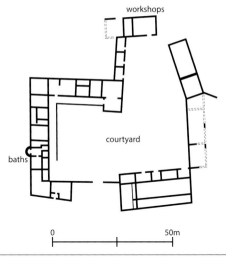

8 Roman villa, Llantwit Major, Glamorgan.

houses had disappeared and had been replaced by a stone-built rectangular building; further rectangular buildings were added in the third and fourth centuries until all four sides of the courtyard within the original earthen banks had been filled with stone-built buildings.

Elsewhere in Wales the local inhabitants either abandoned their hill forts or continued to live much as they had always done. Indeed, It seems 'clear that the Romano-British settlement pattern in rural Wales is closely linked – both in character and extent – to that of Iron Age occupation'.[2] At the Iron Age farmstead at Bryn Eryr, near Llansadwrn, Anglesey, for instance, occupation continued through to the late third or early fourth century AD, during which time a third round-house was added to an existing pair of conjoined round-houses at a time when the protective earthworks were allowed to erode away.[3] Archaeological excavation has shown that the 1.7 m-thick walls of the conjoined round-houses were clay or *clom*, probably using a mixture of clay, coarse aggregate and straw to provide sufficient strength to avoid collapse. The two round-houses were approximately 7 m and 8 m in diameter respectively. The method adopted for roofing these large spans is difficult to ascertain, as so little evidence survives, but the St Fagans National Museum of History has constructed an experimental Iron Age farmstead based on the conjoined round-houses at Bryn Eryr. **(9)** Here, the conical wood and thatch roofs of the round-houses have been linked by a curving ridge, thus avoiding valleys at the meeting points where water could collect.

The dominant settlement type in rural Roman Wales was a farmstead, either lightly enclosed by timber palisades or hedges, or left open. The enclosures themselves could be concentric (circular), rectangular or irregular in shape, with a greater diversity in the fertile soils of the south-west and the Vale of Glamorgan. Remains of both stone and timber round-houses have been found in the north-west. In recent years crop marks recorded by aerial photography have greatly increased our knowledge of the distribution of these settlements. Apparently the majority of single-house settlements were sited above the 200-m contour, while the majority of the enclosed settlements were below this level.[4] The round-houses were generally built in timber except in the north-west and other thinly scattered areas in the uplands, where they were often of dry-stone construction. Many timber farmsteads were later rebuilt in stone. Higher-status settlements often had substantial embankments and ditches and might continue in use well into the Roman period.

Celtic Survival

During the second century AD the garrisons of many Roman forts in Wales were reduced in size or evacuated, and by the end of the fourth century all had been vacated. Thereafter there was growing insecurity in the countryside, and while

9 Reconstructed Iron Age farmstead with timber roundhouses at National Museum of History, St Fagans, based on archaeological excavations at Bryn Eryr, Anglesey.

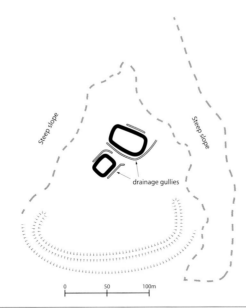

Steep slope

Steep slope

drainage gullies

0   50   100m

10 Dinas Powys hill fort, Glamorgan.

this probably affected the nature, economy and architecture of rural settlements, the two Roman towns continued to act for a while as safe havens. Venta Silurum continued in some form into the fifth century AD, although by then it had already begun to fall into ruins. Meanwhile, 'elements of native tradition with clear Iron Age antecedents [had] remained strong',[5] and in both countryside and town Roman methods of building and sanitation became less and less visible, until they were gradually forgotten and the Roman way of life broke down.

While the way of life of indigenous tribes had certainly been altered in varying ways during the Roman period, it should not be assumed that afterwards the tribes declined into a primitive, uncivilized way of life. The Celts had had, after all, expertise in craftsmanship and distinct artistic styles (as expressed in metalwork and stone artefacts) as creative and beautiful as those of the Romans. Indeed, it is difficult to believe that everything was completely forgotten, especially as many words in the Welsh language – such as *pont* (bridge),

ffenestr (window), *porth* (doorway), *mur* (wall) and *ystafell* (room) – still retain their Latin roots. However, it may well be argued that after Roman authority had ceased to function the native Celts (proto-Welsh) would have seen little reason to perpetuate some of the more idiosyncratic peculiarities of an architecture that had evolved to suit a climate much warmer and drier than theirs and an administration that no longer existed. At the same time, while evidence for material culture is limited during the early medieval period (the so-called 'Dark Ages'), it is clear that Wales continued to be influenced as well as by the building practices adopted by the Anglo-Saxon kingdoms to the east and Christian Ireland to the west. At the same time, links were maintained with continental Europe by trade and travel.

There appears to have been comparatively little organized commerce or development of urban life for much of the early post-Roman period in Wales. People mostly continued to live in very small settlements and isolated farmsteads, while many may have remained or returned to live in the Iron Age hill forts dotted around the country. Apart from those belonging to a *llys* (royal court) of a local king or noble, houses and other buildings were invariably small and made of perishable materials such as wood or *clom* (a mixture of mud, clay and straw) in most parts of the country. Some of the hill forts, such as Dinas Powys and Coygan in the south and Dinas Emrys and Degannwy in the north, appear to have been reoccupied as easily defended *llysoedd*. Dinas Powys, near Cardiff, which was occupied during the fifth- to seventh centuries, stands at the end of a narrow ridge defended by four cross banks. The arrangement of drainage gullies within the triangular enclosure suggests that the *llys* included two rectangular buildings with hipped roofs set at right angles to each other. **(10)** Excavation finds included pottery and glass from the Mediterranean, confirming the settlement's high status. Dinas Emrys at the foot of Snowdon was traditionally linked with Vortigern, a fifth-century British king, and Ambrosius, the son of a Roman consul, and the legendary fight between the red and white dragons around a lake. The hill fort was occupied during the Roman period and strengthened later with additional stone defences. As in the red and white dragons legend, there is a pool in the centre, and again, as at Dinas Powys, there is evidence, in the form of exotic pottery and glass, of trade with the Mediterranean.

In Gwynedd, where stone was easily available, the remains of numerous circular huts – not to be confused with eighteenth-century sheepfolds – are still visible on the hillsides. Examples that have been excavated confirm that many were occupied during the latter part of the Roman period and that they may have continued in use long afterwards. They could be in single, isolated units or scattered in loose groups or grouped together inside enclosures like the hut circles at Tre'r Ceiri hill fort, perched 564 m above sea level. (11) Upright stone slabs probably marked the positions of beds and seats; the huts presumably had conical thatched roofs supported on central poles. (12)

In Anglesey remains of enclosed farmsteads show the influence of both Roman and Irish construction. Pant y Saer, for instance, is a good example of a type of enclosed farmstead common throughout Gwynedd. Its enclosing wall, 2.5m thick, is oval in plan and resembles an Irish *rath*. Inside are two circular dwellings, one of which contains a raised stone bench for sitting and sleeping. (13) Not far away are the remains of Din Lligwy, a fourth-century enclosed hut group that shows the effect of Roman design superimposed on the native tradition. Here the enclosing walls are straight and angular, forming a pentagonal courtyard within which were placed two circular dwellings (one of which steps up to the entrance and was built with large limestone slabs) and six rectangular dry-stone buildings, which may have been stores or workshops. (14)

An unusual form of defended settlement was the crannog, or artificial island, a type unknown in Wales save for a single example at Llangors, near Brecon. Here, about 893, an island was constructed in the comparatively shallow lake with large stones, brushwood and timber planking, ringed around with timber piles and defended by a timber palisade. Although no remains of its timber buildings have been found during limited excavations, its high status is clear from fragments of high-quality embroidered textile and leather found at the site, and it is presumed that the crannog was

11 Tre'r Ceiri hill fort, Caernarfonshire, aerial view.

12 Tre'r Ceiri hill fort, Caernarfonshire, remains of stone round-house.

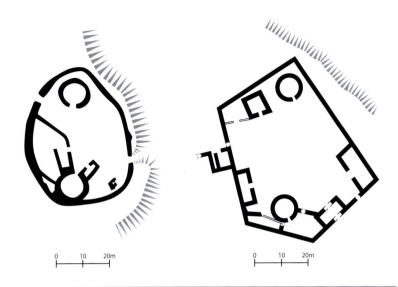

13 Comparative plans of enclosed hut groups at (a) Pant y Saer, and (b) Din Lligwy.

14 Din Lligwy enclosed hut group, Anglesey.

once the *llys* of the Brycheiniog dynasty. The close parallels with the numerous crannogs of Ireland suggest that the Llangors crannog may even have been built to emphasize the dynasty's Irish ancestry.

The remains of secular buildings erected during the later part of this period are rare. Giraldus Cambrensis (Gerald of Wales), writing in the late twelfth century, noted that the Welsh lived in 'wattled huts', and if this was the case generally, it would go a long way to explaining the absence of surviving remains today. An exception to this dearth is an enclosed Viking settlement with a number of rectangular tenth-century buildings discovered in 1998 at Llanbedrgoch, Anglesey. At least three of the buildings used a form of sill-beam. One of the buildings was 11 m long and had low limestone walls (to support the timber superstructure) around a single, partially sunken room where the family ate, worked and slept. In one half of the room there were raised benches characteristic of Scandinavian construction on three sides, around a central hearth set within a rectangle of kerb-stones.

Most remains of this period point to the continued existence of an entirely rural society, though by now this had probably increased in density, particularly in lowland areas where the soil was favourable for cultivation. In general people still lived in hamlets and dispersed homesteads, except where there were larger accumulations of buildings, such as the *llysoedd* (royal courts) and ecclesiastical hubs. The *llys* itself, particularly in the north-west, was the administrative centre of a commote which the regional king would visit periodically to do business and dispense justice. However, there is little to inform us about these larger settlements before the late eleventh century, except what can be gleaned from literary sources like the early lawbooks, such as the tenth-century Laws of Hywel Dda.

The lawbooks – reading between the lines of legal obligations, values and penalties – shed light on the ways in which buildings were arranged and constructed, although the laws themselves were more likely to be ideals rather than to reflect the actual way in which the courts were laid out. The laws dealing with the *llysoedd* specifically stipulate a number of buildings for the king, indicating that each court comprised a collection of separate structures around a main hall and enclosed within a wall. These were the king's hall, his and the queen's chambers, the refectory, the chapel, the stable, the gatehouse, and possibly the brew-houses, as well as other less important buildings. Outside the court were the king's barn and his kiln as well as dwellings for the king's officers and servants. Apparently the king's hall was to be constructed with six columns to support the roof, perhaps indicating an aisled building with two parallel rows of timber posts (or crucks) to form a central living area and side aisles for sleeping, as found in the aisled halls in Ireland. Effectively the laws incorporated early forms of building regulations that included stringent fire decrees, such as that no smithy could be erected within nine paces of adjoining buildings, and forges had to be built with non-combustible roofing materials.

Early Christian

When the Roman armies finally departed at the end of the fourth century, Christianity continued to survive in the towns and settlements that they had established in Wales. However, it was left to the native 'saints'– monks like St Cadog, St Illtud and St David – to consolidate the religion which, in the course of time, became predominantly a monastic Church. During the seventh century the Celtic churches of Ireland and Northumbria accepted the supremacy of the Roman Church, the latter in AD 664 at the Synod of Whitby. Significantly, the Welsh Church did not accept Roman customs or submit to external authority for another century. This happened in AD 768, when Elfoddw, bishop of Bangor and Gwynedd, finally capitulated and, according to the Welsh annals *Brut y Tywysogion*, 'the Easter of [all] the Britons was changed.'[6]

In addition to inheriting Christian traditions from the Romans, the monks in Wales were inspired by the ascetic ideals of eastern Christianity that had spread, via France from Mediterranean areas. At the time it was primarily a monastic religion with an emphasis on meaning and philosophy rather than with its external appearance. This, combined with the rapidity of the religion's spread, meant that in the early days it had little positive influence in the decorative arts. A later source of inspiration came from Ireland, although, paradoxically, many of the Irish monks had been trained in Wales.

When eventually the Christian church did patronize the arts, the traditional curvilinear and elaborately interlaced forms of Celtic art were used both for illuminated manuscripts and for the superb memorial stones. Though very few of the illuminated manuscripts produced in Wales have survived, we can gain some idea of their quality from an eleventh-century manuscript, the *Rhigyfarch Psalter* (now in Trinity College, Dublin), which was written at the Llanbadarn Fawr *scriptorium* and illuminated in the Irish tradition by Ieuan – son of Sulien, bishop of St David's – with colourful animals and Celtic interlace-work.

While the illuminated manuscripts are rare, the memorial stones, be they simply inscribed, cross-decorated or carved stone crosses, have survived in abundance, particularly in the western peninsulas of Llŷn and Pembroke, and in Anglesey, Breconshire and Glamorgan. The great number of stone monuments with their wealth of inscriptions both in Latin and Ogham script make them important records in the history of early Wales and the early Christian Church. The earliest decorated stones, from about the seventh century, were roughly incised with a cross on crude slabs. Later the cross might be set in its own frame. Finally, during the ninth century and later, carved high crosses (of which sixty-nine have survived) were ornamented with intricate curvilinear or rectilinear patterns accompanied by complex designs of interlaced plait work. Later crosses in Wales, such as those at Penally (early tenth century), Nevern (late tenth century), Whitford (late tenth, or early eleventh century) and the 4.1 m high cross at Carew (early eleventh century), differ in type from the well-known Irish high crosses which in general were highly naturalistic in design. (15)

It can, however, be argued that the stylized technique used on the Welsh crosses called for a higher degree of craftsmanship than that required for the Irish crosses. As Nora Chadwick wrote: 'the art which could repeat the same design with an unerring hand over the entire surface argues an astonishing control over the tools. A single false step, a

15 Early Christian Cross, Carew, Pembrokeshire.

slip of the tool, and the entire cross would have been ruined.'[7] Many of the Welsh crosses appear to be very localized in style and grouped around different sites, such as Nevern and Penally in Pembrokeshire, or Llanilltud Fawr (Llantwit Major) and Margam Museum – where there is a splendid collection of crosses in the Stones museum – in Glamorgan, suggesting that there were a number of workshops or schools of craftsmen, each under the patronage of a wealthy monastery.

Unfortunately, the remarkable beauty of the illuminated manuscripts and the stone crosses is not evident in the meagre remains of early Christian churches. In fact there are very few known remains of these early churches or monasteries, although the stone crosses themselves may often indicate the sites where they once stood. Another indicator of the sites of early Celtic churches is the distribution of ancient churches and chapels that were dedicated to Celtic saints. E. G. Bowen identified 614 of these known dedications, spread right across Wales, with a large proportion in relatively isolated places in far valleys and remote moorlands.[8] The unmarked sites of Celtic churches or monasteries are often indicated by the place-name element *llan* (enclosure of cemetery or church) followed by the saint's name, as in *Llan*illtud, or *merthyr* (martyr), as in *Merthyr* Tydfil. Altogether seventy-three sites of known or probable Celtic monasteries have been identified.

In the case of later churches, the circular or oval boundary walls of the *llan* in which they still stand testifies to the antiquity of their sites. Generally the sites chosen by the saints for their first church were new ones, such as at Llangelynin in the Conwy valley, Llanelltud near Dolgellau, Pennant Melangell in the Berwyn Mountains, or Llanilltud in the Brecon Beacons, where the ancient *llan* is an almost perfect circle raised high above the surrounding moorland. Even more isolated is St Cwyfan's church near Aberffro (Aberffraw), Anglesey, where the tiny church (rebuilt in the twelfth century) was built in the centre of circular island no more than 30 m across, the edges of which marked the position of the *llan* wall. Occasionally much older sites were chosen for reuse; the circle of stones at Ysbyty Cynfyn in Ceredigion, for example, has been clasified by some archaeologists as Bronze Age. Others appear to have used Iron Age enclosures, as at Eglwys Gymyn, Carmarthenshire, or rectangular sites like part of the Roman fort at Caerhun, near Conwy.

Eschewing worldliness and material comfort, the earliest monastic cells or churches were simple in the extreme. They appear to be, almost without exception, very small square or rectangular structures built of either timber or stone. The evidence for early wooden churches in Wales is rare, though it would seem natural to have built the earliest in timber except where stone provides an easily obtained building material. Ephemeral remains of two wooden churches have been found in the Gower peninsula. The first, at Llanelen, was identified by nothing more than a couple of slots for timber beams and a fragment of glass giving a date between the sixth and eighth centuries. At the island of Burry Holms traces of a possibly eleventh-century wooden church amounted to four post-holes defining an area of 3.3 m by 3.2 m, similar to some early wooden churches in Ireland. Both churches were later rebuilt in stone as small single-cell rectangles to which chancels appear to have been added later. The later stone church at Llanelen measured 5.7 m by 4.1 m internally, while that at Burry Holmes measured about 5.2 m by 3.3 m. Both of these are similar in size to the foundational remains of a stone chapel (5.5 m by 3 m) discovered under the later St Beuno's chapel at Clynnog Fawr and to St Justinian's chapel (3.4 m by 2.7 m) near St David's. Windows and doorways were probably square-headed, using wooden beams or stone lintels, for the arch was unknown in early buildings. Vaulting between walls was sometimes achieved by using corbelled flat stones.

Again there are no clearly datable remains, so that it is impossible to say where the above buildings come in the development of early church architecture. Indeed, the paucity of remains might indicate that very few churches, timber or stone, were built before the twelfth century. A reference to Trahaearn ap Caradog (d. 1081) in *Brut y Tywysogion* as 'the strength ... and foundation of the churches [in Gwynedd]', however, suggests otherwise. Meanwhile the more important of the early Christian monasteries emerged as *clas* churches, each run by a *clas*, or body of canons under an abbot or bishop, who was often hereditary.[9]

Thirty-four 'clas' churches are known to have existed, among them Ynys Seiriol (also Ynys Lannog, or Puffin Island) and Clynnog Fawr, as well as major centres of learning and scholarship such as Llanilltud Fawr (Llantwit Major) and Llancarfan, both in the Vale of Glamorgan, and Llanbadarn Fawr, near Aberystwyth, together with the later cathedral churches of St David's, Bangor and St Asaph. Very little is known about the buildings of these 'clas' churches, but in some cases they must have been very extensive. The monastic college of Llanilltud Fawr, for instance, was reputed to have had seven halls and several hundred pupils. No remains of Illtud's monastery have been found there, however, for it probably comprised small, individual timber or dry-stone cells clustered around the larger superstructures. Although these have perished, their foundations may still lie under the houses nearest the present church. The remarkable collection of memorial stones and carved wheel-crosses now in St Illtud's Church, but originally found in the churchyard, bear moving testimony to the renown of this important and ancient centre of early Welsh Christianity.

The best example of an early monastic settlement – though difficult to access – is on Ynys Seiriol, off the east coast of Anglesey. The settlement or *llan* was roughly oval in shape and surrounded by a dry-stone wall, with a church in the centre. **(16)** Grouped along the northern side of the *llan* wall are remains of small, rectangular-shaped cells that would have been the living quarters of the early Christian monks. Excavations in 1900, next to a later, early twelfth-century church tower, revealed the foundation walls of a 1.5m square sixth-century oratory generally associated with St Seiriol. The oratory seems to have been destroyed, possibly by the Vikings, and then rebuilt in the eleventh century, apparently slightly off-course, suggesting that the whole arch-shaped building had been erected with horizontal courses as in early Irish oratories.[10] An imprint of its side walls and roof were left on the outer face of the church's tower, showing that the oratory 'had a stone barrel-vault with a sharply pointed roof above'.[11] Other island settlements which may possibly have

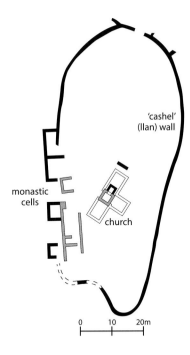

'cashel'
(llan) wall

monastic
cells

church

0   10   20m

16   Ynys Seiriol Celtic monastery, Anglesey. Early remains shown black; later remains shown grey.

been of monastic origin are Bardsey (Ynys Enlli), off the Llŷn peninsula in the north-west, and Gateholm, near St Bride's peninsula in the south-west. The latter settlement has an unusual layout with long, irregular chains of cells that occupy almost the full length of the island. Two of the excavated cells comprised houses, 8 m by 6 m and 15 m by 7 m, with turf walls, one of which was faced with stone internally.

It is unfortunate that there are no standing examples of buildings belonging to the Celtic monastic tradition. Many monastic sites had a number of very small churches dedicated to different saints. As Jeremy Knight has pointed out, 'this was partly an architectural matter', for with limited building skills any monastery 'wishing to honour more than one saint, or to house several altars in a suitable setting, would need to build multiple churches'.[12] The resulting churches may have resembled some of the surviving holy

wells associated with the early saints. Though these well structures may have been restored a number of times, they may still offer clues to the constructional methods and appearance of the Celtic churches and oratories. Many, such as Ffynnon Beuno (Clynnog Fawr), Ffynnon Gybi (Llangybi) and St Seiriol's Well (Penmon), in Gwynedd, Capel Trillo (Llandrillo-yn-Rhos) in Denbighshire, and Higgon's Well (Haverfordwest) in Pembrokeshire, appear to have been in continuous use since the sixth century. One of the best preserved is Maen-du Well (Brecon), which, according to a date-stone, was repaired or reconstructed in 1754. **(17)** Of its history we know very little, but its small size, primitive stone walling and stone vaulting and roof appear basically similar to the oratory on Ynys Seiriol and a number of surviving monastic cells in Ireland (such as Colum Cille's House in Kells), indicating perhaps the preservation of original construction details.

The dearth of remains associated with early Christian buildings in Wales does not imply that the buildings were few or poorly constructed, even when compared with Anglo-Saxon England, where a couple of dozen churches from the eighth to eleventh centuries have survived, including one (Deerhurst) as far west as Gloucestershire. The absence of extant remains is misleading, particularly when one considers the obvious skill and ability of the masons in stone carving, as manifested by the early Christian crosses and beautifully worked church fonts found across Wales.[13] Some early churches will have been replaced by new ones on the same site, others may merely have disappeared only to be discovered by excavation or aerial photography, while others are known to have existed from documents or implied by church dedications, known to have their origins during the pre-Norman period, such as those at St Arvan's and St Kinemark's in Gwent and Llandaf in Glamorgan. At Llandaf a stone church – some 12 m long, 4.5 m wide and 6 m high according to the early twelfth-century *Book of Llandaf* – had been built on the site of a sixth-century early Christian church. Significantly the church had a chancel with a semicircular apse. Even smaller Glamorgan churches with apsidal ends are known from archaeological excavations at

St Barruc's chapel on nearby Barry Island, which probably dated from about 1140, and further afield at Burry Holms, at the end of the Gower peninsula.

It is also clear that churches had begun to multiply in the lowland areas long before the coming of the Anglo-Normans. Twenty-six *ecclesiae*, or churches, dating from c. 620 to c. 1040 have been recorded in the south-east, for instance,[14] while in Pembrokeshire at least twenty-two churches of pre-Norman origin (i.e., *clas* churches or ruins with documentary evidence) have been identified.[15] Some of the larger churches or monasteries, such as Mynyw (St David's) and Llandaf, were known to be seats of bishoprics. There is evidence too that many of these Celtic churches were in use well into the twelfth century and beyond, only for the buildings to be later demolished in order to make way for new churches built more in accordance of the requirements of the day. Perhaps, in a few cases, some remains of the older church could have been buried within the structure of the new building. But if that is the case, nothing has been revealed so far, and to all intents and purposes few remains of early Christian churches have survived above ground ∎

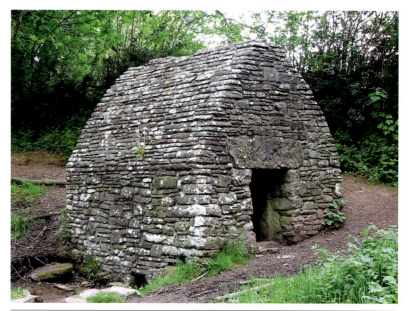

17 Maen Du Well, Brecon.

02 Roman Occupation and Celtic Survival, 47 to c.1080
References

1   Gerald of Wales, *The Journey through Wales*, pp. 114–15.

2   M. Aldhouse-Green and R. Howell, *Celtic Wales*, p. 70.

3   F. Lynch, S. Aldhouse-Green and J. L. Davies, *Prehistoric Wales*, pp. 164, 168; C. J. Arnold and J. L. Davies, *Roman and Early Wales*, pp. 67–8.

4   F. Lynch, S. Aldhouse-Green and J. Davies, *Prehistoric Wales*, p.163.

5   Aldhouse-Green and Howell, *Celtic Wales*, p. 125.

6   *Brut y Tywysogyon*, p. 5.

7   N. Chadwick, *The Celts*, p. 251.

8   E. G. Bowen, *Settlements of the Celtic Saints*, p. 10.

9   *Brut y Tywysogyon*, p. 31.

10   H. H. Hughes and H. L. North, *The Old Churches of Snowdonia*, p. 22

11   Hughes and North, *The Old Churches*, p. 22

12   J. Knight, *South Wales*, p. 107.

13   P. Lord, *Medieval Vision*, pp. 48–52.

14   W. Davies, *An Early Welsh Microcosm*, p. 137.

15   H. James, 'Early Medieval Pembrokeshire', *Pembrokeshire County History*, vol. 1, pp. 394–5.

3

Early Castles of the Middle Ages, 1080 to c.1270

A Land of Castles

Wales is truly a land of castles, numbering hundreds and located in all parts of the country. Their remains, often on dramatic sites, make them striking and melancholy reminders of Wales's turbulent past. The range of fortified structures covers almost all types from small late eleventh- and twelfth-century earthen ringworks and mottes to the massive and complex masonry structures of the late thirteenth and the fourteenth centuries. Thus, within the confines of Wales, it is possible to follow the development of castle building from modest beginnings to those that may be counted amongst the most splendid fortresses in Europe.

The chief reason for the abundance of castles stems from the different reactions of the Welsh and the Anglo-Saxons to the Norman-French invasion of 1066. In stark contrast to the Anglo-Saxon leaders' ready acceptance of foreign rule – despite sporadic rebellions in the north – following William, Duke of Normandy's, *coup de grâce* at Hastings, the Welsh princes refused to submit. Consequently, it took more than two hundred years of irregular warfare to achieve the total subjugation of all Wales, a conquest that was not achieved until 1283. The physical result was the erection of more than 500 castles – of which about 330 were earth-and-timber castles and about 190 stone castles, most of which were on new sites – a striking testimony to two hard-fought centuries. They symbolize on the one hand the persistent pressure of the Anglo-Norman lords' efforts to overrun the country, and, on the other, the determined opposition and tenacity of the Welsh princes in defence of their homeland.

In 1081, some fifteen years after the battle of Hastings, Duke William – or 'William the Bastard' as he is referred to in the *Brut y Tywysogyon* ('Chronicles of the Princes') – embarked on a pilgrimage to St David's in the far western corner of Wales. This was significant in that it turned out to be rather more than a pilgrimage – more a show of strength and an opportunity to agree a peaceful settlement with Rhys ap Tewdwr, ruler of Deheubarth. Meanwhile William had installed powerful Norman barons in strategic positions near the Welsh border at Chester, Shrewsbury and Hereford, and it was from these castles in erstwhile Anglo-Saxon territory that the Normans – or 'French' as they were known to the Welsh scribes – made deep inroads into Wales. In 1093 Rhys ap Tewdwr was killed, 'and then', according to *Brut y Tywysogyon*, 'the French came into Dyfed and Ceredigion ... and they fortified them with castles.' The situation was soon reversed, and in the following years 'the Britons threw off the rule of the French ... destroyed their castles in Gwynedd [and] all the castles of Ceredigion and Dyfed except two ... Pembroke and Rhyd-y-gors.'[1]

The Anglo-Norman lords continued to build their castles, however, with the greatest profusion in the frontier zone known as the March (after the Old French *marche*). This area stretched on either side of the eighth-century Offa's Dyke from Mold in the north-east to Chepstow in the south-east and along the southern coast from Chepstow to St David's in the south-west corner. In areas such as Gwent, the Vale of Glamorgan, Gower and southern Pembrokeshire, the Anglo-Normans were dominant and in more or less full control. Beyond these districts the limit of the March was flexible depending on who – Anglo-Norman lords or Welsh princes – had the upper hand at any one time; the contested areas included northern Pembrokeshire, southern Carmarthenshire, Glamorgan, Breconshire, Radnorshire and Flintshire. The rest of Wales remained under Welsh rule until the end of thirteenth century.

Anglo-Norman Castles of the March

The first castle to be built by the Normans on the Welsh side of Offa's Dyke was on a spectacular site at Chepstow, where the Wye river formed a dramatic frontier between the two nations. The long, slender shape of the site – situated between the high limestone cliffs of the river on one side and a narrow valley on the other – controlled the layout of the castle. It was here, at the slimmest part of the site with barely room to pass, that the Great Tower was built, possibly with ward at either end enclosed by timber palisades. The sturdy tower with its 2.5 m-thick stone walls is a rectangular, two-storey building, looking externally like a keep-tower but with little in the way of residential quarters for the lord. It still stands proudly above the later walls and turrets of the castle. (18) There were entrances at each floor level. The lower round-headed doorway has two bands of voussoirs, and a lintel and semicircular tympanum, all geometrically decorated with chip-carved stones. Neither the date nor the purpose of the Great Tower are very clear. The *Domesday Book* of 1086 states that 'Earl William [fitz Osbern] built the castle of Estriguil' (i.e., Chepstow). This is likely to have been a motte-and-bailey or ringwork structure of earth

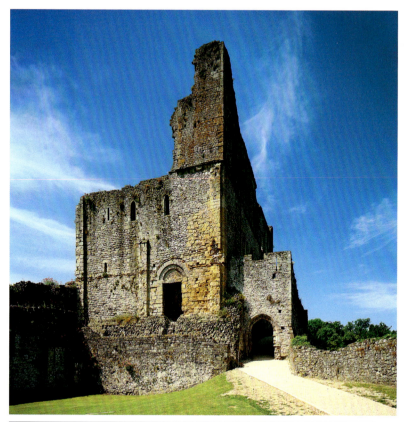

18 Chepstow Castle, the Great Tower.

and timber, hastily built to control the newly won territory. The erection of an ambitious masonry structure like the Great Tower would have taken much longer, and 'it is hard to believe that William fitz Osbern [died 1071] could have presided over the erection of so elaborate a building with so much to occupy him elsewhere.'[3] According to David Bates, 'everything points to the later years of [William] the Conqueror's for the main phase of construction', perhaps as some kind of ceremonial banqueting hall for the king's use while on his 'pilgrimage' to St David's in 1081. In reality the king appears never to have visited Chepstow, and so it seems that the Great Tower was never used for its original purpose.

19 Cardiff Castle, Norman motte and 12th-century masonry shell-keep.

Apart from Chepstow, the earliest castles of the Norman lords were constructed of earth and timber, and were erected as quickly as possible like giant molehills in the landscape. The earth-and-timber castles fell into two basic types: the motte-and-bailey castle and the ringwork castle. The motte in the former type was a huge earthen mound, surrounded by an encircling wet or dry ditch, the excavation of which would have provided most of the earth needed. The top was flattened like a truncated cone, and carried a palisaded timber stockade within which was the wooden keep-tower. In theory a motte could be thrown up in about four to nine months, depending on its size and the number of diggers involved. The bailey lay next to the motte and comprised a large, flat area defended by an earthen bank topped by a timber palisade as a first line of defence; within the bailey there were a number of wooden huts to accommodate the lord's men, supplies and animals. The ringwork or ring-castle was an altogether simpler construction, being a roughly circular enclosure defended by palisaded earthen banks within which stood the wooden keep-tower and various huts.

Starting from Chepstow and following the coastal route to St David's, the way is littered with the remains of these early castles. Within eight miles of Cardiff's centre there are, for example, the remains of twenty-two ringwork and motte-and-bailey castles, all witness to the Normans' frenetic dash to outdo each other in their race to seize the prized land. Most important of these was that at Cardiff itself, where in 1081 William I utilized the late third-century Roman fort and raised an 11 m-high motte-and-timber castle surrounded by a water-filled moat in its corner. **(19)** In order to further strengthen the castle, huge earthen banks were raised over the remains of the Roman outer wall to form a large rectangular bailey, and the outer ditch was deepened. **(20)** Twelve years later the castle became the nerve centre of Robert Fitzhamon's newly established lordship of Glamorgan, and one of the most important fortresses in southern Wales, for it was from this base that the conquering lords attempted to control the rich and fertile lands of the Vale of Glamorgan.

Further west, Banc y Beili at St Clears is another good example of a motte-and-bailey castle, although the ditches which once surrounded both the motte and the square bailey have been filled in. Finest of all is Wiston castle in Pembrokeshire. **(21)** Here Wizo, a native of Flanders serving with one of the Anglo-Norman armies, raised his motte-and-bailey castle by 1112 and possibly earlier. The kidney-shaped bailey, 130 m by 80 m, is defended by a stout earthen bank still 3 m high in places and appears to have been constructed prior to the motte with which it merges on the northern side. The conical motte rises 7 m above the bailey and is surmounted by a later stone shell keep. Surrounding the motte and the greater part of the bailey is a silted-up ditch 2–3 m deep. Presumably the bailey was once filled with huts and storehouses. Other good examples of motte-and-bailey castles exist at Tretower in the Usk valley, Bailey Hill (Mold) in the north-east and along the borders at Hen Domen (Montgomery) which had a double ditch, and at Sycharth (south Denbighshire).

The more important earth-and-timber castles were later rebuilt in masonry. Chepstow castle was an exception to the rule, as the Great Tower had already been built in stone and no further major work was undertaken for another century. When expansion did take place in the late twelfth and thirteenth centuries it led to a most unusual layout due to the restricted nature of the site between vertical cliffs and a steep valley. **(22)** The development could only follow a linear route, with a series of new wards strung out at either end of the Great Tower. The resulting footprint measured

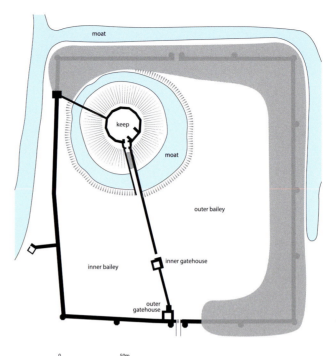

20 Cardiff Castle. The earthen mound above the walls of the Roman fort is shown light grey.

21 Wiston Castle, Norman motte and 12th century shell-keep.

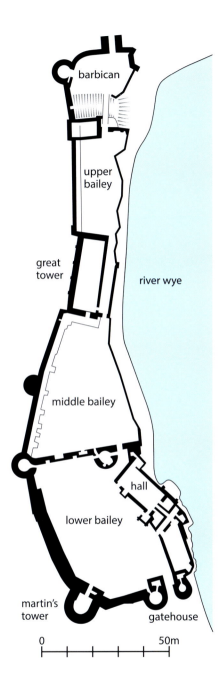

barbican

upper
bailey

great
tower

river wye

middle bailey

hall

lower bailey

martin's
tower

gatehouse

0   50m

22 Chepstow Castle.

210 m in length by only 13 m in width at the narrowest point. Chepstow was, in every sense, a very unusual castle.

Normally the timber stockade of earthen castles would be the first part to be replaced in stone, either with a rectangular tower or a more advanced form of redoubt, such as a polygonal or circular shell-keep. The new keep contained a great hall and the private apartments of the lord, and was usually entered at first-floor level from an external timber stairway. When the masonry keep or shell-keep had been completed the outer defences of the bailey would be reconstructed as a stone curtain-wall, and finally a strong gateway might be added to the curtain-wall in order to defend the main approach to the castle. Stone castles were rarely built in one operation, but were continually altered and extended so that they could take years or even centuries to complete. By the time that a castle was finished it might look very different from the one that had been anticipated at the beginning. Consequently, it is often difficult at first sight to classify castles by type. There are, nevertheless, some pointers to the way castle planning developed over the centuries.

The earliest stone keeps or hall blocks were rectangular in plan and located next to the curtain-wall. A good example, erected in the early twelfth century, and still surrounded by the dry moat of the original c. 1100 ringwork, can be seen at Ogmore Castle. The lower floor of the stoutly built, rectangular three-storey keep survives, complete with a row of joist holes showing the position of the main floor. Though the floor has gone, the handsome fireplace with its round-headed hood still dominates the principal room. Not far away, at Coity, the three-storey, late twelfth-century stone keep was square and inserted into the faceted curtain-wall at a point overlooking the outer ward. The castles at Dinas Powys and Kenfig also had twelfth-century rectangular keeps, although neither is easily visible any longer. Further west, at Manorbier, the rectangular, twelfth-century hall block is situated at the furthest end of the sub-rectangular ward.

An important feature of medieval castles were the defensive mural towers that projected beyond the line of the walls, so allowing archers to enfilade the areas alongside the walls. The earliest towers, like the early keeps, were usually square or rectangular in plan. The Newcastle at Bridgend has, for instance, two square towers embedded into the curtain-walls on its weaker west and south sides, the east and north-east sides being protected by a steep escarpment above the river. Unusually, the remains at Newcastle are all of one build, in this case of the late twelfth century. The most remarkable feature of the castle, however, is the striking Romanesque doorway standing alongside the south tower. It has a round-headed arch with a plain outer band and an inner roll moulding that carries down to moulded pilasters; within this frame the lower, segmental arch and jambs are embellished with small sunken rectangular hollows.

Masonry curtain-walls that followed the line of the original palisade on top of a motte are known as shell-keeps, for though they were not in the true sense keeps (which were towers), they acted as the inner stronghold of the castle. One of the finest and best-preserved examples of a shell-keep stands within the remains of the Roman fort at Cardiff, where about c. 1140 the Normans replaced the earlier timber keep with a polygonal, high-walled shell-keep on top of Fitzhamon's earlier motte. The new structure was built with twelve sides, presumably because it was easier to build a sequence of flat sides than a continuous curved wall. Even precautions of this magnitude were sometimes insufficient to prevent intruders, as in 1158, when Ifor Bach of Senghenydd and his followers scaled the walls at dead of night to kidnap Earl William, lord of Glamorgan, and his countess and son, and hold them captive in the hills until his political demands were met. Another good example of a shell-keep is at Wiston, Pembrokeshire, where a fifteen-sided wall was erected on top of the 7 m-high motte sometime after 1220. The broken remains of a late twelfth-century shell-keep can also be seen at Tretower in the Usk valley.

One of the problems of building walls with rubble stone was that the corners of walls were structurally and militarily weak, being vulnerable to ramming and collapse. From the late eleventh century onwards it became possible to reinforce the corners where two adjacent sides met by 'stitching' the angle with long and short ashlar-work. A still better answer was to build rounded corners or rounded towers where battering rams

23 Cilgerran Castle.

could have little purchase. The earliest example of this in Wales appears to have been at Chepstow Castle where during the last decade of the twelfth century rounded towers were attached to the outer face of the walls of the Middle Bailey. The initiator of rounded towers in Wales appears to have been William Marshal, who in 1189 came into possession of Chepstow as part of the vast de Clare estates through his marriage to Isabella, daughter of Richard de Clare (known as Strongbow). Amongst his other castles were Pembroke and Usk, both of which were given rounded wall towers.

During the early thirteenth century rounded wall towers were being included with castle defences all over southern Wales, as at Grosmont and Skenfrith in Monmouthshire (both before 1232), and at Manorbier in Pembrokeshire. By the mid-thirteenth century rounded wall towers are found at White Castle (Monmouthshire), by 1257, and at Laugharne Castle (Carmarthenshire), where the inner ward was rebuilt before 1268 with two bold towers, one of which was domed like that at Pembroke Castle. By the end of the thirteenth century the castle at Carew, originally founded by Gerald of Windsor in about 1100, was rebuilt on a lavish scale to a courtyard plan with two massive round towers, strengthened at lower level by spur buttresses at

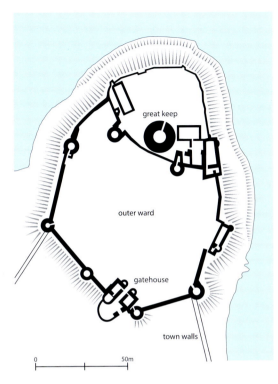

24 Pembroke Castle.

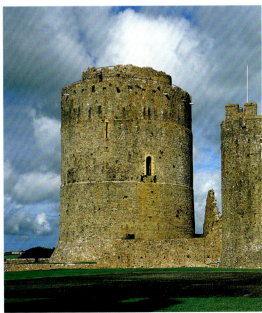

25 Pembroke Castle,
the Great Tower.

either end of the great hall.

Another of William Marshal's innovations was the twin-towered gateway, the first in Wales being the massive gatehouse with flanking round towers built about 1190 at Chepstow. The gateway was moreover equipped with arrow loops at two levels thus enabling the bowmen to shoot their arrows without being seen instead of from exposed positions on the wall-heads as had previously been the custom. Another good example of an early twin-towered gatehouse can be seen at Montgomery, where a new stone castle was begun in 1224 by Henry III to replace the motte-and-bailey castle at Hen Domen. During the thirteenth century, twin-towered gateways would soon be the norm.

An unusual example of round towers can be seen at Cilgerran Castle, Pembrokeshire, where a pair of similar, but not quite identical, three-storey towers were built close together. **(23)** The east tower has an external diameter of 12.8 m and stands at the junction of the outer curtain wall, with the cross-wall separating the inner and outer wards. This is the tower with which William Marshal, Earl of Pembroke, according to the *Brut y Tywysogyon* ('Chronicles of the Princes'), 'began to build the castle of Cilgerran', in 1223 after recovering lands in the area. The west tower, standing astride the cross-wall, was probably built a decade or so later by William's son, Gilbert (d. 1241), at much the same time as he was extending his castle at Chepstow. It differs from the east tower in being slightly larger, with a diameter of 13.7 m, and is slightly tapered. Interestingly, both towers were built so that their outward-facing walls were twice as thick as the walls facing into the inner ward. The reason for two round towers so close to each other is unclear: it may have been that the east tower (with only one fireplace) was originally intended as a keep-tower, but when the west tower (with two fireplaces) was completed the roles were reversed.

Round keep-towers were not new. Once again, Earl William Marshal seems to have been the initiator, soon after 1200, with his mighty, free-standing keep at Pembroke Castle. **(24)** As at Cilgerran's west tower, it stands close to the mid-point of the curtain-wall of the inner ward, although in this case just behind the wall instead of astride it. Standing almost 23 m high, with walls 4.2 m thick, the tower is slightly tapered and has a sloping plinth, above which are the entrance doorway and four storeys of accommodation. (25) Unusually, the ceiling of the upper, attic-like floor is dome vaulted, apparently 'the first building in Britain to have had a domed upper storey'.[2] A row of square holes below the parapet indicates the former position of a projecting timber hourd, or shooting gallery, that once encircled the top of the tower. The most likely source for the round keep-towers with domed upper storeys seems to have been the French castle *donjons* – such as the one at the Louvre, Paris, built less than a decade earlier – with which William Marshal would have been familiar.

A free-standing round keep had considerable advantages over the old square or rectangular keep. Apart from being structurally stronger with no corners to be rammed, they offered a much better all-round view and field of fire and had no 'dead' areas that might obstruct the viewing of attackers. In time, Wales and the Marches would come to have the greatest concentration of round keeps in Britain. (26) There were twenty-one Anglo-Norman round keeps in southern Wales alone, plus two which were not free-standing (Cilgerran and Penrice), together with five round keeps built by the Welsh princes. A good example of a free-standing round keep which was built (1219–32) at the same time as the rest of the castle is at Skenfrith, Monmouthshire. Here the three-storey keep stands in the centre of a quadrangular ward enclosed by curtain walls with round towers at each corner. Access to the upper floors of the keep is by a spiral staircase contained within a slightly protruding semicircular buttress. Otherwise the keep is like that at Pembroke, with a battered plinth at the base. Another fine free-standing round keep survives, this time on a steeply inclined earthen motte, at Bronllys, Breconshire. A few miles away, at Tretower, the local lord managed to squeeze a round keep into the ruins of an earlier shell-keep, thereby destroying the old hall. At Caldicot, Monmouthshire, the four-storey keep stands on an earthen motte at the corner of the curtain wall surrounding the castle. The round keeps at Caldicot and Tretower suggest that the type may ultimately have been derived from the multi-angular shell-keeps.

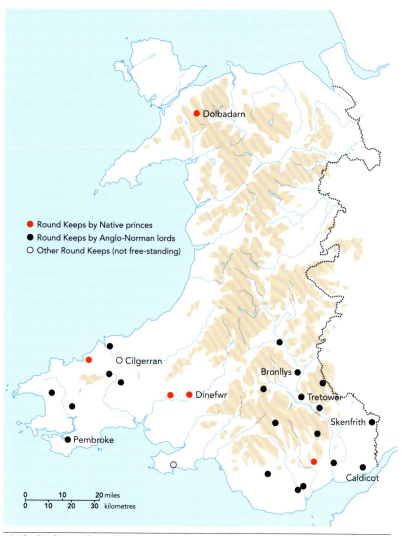

26 The distribution of Round Keep-towers in Wales (After D. F. Renn, 'The Round Keeps of the Brecon Region' with additions by author).

27 Tomen y Rhodwydd (Castell yr Adwy), Denbighshire, motte and bailey castle.

Castles of the Welsh Princes

While the incoming Anglo-Norman lords needed to erect castles in order to control their newly won territories in Wales, this was not in the same way necessary for the princes of Wales whose lands were, by and large, hereditary. While often at war with each other, 'there was only a limited tradition of physical defences, conflict being based on open armed combat.'[3] As a result, it was to be some time before the Welsh began imitating the earthwork castles of the Anglo-Normans. One of the earliest may have been Domen Castell at Welshpool, possibly built by Cadwgan ap Bleddyn, prince of Powys, before he died in 1111. Soon after that, and before 1116, Uchdryd ap Edwin built a short-lived motte-and-bailey at Cymer, near Dolgellau. By the mid-twelfth century native Welsh earth-and-timber castles had become relatively numerous and could be found in Deheubarth (in the south-west), Gwynedd (in the north-west), and Powys (in the centre). Two of the best examples, both erected

in 1149, are to be seen at Tomen y Rhodwydd, **(27)** in Denbighshire, and Caer Penrhos, in Ceredigion. The first was a fine motte-and-bailey castle, built by Owain Gwynedd. However, within a few years of its erection the timber keep was burnt by a neighbouring Welsh lord in a bid to reclaim his land. The second, near Llanrhystud, is a ringwork with a ditch and what appears to be a curving bailey, all built within the remains of a prehistoric hill fort.

The first masonry castle built by any of the Welsh princes appears to have been that at Cardigan, where in 1171 Rhys ap Gruffudd (known as the Lord Rhys, d. 1197) of Deheubarth began to rebuild 'with stone and mortar the castle at Cardigan, which he had before that demolished' prior to retrieving the site from the Anglo-Normans.[4] It then became Rhys's chief stronghold, replacing the ancestral base at Dinefwr. In 1176, in a show of pomp and stateliness, he 'held a special feast at Cardigan, and he set two kinds of contests'– the forerunner of the *eisteddfod* as we know it today.[5] Unfortunately for us, little, if anything, of the first masonry castle has survived beneath later additions and alterations. Rhys went on to build a castle at Rhayader, in Radnorshire, in 1177, and to build it again in 1194, suggesting that the first may have been an earthwork castle and that the second was built in stone. Again there is nothing left to be seen apart from some rock-cut trenches. In 1190 he rebuilt the castle at Kidwelly, according to the *Brut*, and a year later he seems to have been responsible for the round stone tower that replaced the timber keep at Nevern, possibly the first round tower erected by a Welsh prince. He may also have rebuilt Castell Dinefwr in stone, for the *Brut* refers to a later occasion (1213) when Rhys leuanc laid siege to the castle and 'made ladders against the walls for his men to climb over the walls'.[6]

The map shows the masonry castles that are known to have been built by the Welsh princes in the twelfth and thirteenth centuries. **(28)** In the north-west, masonry castles had been erected at Carn Fadryn, near Pwllheli, and Deudraeth, near Porthmadog, by 1188, according to Giraldus Cambrensis. Built respectively by a son and grandsons of Owain Gwynedd, there is little to see of these castles now and even less to indicate how they once looked. It is not until we come (in a figurative sense) to the early twelfth century that we can see what some of the masonry castles of the Welsh princes looked like. It was during the first decade of the thirteenth century that Llywelyn ab Iorwerth (d. 1240) – or Llywelyn Fawr ('the Great') as he is often referred to – emerged as the undisputed ruler of Gwynedd and with it he became the leading Welsh prince. In the next thirty years he was responsible for the building of at least five castles in Gwynedd.

The first of Llywelyn's castles was probably Castell Deganwy, which he built in 1213 on the site of an earlier Welsh fortress guarding the important Conwy river crossing. Apart from fragments of a round tower and a length of curtain-wall there is little to see now. Far more spectacular is Castell y Bere, where in 1221, after seizing the cantref of Meirionnydd from his son, Llywelyn began, according to the Brut, 'to build a castle ... for himself'.[7] (29) It occupies a strong defensive position on a high, rocky ridge beneath the mass of Cadair Idris, where it 'must have presented the ideal picture of an eagle's nest dominating its valley'.[8] The castle was defended by formidable D-shaped towers soaring above the cliffs at either end, and, like many castles of the princes, its ground plan is irregular and closely related to the topography of the site, hugging the contours and emphasizing the topography of the hill itself. (30) The entrance is unusually elaborate for a castle of this period, with two deep ditches and two gatehouses with drawbridges separated by a rocky barbican all overlooked by a round tower. The rectangular middle tower, at one end of the triangular courtyard, served as the keep, though smaller than either of the two D-shaped towers.

The castles of Dolwyddelan and Dolbadarn, guarding important valleys leading into the heart of Eryri – the last stronghold of the Gwynedd princes – also crown rocky outcrops. Castell Dolwyddelan was built sometime between 1210 and 1230 to replace the nearby twelfth-century tower at Tomen Castell, probable birthplace of Llywelyn Fawr. (31) The tall rectangular keep tower (partially restored during the nineteenth century) which stands like a lonely sentinel in the rugged landscape, was the earliest part to be built. The angular curtain-walls were built next, followed by the

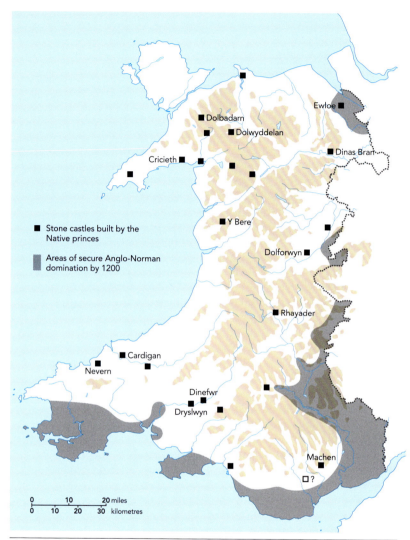

28 The distribution of masonry castles built by the Welsh Princes. (Note: 'area of secure Anglo-Norman domination' is based on R. R. Davies, *The Age of Conquest*).

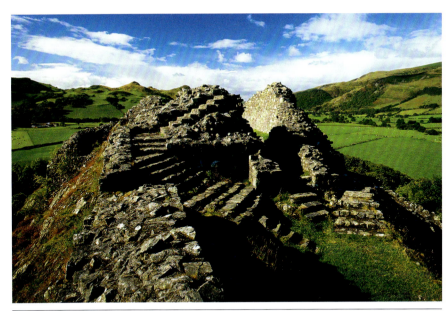

29 Castell y Bere, Meirionnydd.

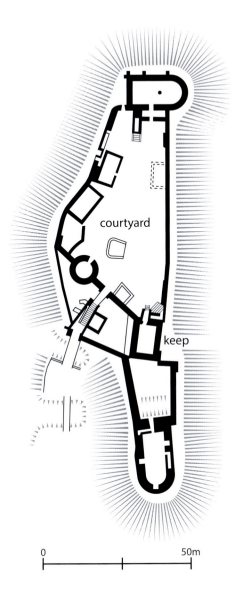

courtyard

keep

0   50m

30 Castell y Bere, Meirionnydd.

now ruined, rectangular west tower. Castell Dolbadarn, 16 km away, stands in romantic surroundings at the edge of Llyn Peris and in the shadow of Yr Wyddfa (Snowdon). **(32)** Its scant remains of curtain-walls and two smallish rectangular towers appear to date from the same period as Dolwyddelan, while the fine three-storey round keep tower built astride one of the curtain-walls was clearly added later, perhaps in the 1230s. The curved stairs that follow the outer curve of the tower lead to a traditional first-floor entrance and must have been built to replace earlier timber stairs. The round tower – with an internal diameter larger, at 8.1 m, than that at Pembroke, was presumably modelled on earlier round towers elsewhere, but whether these were the round towers of Deheubarth or English examples is an open question.

Later than any of the above was the castle at Cricieth, probably built between 1230 and Llywelyn Fawr's death in 1240. The original castle has a five-sided curtain-wall with a rectangular keep-tower and an imposing, but massively overscaled double gateway similar in design to the English gateway (completed in 1232) at Montgomery castle. An outer ward with two additional rectangular towers was added by Llywelyn's grandson, Llywelyn ap Gruffudd, sometime between 1255 and 1280.

The only known stone castle built by a prince of Powys was that near Welshpool, known as either Castell Coch (Red Castle), because of the red colour of its stonework, or Powis Castle. It crowns a rocky ridge, and the three- and four-storey structure that we see today belongs mainly to the fourteenth century. The earliest stonework, 'possibly dating to about 1200' appears to be a curving wall on the south side that may have been a curtain-wall or shell-keep erected by Gwenwynwyn ap Owain Cyfeiliog (d. 1216) or his son Gruffudd.

By the early thirteenth century the Tywi valley had become the main stronghold of Deheubarth. Here stood the castles of Dinefwr and Carreg Cennen, both on commanding sites and both possibly the work of the Lord Rhys during the latter part of the twelfth century. Castell Carreg Cennen fell to the English in 1277 and was largely rebuilt by them; Castell Dinefwr was rebuilt by the Lord Rhys's son, Rhys Grug, in the early 1220s. After falling foul of his nephew Rhys Ieuanc in 1213, Rhys Grug had become a supporter of Llywelyn Fawr and was rewarded in 1216 by confirmation of his Ystrad Tywi possessions and, in the following year, by entrustment of areas around Kidwelly and Gower. However, he was compelled to surrender these areas in 1220 and destroy part of his own castle as part of Llywelyn's improved relations with Henry III. Humiliated, but apparently undaunted, Rhys Grug set about rebuilding Dinefwr in stone soon afterwards. The inner ward of the new castle had a polygonal layout and was dominated by a massive round keep tower with internal dimensions similar to those at Dolbadarn. **(33a)** The base of the tower is flared, and where the sloping part meets the cylindrical upper part there is a roll-moulded string course of imported Bath stone. The tower was probably three storeys high, with an entrance at first-floor level accessed by timber stairs. **(34)** Any putative upper floor would have been

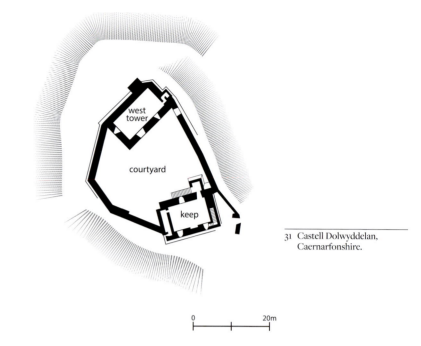

31 Castell Dolwyddelan, Caernarfonshire.

32 Castell Dolbadarn, Caernarfonshire.

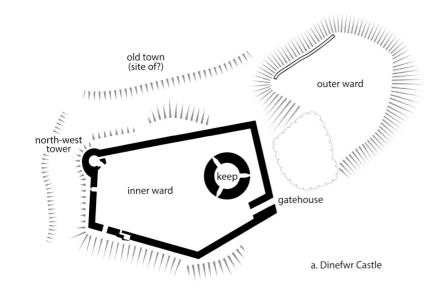

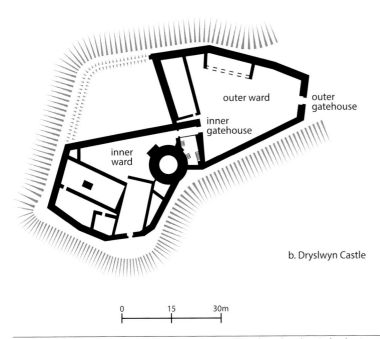

33 Comparative plans of (a) Castell Dinefwr, and (b) Castell Dryslwyn (based on Cadw plans).

destroyed during the construction of a summerhouse in the seventeenth century. Similarly the form of the outer ward is unclear, as apart from the levelled area little remains to show the position of the defensive walls or buildings.

Soon after completing Dinefwr, Rhys Grug (about 1225/6) began building a new castle a short distance away at Dryslwyn. The layout of the castle was remarkably similar to that of Dinefwr, with entrances and massive round keep-towers in comparable positions. The castle was extended in the mid-thirteenth century with the addition of a large outer ward. **(33b)** As at Dinefwr, there was also a small town alongside. Until the castle was archaeologically excavated in the 1990s, it was difficult to make any sense of the site. The excavations revealed, amongst other things, that the lower parts of the keep tower were still covered externally in a thick coat of white, lime plaster, a technique that was used to ensure greater visibility from a distance. The discovery was confirmation of the importance of display by medieval castle builders. Rhys ap Maredudd inherited the castle in 1271, and began to improve its accommodation, including a new outer ward with a strong gatehouse (not shown on plan). After the unsuccessful war of independence in 1282–3 (see Chapter 4), Rhys rebelled against the English king. This resulted in an English siege of the castle in 1287 by 11,000 men; during the siege Castell Dryslwyn proved strong enough to withstand all attempts to capture it for three weeks, before eventually capitulating.

In the south-east there are remains of two masonry castles apparently begun by native Welsh lords during the thirteenth century. The earlier, Castell Meredydd at Machen, near Newport, was captured in 1236 by Gilbert, Earl of Pembroke, who was then forced to restore it to its rightful owner, Morgan ap Hywel, 'for fear of Llywelyn ap Iorwerth', prince of Gwynedd.[9] The remains of Castell Morgraig, sited at the head of a steep scarp slope overlooking Cardiff at the southernmost point of Senghenydd territory, are more intriguing. Excavations in 1903 confirmed an ambitious design of mixed English and Welsh building styles based on a geometric, five-sided star-shaped layout with projecting D-shaped towers at four corners and a rectangular keep tower at the fifth. The castle's history is obscure and is barely referred to in the records. Consequently, opinions as to its origin have varied. On the face of it there seems to be no real reason why the powerful lords of Glamorgan should have needed to build such a large castle so close to and just a few years earlier than their castle at Caerphilly. On the other hand, the Welsh lord of Senghenydd, Gruffudd ap Rhys, might have had every reason to build the castle (between 1262 and 1266) – if supported by Llywelyn ap Gruffudd, who by now had adopted the title 'prince of Wales' – in order to prevent further intrusion into Welsh territory by English descendants of Norman lords.

Further important castles were built by the Welsh princes in the north-east during the latter part of the thirteenth century. The earliest, Castell Ewloe, near the mouth of the Dee river, appears to have been built by Llywelyn ap Gruffudd, in or about 1257, after having regained much of the territory that he had lost a decade earlier. The castle is defended by deep ditches on two sides and at the centre of the upper ward there is a strong, elongated D-shaped keep tower. As at Bere, the lower or outer ward is connected to a round tower. Castell Dinas Bran, was built about 1260 within the remains of an Iron Age hill fort on the crest of the mountain overlooking Llangollen and the Dee valley. It comprised a large rectangular courtyard with a twin-towered gatehouse and square keep at one end and a typically Welsh D-shaped tower protruding from the middle of one of the long sides overlooking a formidable rock-cut ditch. By now Llywelyn was master of native Wales and was able to agree a treaty in 1267 with Henry III that recognized his possessions (including virtually all of Wales apart from Glamorgan, Gwent and Pembrokeshire) and confirmed his position as Prince of Wales.

However, the peace brought about by the Treaty of Montgomery was not to last long, as disputes arose between Llywelyn and the new English king, Edward I. One source of dispute was Castell Dolforwyn, which Llywelyn had begun to build about 1273 on a rocky ridge a few miles from the royal castle at Montgomery and on the opposite side of the Severn valley. Work began with two free-standing towers, one a strong rectangular keep tower and the other a round

34 Castell Dinefwr, the Inner court and Keep Tower.

tower at the furthest end of the site. Both towers were then linked by curtain-walls around a rectangular courtyard in a layout similar to that used earlier at Castell Dinas Bran, with a small D-shaped tower half-way along the north-west curtain. In November 1276 Llywelyn was declared a rebel by Edward I. War followed, and in April 1277 Dolforwyn capitulated after an eight-day siege. Castell Dinas Bran was abandoned and burnt in May when the hopelessness of resistance had become apparent.

Caergwrle, the last Welsh castle to be built, was surprisingly close to the border and the English stronghold at Chester. Apparently it had been built by Dafydd ap Gruffudd with Edward I's permission, as a reward for turning against Dafydd's brother, Llywelyn ap Gruffudd, in 1273. The castle had a roughly semicircular layout with a large round tower at one corner and two smaller D-shaped towers. Later (and possibly before the castle had been completed) Dafydd rebelled and attacked the English castle at nearby Hawarden, while other discontented Welsh lords captured – in what appears to have been a coordinated pan-Welsh uprising – the castles at Aberystwyth, Carreg Cennen and Llandovery, thus precipitating the 1282–3 war of independence ∎

03 Early Castles of the Middle Ages
References

1   *Brut y Tywysogyon*, p. 33

2   Malcolm Hislop, *Castle Builders*, p. 72

3   C. Capel, *Excavations at Dryslwyn Castle*, p.14.

4   *Brut y Tywysogyon*, p. 155.

5   *Brut y Tywysogyon*, p. 167.

6   *Brut y Tywysogyon*, p.197.

7   *Brut y Tywysogyon*, p. 221.

8   Morris, *The Welsh Wars*, p. 310.

9   *Brut y Tywysogyon*, p. 235.

4

Later Castles of the Middle Ages, c.1270 to 1535

Later Lordship Castles

Llywelyn's ambition to become the accepted ruler of the whole of Wales had made him powerful enemies among the by now fully anglicized Marcher barons and the king, a situation that was worsened by Dafydd's dramatic volte-face in 1282. The most obvious early reaction to this state of affairs was in the Marches, with the construction of the castle at Caerphilly by the Glamorgan baron, Gilbert de Clare, Earl of Gloucester. First begun on a massive scale in April 1268 as a reaction to Llywelyn ap Gruffudd's growing power, work

went ahead quickly, only to be stopped in October 1270 when 'Llywelyn gained possession of the castle at Caerffii' and burnt it.[1] Earl Gilbert mounted a counter-attack and was able to restart building work in June 1271.

When completed in 1290, the castle covered an area of 12 ha, making it the largest medieval fortress in Britain after Windsor Castle. Possibly designed by Robert of Beverley,[2] keeper of the works at Westminster Abbey and the Tower of London, it was probably the first fully concentric castle in Britain (followed by the Tower of London between 1275 and 1285), where the inner ward is surrounded by an outer ward which in turn is surrounded by water, like a box within a box. **(35)** The inner ward of the island citadel, with its great hall and other residential accommodation, was defended by round towers at the four corners and by two impressive, twin-towered gatehouses, all of which overlooked the lower outer ward with another pair of twin-towered gatehouses. **(36)** To the west of the citadel a second, smaller island – originally with gatehouses on either side and known in Welsh as Caer y Werin ('people's fort') – may have provided a refuge for townspeople from the borough. The citadel and Caer y Werin were surrounded by an artificial lake, the water being held back on the eastern side by a long dam that formed a fortified barrage wall unique in Europe, 160 m in length, with two entrances via twin-towered gatehouses approached by drawbridges.

Complex in design and bold in appearance, it was a stunning castle by any standard and paved the way for the design of later Edwardian castles. Above all, it was a measure of Earl Gilbert's concern regarding the possibility of a Welsh resurgence. In the late 1270s a second lake with a further 125 m-long dam was added north of the castle. During the early fourteenth century (1317–26) the Great Hall in the inner ward was rebuilt on grander lines, probably to the design of master mason Thomas de la Bataille.[3] Conserved and restored by the fourth Marquess of Bute between 1928 and 1939, the Great Hall survives as a structure of some architectural distinction with graceful ogee-pointed windows and rich interior mouldings.

The next concentric castle to be erected in Wales was

at Kidwelly in Carmarthenshire, where another Marcher lord, Payn de Chaworth, began rebuilding it on a massive scale after returning from one of the Crusades in 1274. Though concentric in spirit it is not a true concentric design as the outer ward does not completely surround the inner ward, its place on the eastern side being made unnecessary by virtue of the steep river bank on which the castle sits. Thus the square inner ward with its great round corner towers overlooks the D-shaped outer ward on the west side, but the river on the east side. The lower section of the semicircular outer curtain-wall appears to be a survival from the original stone castle of the late twelfth or early thirteenth century. The massive twin-towered main gatehouse facing the borough was added at the end of the fourteenth century.

Edwardian Castles

So far the major new castles had been built by the Marcher lords, but even before the 1276–7 war of independence had come to a conclusion, Edward I had begun erecting a chain of castles in areas newly acquired by the crown, at Aberystwyth,

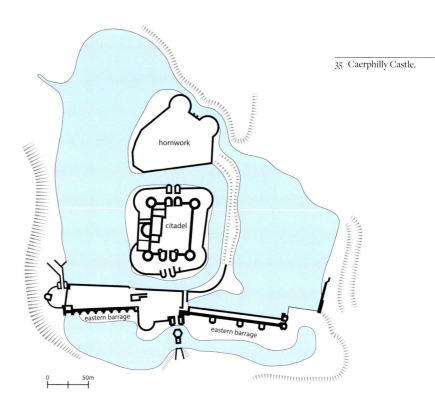

35 Caerphilly Castle.

36 Caerphilly Castle, seen across the lake.

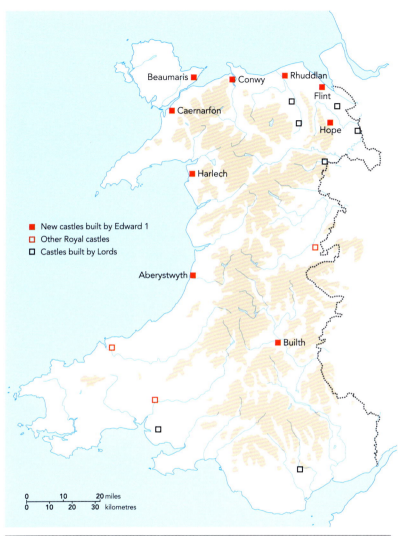

Beaumaris ■
Conwy ■
Rhuddlan ■
Flint □
Caernarfon ■
Hope ■ □
Harlech ■
■ New castles built by Edward 1
□ Other Royal castles
□ Castles built by Lords
Aberystwyth ■
Builth ■

0   10   20 miles
0 10 20 30 kilometres

37   The distribution of Edwardian and Lordship Castles in Wales in the late 13th century.

Builth, Flint and Rhuddlan, each threatening the borders of a diminished Gwynedd. **(37)** They provided him with an opportunity to put into practice lessons that he had probably learnt from observing the most up-to-date developments in military architecture while crusading in the Holy Land. Edward's castle at Builth was begun in May 1277, on the site of an earlier motte-and-bailey castle, and appears to have been quite unlike any of his other castles in Wales. Documentary evidence refers to the existence of a 'great tower [possibly a shell-keep], a stone wall with six lesser towers surrounding the castle'.[4] Little remains apart from the original motte, any masonry remains now being hidden under earthen mounds. The castle at Aberystwyth, begun three months later, stands on a rocky headland overlooking the sea. Although probably intended to have a symmetrical layout, like many of Edward's castles, its nearness to the coast seems to have thwarted the original idea, so that both the inner and outer curtain-walls on the south-west side were built at slightly different angles (and dates) from the rest of the diamond-shaped, concentric plan. The main entrance on the east was a twin-towered gatehouse, with D-shaped towers large enough to provide residential accommodation. Most of the corner towers appear to have been round, with D-shaped interval towers on the south-west and north-east inner curtain-walls.

The castle at Flint had a square inner ward with strong round towers at three corners and lofty curtain-walls backing onto the Dee estuary. A grand round keep-tower stands just outside the fourth corner – separated from it by a circular moat – rather in the manner of a French *donjon* such as at Aigues Mortes, which Edward is known to have visited on his way to the Crusade in 1270. The 7 m-thick walls of the keep-tower comprise, in fact, two circular walls, one within the other, connected by a stone vaulted passageway. A large outer ward lies between keep-tower and the town ditch. Rhuddlan Castle was built to a concentric layout and, as at Aberystwyth, has a diamond-shaped inner ward, but this time with two strong twin-towered gatehouses opposite each other and two round towers at the intervening angles. The outer ward has a more irregular shape and was protected by a low curtain-wall, surrounded by a wide moat fed from

38 Conwy Castle,
Caernarfonshire.

the Afon Clwyd. In order to ensure that the castle could be provisioned in the event of a siege, the Clwyd was canalized and deepened to make it navigable to sea-going ships.

Llywelyn was ambushed and killed near Builth in December 1282. Despite the setback, the Welsh resistance to Edward continued for many more months under Dafydd, Llywelyn's brother and successor. Eventually Dafydd was captured on the slopes of Cadair Idris in June the following year, and died in captivity in October. After the Edwardian conquest the royal *llysoedd* fell into disuse, some immediately and others more gradually, or were reused for other purposes. In the case of the prince's halls at Aberconwy and Ystumgwern, Meirionnydd – which had evidently been fabricated in timber, rather than built in stone – they were later dismantled on Edward I's instructions and re-erected at his castles of Caernarfon[5] and Harlech.[6]

Following the 1282–3 war of independence, Edward began to build a second chain of mighty castles, this time in the heart of Gwynedd at Beaumaris, Caernarfon, Conwy and Harlech. The scale of the castles and the speed at which they were built was astonishing, as much an act of revenge for earlier humiliating defeats as a need 'to contain and thwart the attacks of the Welsh'.[7] To carry out the work, almost 3,300 workmen – numbering 150 masons, 415 carpenters, 1,120 diggers, and 1,600 woodcutters – were impressed from every county in England save Cornwall and Devon during 1282 and 1283 alone.[8] The master mason in charge of the whole project, Master James of St George, came from Savoy in the Alps; he had been borrowed by Edward from his great-uncle, Count Philip of Savoy. Many of the other master craftsmen were also from Savoy or other parts of France, such as Philip the carpenter, Stephen the painter, William de Seyssel, Gillot de Chalons, Albert de Menz (all from Savoy), and Bertram de Saltu, a military engineer probably from Gascony.[9] However, not all had travelled so far: Richard the engineer was from Chester.[10]

The largest of the new Edwardian castles were at Conwy and Caernarfon. Work at the former seems to have begun in March, 1283, just a few weeks after the capture of Dolywddelan and the Welsh defeat. Three months later, ditching work was begun at Caernarfon. Because of their elongated rocky sites, neither castle was built to a concentric layout, but each was built with a single encircling curtain-wall. Conwy had eight bold, circular towers and was subdivided into an outer and inner ward by a cross-wall. (38) The outer ward is the larger of the two wards and is approached by way of a barbican and through the main gate. On the north side are remains of the large kitchen block, and on the south side the walls of the long, curved hall range which was originally divided by a passage with the great hall on one side and a chapel on the other. The middle gate and drawbridge at the farther end of the outer ward gave access to the square inner ward, which contained the royal apartments. These included the king's great chamber, king's chamber and queen's chamber, all on the first floor. Accessible from the great chamber was the stone-vaulted royal chapel, built into one of the towers and lit by three lancet windows. At ground level a small gate gives access to another barbican, where stairs lead down to a water gate and the Conwy river.

Whereas Conwy is massive and rounded, Caernarfon is massive and angular, tall and perhaps more aesthetically pleasing. It is even more irregular in plan, but was similarly divided into two wards and protected by colossal curtain-walls and seven immense polygonal towers, two twin-towered gateways (also polygonal in plan) and one smaller tower. (39) The main towers at Caernarfon are topped by octagonal turrets, and the curtain-walls are threaded with a complicated array of internal passageways that act as shooting galleries. The formidable strength of Caernarfon is nowhere more apparent than in the main entrance, the King's Gate, which comprised two octagonal towers approached by a drawbridge and protected by five gates and six portcullises with arrow-loops between the divisions and 'murder holes' in the vaulting above. The architectural treatment throughout is unusually sophisticated for a military structure, with fine coursed masonry in bands of different colours and subtle offsets to the walls and towers. (40) Clearly no expense was spared in building this spectacular fortress, for it was from

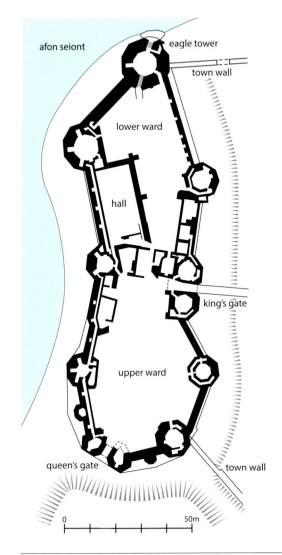

39 Caernarfon Castle, Caernarfonshire.

the beginning intended to be seen as a palatial status symbol of the conqueror and the administrative headquarters of the king's principality of Wales. Altogether it took almost half a century to build, at a cost of more than £20,000, the equivalent of about £16,000,000 in today's money.

Although strategically part of a chain of fortresses, tactically Caernarfon seems to have been a special case. The siting of the castle and the extravagant nature of its design confirm its emblematic nature by recalling Caernarfon's legendary past, not so much as a way of glorifying Welsh tradition, 'but rather to symbolize the appositeness of the repossession of Caernarfon by an imperial power'.[11] The fact that the castle was raised on a site almost within a stone's throw of the Roman fort of Segontium – a place traditionally associated in *The Mabinogion* with Macsen Wledig (Magnus

Maximus) and his wife Elen (Helena) and son Cystennin (Constantine) – is immediately telling. The castle as built reminds one of Macsen's dream, where 'he saw a great city at the mouth of the river, and in the city a great castle, and he saw many great towers of various colours on the castle.'[12] Again, one of the Welsh names for Caernarfon was Caer Cystennin (i.e., the 'fort of Constantine'), the same as the Welsh name for Constantinople itself. The capture of one of the chief places of the Welsh princes – the Constantinople of Wales – must therefore have been of great importance to Edward I, and this is reflected in the castle's design. Most obvious are the hexagonal towers with their contrasting bands of stone, towers that – despite the military disadvantage of their vulnerable corners – are evocative of the towers of the town walls of the other Constantinople

40 Caernarfon Castle, Caernarfonshire.

41 Harlech Castle, Meirionnydd.

on the Bosporus. The alternative view that the wall banding was copied from French castles, such as Château Galliard, or even from Roman remains in England, is less convincing, if only because it is not the only symbolic feature connected with the castle. One such was the deliberate arrangement for Edward I's fourth son, Edward (later the first English prince of Wales, and future king), to be born in the castle in April, 1284; another was the raising of three sculpted eagles on the topmost turrets of the principal (Eagle) tower in 1317, presumably as a tribute to the Roman Segontium, which can be clearly seen from the tower (ironically, the eagle was also the symbol of Owain Gwynedd, great-great-grandfather of the last Llywelyn).

The lavishness with which the castle was built did little, however, to cow the Welsh into abject submission, as shown by the violence of the insurrection led by Madog ap Llywelyn in September 1294. During the rising the borough was overwhelmed and occupied and the incomplete north walls of the castle thrown down. For six months the great castle that had been built to overawe the natives was in Welsh hands and towards the end of the following year the builders had to start again from the bare lower walls.

For Edward I's fully developed concentric castles we must turn to Harlech and Beaumaris. Both are superb examples of the type. Harlech, started in the spring of 1283, is splendidly situated high above the sea on a steep, rocky cliff with a dry moat cut into the rock on the landward side. (41) The castle has a strikingly symmetrical plan, comprising a quadrangular inner ward surrounded by a narrow outer ward. The inner ward has massive round towers at the four corners linked by high curtain-walls with, in the centre of the eastern curtain, a majestic twin-towered gatehouse with residential accommodation on the two upper floors. After Madog's rebellion in 1294 a large area of land to the north of the castle, on Castle Rock, was enclosed by an additional curtain-wall as a further protection.

The last of the castles to be built for Edward I was at Beaumaris on the isle of Anglesey. (42) Work on the new castle began early in 1295, in response to Madog's capture of Caernarfon, and it was mostly erected within eighteen months. The castle lies on a flat site close to the shore and was built to a concentric layout with inner and outer wards surrounded by a wide water-filled moat. (43) Possibly inspired by Caerphilly Castle, it is a masterpiece of medieval planning, the epitome of the concentric ideal with every part covered by cross-fire from the towers. The square inner ward has imposing twin-towered gatehouses on both the south and north sides and six round and D-shaped mural towers along the east and west curtain-walls, all of which overlook the octagonal outer ward with its twelve comparatively small towers. The polygonal chapel in one of the towers has been restored, complete with (modern) stained glass windows. The outer ward was built with two gatehouses, the Llanfaes Gate on the north side and the Gate Next the Sea on the south side, next to a dock for seagoing ships. Though conceivably overshadowed by Caernarfon and Harlech in grandeur and drama, it is perhaps today the most attractive of all Edward's castles.

Finally, mention should be made of the lordship castles at Denbigh and Chirk, which, if not royal castles, were at least built with the sanction and approval of Edward I and may even have been designed by James of St George. After starting in late 1282, work on Denbigh Castle seems to have either slowed down or stopped, so that by the time of Madog ap Llywelyn's rebellion in 1294 only part of the curtain-wall and four D-shaped mural towers had been completed. When building work resumed it was to a new scheme with north and east curtain-walls built twice as thick as the original, together with three large polygonal wall towers and a gatehouse – consisting of an octagonal vaulted hall within a triangular framework of three octagonal towers – that was even more ambitious in design than the King's Gate at Caernarfon. Work on Chirk Castle was begun by Roger Mortimer in 1295. It was intended to follow a symmetrical layout like Beaumaris Castle, with round towers at each corner and half-round towers in the middle of each curtain-wall except the south curtain, where a lavish gatehouse had probably been planned. In the event work appears to have stopped in 1322 – after Mortimer had taken up arms against the king and was later thrown into the Tower of London – leaving the south curtain and gatehouse unbuilt and the towers uncompleted.

The Last Castles

The economic decline and poverty experienced throughout northern Europe for much of the fourteenth century as a result of desperately poor harvests and widespread plague, continued into the fifteenth century. In Wales, agricultural depression, continual poverty and hatred of oppressive officialdom that often flew in the face of age-old Welsh customs, nurtured the seeds of rebellion. These grievances, together with friction following privileges given to English burgesses in the new 'planted' boroughs, culminated in Owain Glyndŵr's country-wide revolt between 1400 and 1415. For a few brief years castles came into their own again, as one by one Edward's castles were besieged or captured by Glyndŵr's forces. Among those captured were the great castles of Aberystwyth, Conwy, and Harlech. Glyndŵr was able to hold Welsh parliaments at both Machynlleth and Harlech, but then, as English forces gathered in strength, the castles fell and Glyndŵr disappeared into the wilderness.

A Penal Code was introduced in 1402 prohibiting

42 Beaumaris Castle, Anglesey.

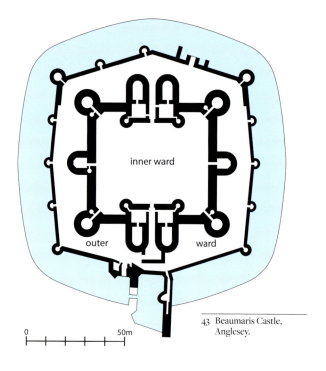

inner ward

outer   ward

0   50m

43 Beaumaris Castle, Anglesey.

Welshmen from gathering together, dwelling in fortified towns or gaining high office, and for two centuries after the Edwardian invasion the land remained relatively calm except during the Glyndŵr Revolt. As a result the art of castle building fell into decline and hardly any new castles were erected in Wales. Throughout this period castles were being abandoned – especially the older, earth-and-timber castles – for one reason or another. Once abandoned, they became uninhabitable and unusable, and gradually deteriorated into ruins. Sometimes, in order to speed things up or remove the possibility of the ruins being used illegally, they were demolished – either by brute force as happened at Castell Carreg Cennen in 1462, or by way of controlled explosion. If not abandoned, then a castle might be altered – as was the case at Swansea between 1328 and 1347, when elaborate arcaded parapets in creamy white Sutton stone were added to the external wall of the castle's south range (44) – or recconstructed to make them even more formidable, as at Cilgerran where a new north tower and domestic buildings were added in about 1377, and at Kidwelly

44 Swansea Castle, showing arcaded parapet.

where a powerful new south gatehouse was added between 1390 and 1402. Alternatively, it might be to make it more liveable, as at Cardiff, with the addition of the Beauchamp Tower and a new hall during the early fifteenth century, and at Carew and Laugharne, where more comfortable accommodation was added to each in the sixteenth century, or transformed into a great country house, as happened at Chirk and Powis. If not altered or reconstructed, then the old castle might be replaced by an entirely new building, either on the same site, as at St Fagans about 1590, or nearby, as at Tretower in the fifteenth century and at Penrice in 1773. Rarely, if ever, did a castle remain the same and continue to be lived in. Not surprisingly, few castles continued in residential use through the centuries by the same family.

Two castles that were built after the thirteenth century offer a complete contrast with regard to size and style. At one end of the range is the lightly fortified castle at Weobly, dramatically sited near the end of the Gower peninsula. Built in two phases by the de la Bere family between 1304 and 1327, it stands solid and compact and appears generally well preserved, except on the south side. The initial phase had a U-shaped layout around a small, quadrangular courtyard with a stout, rectangular tower at the south-west corner and an octagonal tower at the south-east corner. To this was then added the west range incorporating a gatehouse with a simple, slightly pointed doorway and, at the north-west corner, another square tower. All the main rooms, including the hall, solar, guest chamber and chapel, were at first-floor level.

With the building of Raglan Castle, in Monmouthshire, the long era of castle-building in Wales can be said to have come to an end. Originally a Norman motte-and-bailey castle, it was entirely rebuilt on a grand scale during the mid-fifteenth century to withstand not arrows but cannon-fire. The main rebuilding was begun in the 1430s by William ap Thomas, and included a remarkable great tower known as the Yellow Tower from the colour of the stone used. Hexagonal in plan and originally five storeys high with six turrets, the tower was separated from the rest of castle by an encircling moat so that in the event of a siege it could be held independently.

But even these precautions were considered insufficient and further defences in the form of a walkway with an apron wall with gun-turrets was later added around the base of the tower. The remainder of the castle, comprising a large double-court building with sumptuous apartments on the perimeter and a great hall, parlour, chapel and long gallery in the central wing between the two courtyards, was largely built by William's son William Herbert, Earl of Pembroke, between 1460 and 1469. The main entrance to the castle was by way of a stoutly defended twin-towered gatehouse leading into one of the courts. (45) The main hall and long gallery were rebuilt during the mid-sixteenth century along with a brand-new north wing lying between the north and north-east towers. Eventually the life of this splendid castle-palace came to an end with the surrender of Raglan in 1646 after a two-month siege during the first Civil War. The great tower, which had survived almost unscathed the siege's gun-fire, was then partially destroyed by Cromwell's mines so that it would never again threaten the peace of Parliament.

By the middle of the fifteenth century, the gentry and owners of castles were generally more concerned with comfort and convenience than defence. Two castles can illustrate the change in attitudes. At Chirk Castle, Clwyd, the south curtain-wall of this rather forbidding-looking border castle was rebuilt during the fifteenth century to complete the circuit of walls and provide a chapel. A century or more later the remaining rooms behind the south curtain, including the Great Chamber on the first floor with mullioned windows instead of arrow-slit openings, were completed. At St Donat's Castle, Glamorgan, the whole of the inner court was rebuilt in the late fifteenth century, apart from some of the twelfth-century exterior walls. Amongst the new buildings was a Great Hall complete with a deeply projecting porch, screens passage and, at the dais end, a three-light window with panel tracery. The Great Hall has a high timber roof with three tiers of wind-braces and is decorated with Tudor roses ∎

04   Later Castles of the Middle Ages, c.1270 to 1535
References

1   *Brut y Tywysogyon*, p. 259.

2   N. Coldstream, 'Architects, Advisers and Design at Edward I's Castles in Wales', *Architectural History*, 46 (2003), 27.

3   Renn, *Caerphilly Castle*, p. 41.

4   Taylor, *King's Works in Wales*, p. 296.

5   Taylor, *King's Works in Wales*, p. 354

6   R. Davies (1991), *The Age of Conquest*, p. 355

7   Quoted by Davies, *The Age of Conquest*, p. 158.

8   Taylor, *King's Works in Wales*, p. vi.

9   Taylor, *King's Works in Wales*, pp. 1036–7.

10   R. Turner, 'The Life and Career of Richard the Engineer', in Williams and Kenyon, *The Impact of the Edwardian Castles in Wales*, p. 46.

11   J. Davies, *A History of Wales*, p. 170.

12   'The Dream of Macsen Wledig', in *The Mabinogion*, p. 71.

5

Romanesque Churches of the Middle Ages, c.1080 to c.1180

Although sections of the Welsh Church had recognized the papal authority of Rome in certain matters as far back as the eighth century, the Church had remained generally independent of the Anglo-Saxon Church in England. Given its history, it is not surprising that the Welsh Church was in many ways closer to the Celtic Churches of Ireland and Scotland in its organization. The Anglo-Normans, however, when they arrived during the latter part of the eleventh century, were determined to alter the situation. The *clas* or 'mother' churches, formerly the most characteristic institution of the pre-Norman Church in Wales, were gradually squeezed out of existence. A few were transformed into cathedrals or were taken over by the foreign monastic orders that arrived with the Normans; others became 'collegiate' churches or simple parish churches while the rest were suppressed and their possessions transferred to monasteries in England. Eventually the Anglo-Normans succeeded in obtaining the allegiance of the Welsh Church to Canterbury. Naturally this did not happen without strong opposition from the Welsh princes – who, understandably, preferred their spiritual welfare to be in the care of Welsh rather than foreign bishops – nor from some of the bishops themselves – who, for whatever reason, cherished their own independence.

The Anglo-Normans replaced the loose-knit organization of the native church with a continental pattern of hierarchical ecclesiastical government, firstly establishing four dioceses in Wales – three of which (St David's, Llandaf and Bangor) had already emerged as episcopal centres of prominence – and then subdividing these into parishes. The process was extremely slow, for much of the country was sparsely inhabited, and in the areas remaining under native rule (particularly in the north) large parts were still unregimented by the time of the Edwardian Conquest in the late thirteenth century.

Monastic Wales

Perhaps the most important influence on the shape and design of churches in Wales during the Middle Ages was the emergence of a new type of monastery based on French institutions that were organized and planned on entirely different lines from the Early Christian monasteries that had previously been such a feature of Welsh religious life but had now largely outlived their usefulness. The new monasteries followed the rules of the sixth-century monk, St Benedict, and were introduced here in the late eleventh century, soon after the dramatic arrival of the Anglo-Normans in the Gwent borderland. The first of the new French-style monasteries to be founded in Wales was the Benedictine priory at Chepstow, by 1071. This was followed before the end of the eleventh century by other Benedictine priories in the south-east, such as those at Abergavenny, Brecon and Monmouth, and in the west at Pembroke. **(46)** During the twelfth century, the Benedictines founded further priories at Ewenni, Kidwelly and Cardigan.

The Benedictines were followed by other religious communities in southern Wales. The Augustinians were first off the mark when, in about 1118, they adopted a tiny, existing monastery at Llanthony in the Black Mountains. Next came the Tironensians when they established an abbey at St Dogmaels (1120), followed much later by an abbey for the Premonstratensians at Talyllychau (Talley) in the late 1180s.

The Cistercians were a reformed order that had been founded in 1098 at the new monastery of Cîteaux, France. From Cîteaux daughter houses were founded in other parts of northern France, and from these further abbeys were established in the Marches, including Tintern (1131), Neath (1130), Basingwerk (1131) and Margam (1147). Although all the above were founded in the first half of the twelfth century, none, apart from Chepstow and Margam, have more than fragmentary Romanesque remains. In the Welsh heartland, in areas ruled by the native princes, a further and later group of Cistercian abbeys was founded. The first, founded in 1140 in Pembrokeshire, was a daughter house of Cîteaux itself. This was later resited at Hendy-gwyn (Whitland) in Carmarthenshire, and from there daughter houses were established at Ystrad Fflur (Strata Florida) in 1164, Strata Marcella (1170) and Cwm-hir (1176), and from these further daughter houses at Llantarnam, Cymer, Aberconwy and Valle Crucis. As a result of their close links with the princes, many of these abbeys became important centres of Welsh learning and literature.

The most important part of the monastic layout was of course the church, which, except in the smallest communities, was usually cruciform in plan with a number of small chapels attached to the transepts. The other buildings – such as the chapter house, sacristy, monks' dormitory and refectory – were generally arranged around a cloister, as at the Augustinian priory at Haverfordwest. **(47)** The cloister was an enclosed court facing an open area or *garth*, which was

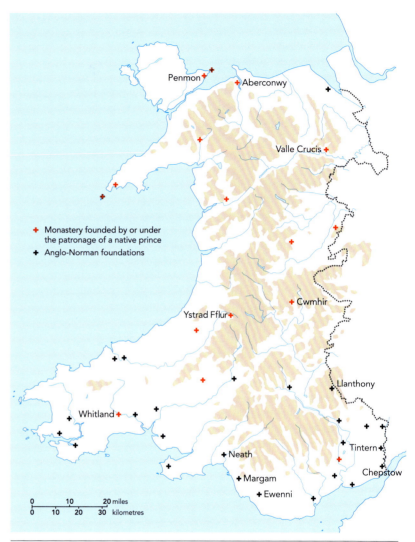

+ Monastery founded by or under the patronage of a native prince
+ Anglo-Norman foundations

46 The distribution of Monastic Houses in Wales.

83 Pembroke, aerial view of town and castle.

equal parts. The cross streets lie parallel to the probable course of the town wall and ditch and streets on the far side of these. At Newport, the town forms a long rectangle between two parallel streams with the estuary and 'old castle' (possibly an early medieval earthwork) at one end and the new masonry castle at the other. Between the two castles are two streets that lie parallel to each other and the two streams. Again, the main street begins just outside the new castle. Elsewhere the internal layout of streets appears to have been largely fortuitous and dependent on the topography of the site, so that no two new towns are alike. Thus the new boroughs have no standard layout pattern, and each is different. Nevertheless, in a number of cases there appears to have been a similar approach to town planning.

Over time a town's core would be redeveloped with newer buildings, although the medieval street layout survived more or less intact. Cowbridge and Llanidloes, for instance, were based on cruciform street plans with gateways at the centre of the wall on each side. In Cardiff, where the western boundary was formed by the line of a curving river, the main streets still retain their original T-shaped layout. Both Welshpool and Pembroke have linear plans, but whereas Welshpool's main street followed the river valley, Pembroke's is aligned along a ridge of high ground between parallel river valleys. (83) Brecon, Carmarthen, and Montgomery have irregular block plans within tightly restraining town walls. In Brecon it is the large parish church which dominates the town rather than the castle, which is on the opposite side of a narrow valley. Tenby, situated on a rocky promontory that juts out into the sea, has a vaguely gridded street layout confined between the sea and a severely rectilinear town wall.

Many of the early boroughs have lost their enclosing walls, either through decay and lack of maintenance or as a result of nineteenth-century expansion. Fortunately, the remains of town walls and their integral gateways can still be seen in former Marcher towns such as Chepstow, Cowbridge, Pembroke and Tenby. Monmouth still retains its fortified gatehouse astride a bridge, once a common feature of European towns and now the only one its kind in Britain.

the proportion was only 33 per cent, and in Scotland, where towns developed later, the proportion was only 5 per cent.[9] The form of layout noted above can be seen in the south-west at Kidwelly and Laugharne in Carmarthenshire and at Newport in Pembrokeshire, where in each case the castle is situated in a dominant position at one end of the town, looking down the main street and asserting its power and importance. In Kidwelly the half-circular castle is at a slight angle to the town causing the main street between the castle entrance and the town's west gate to cross the town at an angle to its other main street and the general mass of the town. In Laugharne the main street starts outside the castle's entrance and goes directly to the town's main gateway, thus dividing the urban area into two more or less

84 Monnow Bridge, Monmouth.

any remains above ground. In the Severn valley Llywelyn ap Gruffudd endeavoured to set up a new town and market in 1273 alongside his new castle at Dolforwyn, but because of its nearness to Montgomery and the threat it posed to the English borough's trade, its development was prevented by Edward I. Less than a decade later other boroughs were established across mid-Wales by the princes of Powys at Caersws, Llanidloes, Newtown and Machynlleth. Their regular street patterns indicate that the planning of these new towns had been strongly influenced by Norman precept. In the north, Llywelyn's *llysoedd* at Aberffro and Llan-faes, in Anglesey, appear to have attracted civil settlements around them, but the ending of Welsh rule in 1284 and the development of Edward I's new towns at Newborough and Beaumaris destroyed any future that these embryonic town might have had.

The outstanding examples of medieval town planning are undoubtedly some of the towns, mostly in the north, that were built by Edward I or under his auspices between 1277 and 1307. The towns were built in two waves: the first, including Aberystwyth, Flint and Rhuddlan, after the first war of independence in 1277; the second wave were all begun during or after the second war of independence: Holt in 1282, Caernarfon, Conwy and Harlech in 1283, Cricieth in 1224, Caerwys in 1290, Overton in 1292, Beaumaris in 1295 and Newborough in 1307. As Flint and Rhuddlan were the first of Edward's castle-towns in Wales, much has been made of the claim that 'it is natural to look for French and Gascon models; in 1277 it was only three years since he [Edward I] had been in Gascony.'[11] The Gascon models referred to are the *bastides*, or 'planted' towns that proliferated in south-western France between about 1250 and 1300.[12] Yet, as has been pointed out, 'the layouts of the new towns in north Wales do not share much in common with those of Gascony.'[13] Just as the *bastides* of Gascony varied considerably in both size and layout, so did the Edwardian towns in Wales. Whereas Cricieth and Harlech were both less than 3 ha in extent, Aberystwyth, Beaumaris and Flint were more than four times their size at almost 12 ha.[14] In most of the towns there appears to have been a clear attempt at a chequered, grid-like layout, while at Harlech and Newborough the layout was based on a straightforward

(84) The triple-arched, red sandstone Monnow Bridge dates from the late thirteenth century, and the tall gatehouse – with rounded ends and portcullis chamber above the main arch – was added, along with the town walls, between 1297 and 1315.[10] The neat, stone-tiled and hipped roof was added in the early eighteenth century.

Of the almost ninety medieval boroughs, comparatively few were of Welsh origin, and fewer still were destined to become fully fledged towns. Of those established by the Deheubarth princes besides the castles of Dinefwr and Dryslwyn in the Tywi valley, there are scarcely crossroads, and at Cricieth the main street simply follows the contours. Finally, eight of Edward's towns had castles, but only five had surrounding, fortified walls.

The earliest of Edward's new fortified towns – apart from Holt, which was the work of a Marcher lord – were each built, along with their supporting castles, during a time when the English builders must have been constantly alert to the danger of Welsh insurrection. Each town was surrounded by sturdy defensive walls with strong gatehouses and, in the case of Caernarfon and Conwy, projecting round wall-towers as well. Internally, the layout of each was based on a gridded system of straight streets and rectilinear blocks (chequers) of burgage plots. English exiles, particularly craftsmen, were encouraged to settle in the towns by the grant of a plot within the encircling town walls and farming land outside, along with other economic and social privileges; the Welsh were specifically excluded, for the whole point of the settlements

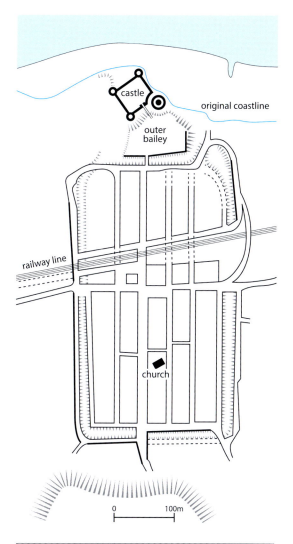

85   Flint. Plan of the Edwardian new town of 1277 with 19th-century additions.

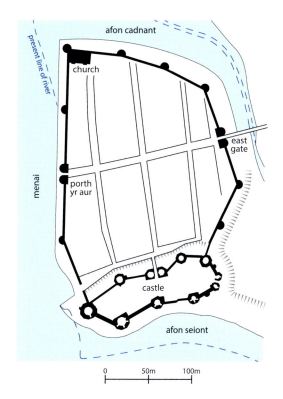

86   Caernarfon. Plan of the Edwardian new town of 1283.

were to secure English dominion over the Welsh nation.

Of the five towns, Flint most resembled the ideal layout, its severely oblong shape contained within a rectangle of walls and ditches and divided lengthways by four straight roads – one of which led to the castle at the sea end of the town – and crossed by a single street near the half-way point. (85) There was an open market square at the junction of the main street and the cross street, and a church further along the main street. The layouts of Aberystwyth and Rhuddlan were constrained by their positions, the former being almost circular on a headland formed by the Rheidol estuary and the sea, while the latter was a triangle alongside the canalized Clwyd. At both Caernarfon and Conwy, each begun in 1283, the castle and town are more closely linked and integrated. (86) Caernarfon was laid out on a level promontory between two rivers with its castle defending the neck of the isthmus. Here the chequerboard street pattern and the complete length of town walls have survived to this day, along with the new church tucked into a corner of the town walls. (87) Conwy is on a hilly site and, like Caernarfon, close to the sea. The town's outline is more irregular, but within the walls an attempt was made to maintain a gridiron layout. Altogether the walls have twenty-seven wall-towers spaced at 50-m intervals and three twin-towered gateways. The walls and towers of Conwy are, if anything, even more complete and threatening than those of Caernarfon. (88) They are surprisingly unmodified by later additions or alterations, and perhaps the most perfect surviving example in Britain – a kind of Welsh Avila or Carcassonne!

Despite the surviving perfection of these two Edwardian towns, they are no longer, as Thomas Pennant once wrote, 'the badge of our subjection', for ironically Edward I's policy of conserving their English character failed. Caernarfon, for instance, is today one of the strongholds of Welsh culture and it is Welsh rather than English that is heard and spoken in its streets (particularly when the tourists have gone home). The Edwardian settlers became assimilated within the Welsh community and in a few generations became Welsh themselves. The East Gate and the West Gate became Porth Mawr and Porth-yr-Aur respectively, and the Eagle Tower at the royal castle became Tŵr-yr-Eryr! ∎

87 Caernarfon, aerial view of town and castle.

88 Conwy, the Edwardian town walls.

07 Other Secular Architecture and Towns, 1200 to 1535
References

1   R. Avent, *Castles of the Princes*, p. 6.

2   D. Longley, 'The Royal Courts of the Welsh Princes in Gwynedd', p. 53; N. Johnstone, 'The Locations of the Royal Courts of Thirteenth-Century Gwynedd', p. 61, both in N. Edwards (1997).

3   N. Johnstone, 'Location of the Royal Courts of Thirteenth-Century Gwynedd', in Edwards (1997), p. 65.

4   N. Johnstone, 'Cae Llys, Rhosyr: A Court of the Princes of Gwynedd', *Studia Celtica*, 33 (1999), 255, fig. 2.

5   M. Wood, *The English Mediaeval House*, pp. 36–7.

6   Quoted by John H. James in *Cathedral Church, Llandaff*, p. 8.

7   I. Soulsby (1983), *Towns of Medieval Wales*, pp. 16–17.

8   M. Beresford (1967), *New Towns of the Middle Ages*, p. 199.

9   O. Creighton and R. Higham, *Medieval Town Walls*, p. 218.

10 M. L. J. Rowlands, 'Monnow Bridge and Gate, Monmouth', p. 265.

11 Beresford, *New Towns*, p. 40.

12 Beresford, *New Towns*, pp. 357–66.

13 K. Lilley, 'Landscapes of Edward's New Towns' (2010), p. 109.

14 Lilley, 'Landscapes of Edward's New Towns', p. 106.

8

Tudor and Renaissance Architecture, 1536 to 1700

For much of the Middle Ages the Welsh architectural scene had been dominated by castles and monasteries. Eventually castle building had given way to the construction of new churches and the extension of older ones. By the end of the fifteenth century the spate of church building was also largely over. Now too, in the sixteenth century, came the demise of the monasteries, and for the next three centuries the dominant form of building was to be domestic in character. The change of emphasis from military fortifications and churches to domestic buildings coincided with the

development of generally more settled conditions. Castles had outlived their purpose and a slowly growing affluence enabled more attention to be paid to house building.

When the partly Welsh Henry Tudor (great-great grandson of Tudur ab Ednyfed, and grandson of Owain Tudur of Penmynydd) landed in Pembrokeshire in 1485 on his way to capture the English throne, he had needed to rely on the help of Welsh landowners during his long march to Shrewsbury. For this 'and their services at Bosworth Field' he was appreciative.[1] Afterwards there seems to have been some decrease in the oppressive feudal power of Marcher lords. The so-called 'Acts of Union' of 1536 and 1542, in which the Principality of Wales was united with the kingdom of England, took further steps forward in this respect by ending the harsher penal laws inflicted upon the Welsh and by abolishing the Lordships of the March. Welshmen were now accorded 'equal rights' (other than in the spheres of culture and language) with the citizens of England, including the right to vote and send members to the English Parliament. On the downside, the incorporation of Wales within a much larger state prevented the possibility of her developing any further a national culture based on her own administrative, ecclesiastical and educational institutions, such as no doubt would have evolved if Glyndŵr's bid for independence had been successful. Nevertheless, the result was an improvement in trade and greater opportunities than had hitherto been the case for individual Welshmen – particularly the Welsh gentry – to make their fortunes, accumulate more property (especially after the dissolution of the monasteries in 1536) and build bigger and better houses for themselves.

The total population of Wales in the middle of the sixteenth century was probably not more than 300,000 inhabitants, but on the increase. Agriculture, in the form of sheep and cattle rearing, was still the main source of livelihood, and the country was, by the standards of the day, relatively prosperous. Wool was highly priced and exported to England in great quantities. The cattle drovers were important members of the community, and helped in the spreading of new ideas and fashions. Evidence of the long journeys travelled by Welsh drovers can be seen in distant Hampshire, where a painted inscription on the side of an inn still offers 'Gwair tymerus, porfa flasus, Cwrw da a Gwal cysurus' ('Seasoned hay, tasty pasture, good beer and comfortable bed').

As a result of the breakdown of the manorial system in the Marches, along with the decay of the old native system of land ownership, some individuals were able to acquire large estates. Others enriched themselves through trading activities in the towns. In this way, a new class of squires and merchants emerged which was to dominate Welsh life until the nineteenth century. The changes were reflected in Welsh architecture by an intense period of house building (known as 'the Great Rebuilding'), which, though later than in much of England, seemed, according to Peter Smith, 'to have crossed the country like a wave beginning early in the east and arriving later in the west ... passing from a seventeenth century to a nineteenth century landscape'.[2] The greatest concentration of building in the seventeenth century was along the eastern borderland areas, and slightly later in Glamorgan, where it is estimated that the 'Great Rebuilding' took place between 1680 and 1730, almost a century later than in the English Midlands.[3] This did not mean, however, that no important houses were erected before these dates; it was just that there were fewer.

During this time older substandard houses were either deliberately demolished and rebuilt or were altered and enlarged by adding another floor, or extended with an extra wing. Fireplaces with chimneys replaced open hearths, and, as in other parts of Britain, glass was used extensively for the first time in windows. By the end of the seventeenth century, improvements in communications enabled the gentry to travel further and more quickly than before. Their greater mobility allowed them to become acquainted with new ideas and new fashions in architecture. At the same time, professional architects working with drawing boards and pattern books began to replace the old master craftsman working with his hammer and chisel.

Tudor Houses

The architecture of the Tudor period was transitional in style between the indigenous manner of the late medieval period and the gradual introduction of foreign ideas based ultimately on the Italian Renaissance. It was part of the transition from military and ecclesiastical buildings to the more sedate compositions of classically inspired country mansions. The process was protracted, and for a long time was little more than a continuation of late Gothic methods of building, in which large windows, gabled roofs and an overall emphasis on the vertical became prominent features. Security remained an important factor throughout the sixteenth century and gatehouses were added to many of the larger houses as an extra line of defence, or just to impress. These included three-storey gatehouses at Pencoed Castle and St Pierre in Monmouthshire (both early to mid-sixteenth century). Other early gatehouses were built at Gwydir Castle in the Conwy valley and at Oxwich Castle on the Gower peninsula. Gatehouses were still being added to houses such as Old Beaupre, Glamorgan, and Plas Mawr, Conwy, later in the same century, and well into the seventeenth century in Gwynedd, at Cefnamlwch (1607) and Cors-y-gedol (1630), the latter a rugged but pleasing design with a three-storey, cross-gabled clock-tower rising from short wings with dormers.

The hall was still retained as the main living space in large houses, but more often than not this was now on the first floor, as at Llancaiach-fawr, Gelli-gaer, a tall, three-storey house on the edge of the Glamorgan uplands. It was built by the ap Richard (Prichard) family, descendants of the lords of Senghenydd, during the early sixteenth century. The walls of the house and its two-storey entrance porch are battered at ground-floor level and apart from a few large, mullioned windows on the first floor, the building has a severe, unsophisticated look. The ground floor rooms were all used for service or storage, the main living area being on the first floor, where there is a large hall and parlour, with back-to-back fireplaces, and a bedchamber. Although there is no sign that there was ever a gatehouse, the house itself was designed for defence, with drawbar sockets to doors

89 Bach-y-graig, Tremeirchion, Denbighshire, drawing from *Houses in the Welsh Countryside* based on painting by Moses Griffiths, 1786.

90 Plas Clough, Henllan, Denbighshire, the main elevation based on drawing by Moses Griffiths, 1770.

and numerous mural stairs allowing alternative means of escape in the event of a surprise attack. Llanwenarth House, Govilon, in the middle Usk valley, is a similar but smaller three-storey house. It was built a few years later for the Morgan family, and has a number of four-light, mullioned windows as well as upper-cruck roof trusses.

Further west, at Neath Abbey, the need for ostentation as well as privacy was ingeniously met by adapting the old Abbot's Lodging (which had earlier been adapted from the former Monks' Dormitory and Undercroft) to form a new two-storey mansion with an attic floor. The result was an unusual layout, with a spacious first-floor hall (above the old undercroft) connected at right angles to what appears to have been a long gallery, 25 m long by 6 m wide, spanning the space between two undercrofts. Both the hall and long gallery were lit by large mullioned windows, one of which was a wide bay window. A new three-storey building with a symmetrical front was added at the north-east corner of the complex, facing the original approach. Though now much ruined, the corner building was clearly meant to impress, and this, together with some imaginative planning of the main part of the house, suggests that no ordinary builder was responsible for its design, but rather a professional skilled in such matters.

Although many large houses were being built or extended during the middle decades of the sixteenth century, there seems to have been little awareness of what was going on outside Wales. There was, however, one remarakable exception to the general run of things in Bach-y-graig, a house built for Sir Richard Clough (d. 1570), where new architectural ideas based on continental designs first made their appearance in Wales. Clough, the son of a Denbigh glover, had settled in Antwerp in 1552 as a merchant and agent to Sir Thomas Gresham. When in 1567 Clough returned to Wales, he married Katheryn of Berain – known as *Mam Cymru* (the Mother of Wales), following her four marriages and numerous descendants – and began building two houses, Bach-y-graig, near Tremeirchion, and Plas Clough, near Denbigh, both in 1567. Clough, as Gresham's agent, had supplied building materials from

Holland for the Royal Exchange, the construction of which had been supervised by Hendrik van Passe, 'who may also have designed Bach-y-graig.'[4] Aptly described as a Flemish château, the house occupied one side of a courtyard and was unusual in being square on plan with a tall first floor above a semi-basement, all covered by a pyramidal roof with two tiers of dormer windows, very tall chimneys and (at the apex) a single square room under a cupola. **(89)** Except for a much altered gatehouse (with a central tower and side wings, each formerly surmounted by pyramidal roofs) and stables, nothing of the complex has survived.

Plas Clough, the second of Clough's houses, was apparently built at the same time as Bach-y-graig and was also constructed in brick (but now covered in plaster). Though less remarkable than Bach-y-graig, it was also influenced by Dutch architecture in that it had a symmetrical layout with a central, storeyed porch and, intriguingly, crow-stepped gables on the front facade, entrance porch and projecting rear wings. **(90)** Crow-stepped gables had been commonly used in Dutch buildings in and around Antwerp, but seem to have been unknown in Wales before their introduction at Plas Clough. Bach-y-graig and Plas Clough were probably the first houses in Wales to be constructed in brick – reputedly with materials and craftsmen specially imported from Holland – although brick houses had been relatively common in the eastern counties of England for a century or more. **(91)**

Clough's houses had some limited influence on subsequent houses, especially in the north. The Middleton Arms at Ruthin, for instance, was built in the same year as Bach-y-graig and traditionally associated with Clough, possibly because of its high Flemish roof with its three tiers of dormers. Other square houses, reminiscent of Bach-y-graig, but with central fireplaces and considerably later, are Cemaes Bychan (1632), near Machynlleth, Trimley Hall (1653), Flintshire, and Edwinsford (c.1635), near Talley. Following the success of Plas Clough, crow-stepped gables soon became a popular feature of other large houses in the north, such as Plas Mawr (1576), Conwy, Golden Grove (1578), near Prestatyn, and Bodelwyddan (1597),

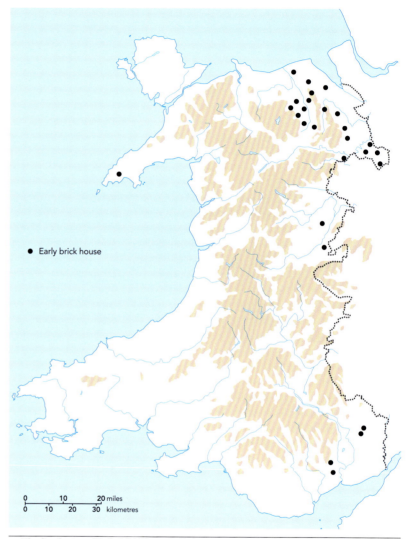

● Early brick house

0   10   20 miles
0   10   20   30 kilometres

91 The distribution of Early Brick Houses in Wales.

92 Oxwich Castle, Gower, bird's-eye-view drawing by John Banbury.

near Rhuddlan. The fashion for decorative stepped gables eventually spread west to Anglesey and the Llŷn peninsula, and south-west to Meirionydd, but apparently never any further south.

Returning to the south, the next house of importance is Oxwich Castle, on the Gower peninsula, which began (between 1520 and 1538) as a two-storey house with adjacent mock-military gateway, and probably replaced a medieval castle of which only a fragmentary tower now remains. A generation later a vast, four- to five-storey block was built at right angles to the original house, from about 1560 onwards. (92) A straight, vertical joint between the two buildings might suggest that it was intended to demolish the earlier block once the new block had been completed, although this in fact never happened. The new block fronts onto a large, sloping courtyard bounded by the earlier house and two curtain-walls, one of which is a modern replacement. The new wing, now roofless and ruined, was E-shaped in plan with two bold, projecting towers at the rear forming the outer wings. The ground floor comprised stone-vaulted undercrofts, above which were the main rooms. The foundations of a two-storey porch with a blocked opening above indicate the former first-floor entrance to the imposing, double-height hall, which was lit by two massive windows high above the ground, one of eighteen lights and the other (now blocked) of twenty-four. Above the hall there would have been a majestic, full-length long gallery, approximately 33 m long by 7 m wide, lit by four large windows on the long wall with larger windows at either end. The long wall, facing the courtyard, was probably finished with gables above the windows in the manner of the day.

On a smaller scale, St Fagans Castle, now the home of the National Museum of History, was erected in 1580 within the stout curtain-walls of a medieval castle, The internal layout of the three-storey mansion, still followed the hall-house tradition with the hall (and withdrawing room beyond) on one side of a central cross-passage and the buttery and kitchen on the other side. Care, however, was taken to ensure that these were arranged symmetrically with projecting wings and a central, storeyed porch to form a letter E on plan. (93) The resulting main facade is reminiscent of Oxwich Castle, with large windows (on both ground and first floors) and multiple gables above, but here more regulated and, at the same, time more domestic in appearance (94)

It was during the last decades of the sixteenth century that a number of large houses were partly reconstructed, as at The Van (c.1580s), Glamorgan, or extended, as at Llanfihangel Court (c.1600), Monmouthshire, and in the process the fashion spread for multiple gables, often enclosing dormer windows. Interestingly, the same kind of thing had already been done at Trevalyn Hall (1576), Denbighshire, which, like St Fagans Castle, was all of one build, but with more awareness of Renaissance ideals. It was built in brick (later rendered apart from quoins) to an H-plan and a strictly symmetrical design, with a central, storeyed porch, multiple gables with finials and a multitude of tall chimneys. But whereas St Fagans Castle had plain door and window heads, the windows and entrance doorway at Trevalyn Hall were all crowned with triangular pediments.

One of the most interesting houses in Wales is Plas Mawr, Conwy, which was built for Robert Wynn of Gwydir between 1576 and 1585. Robert Wynn was the third son of John Wyn ap Maredudd, the builder of Gwydir Castle, and was probably familiar with the architecture of Bach-y-graig through his sister-in-law Katherryn of Berain, who had married his elder brother Morus by 1573 after Sir Richard Clough's death. The house and its gatehouse are on a sloping site and were built in phases as land was acquired piecemeal. Construction began with the north wing on the uppermost part of the site; a few years later an existing mansion to the south was demolished, and the central part and south wing were built; finally the gatehouse was built at the lowest end. **(95)** Despite the extended period of construction both the H-plan house and the gatehouse have a unified character, although there are variations in detail. Externally both have rubble-stone walls, wide mullioned windows capped by 'classical' stone pediments, and elaborate crow-stepped gables to the roofs. **(96)** The overall appearance is very rich, yet uncertain in style, as though trying to prove itself to be *avant-garde* Renaissance. Indeed, Plas Mawr reflects an architecture in trauma – the 'classically' transitional house. At the same time, it exudes the pride of the Wynns in their noble ancestry, being directly descended from Owain, king of Gwynedd, and their pride also in the Tudor inheritance of the British throne. Inside, a central cross-passage leads through to an open, cobbled court at the rear. On either side of the passage are the kitchen and pantry, and beyond these a parlour in the north wing and a large hall in the south wing with wide windows overlooking the lower courtyard. Hidden away at the rear of the central part are two spiral staircases, medieval in feeling, one of which leads to a watch-tower. Above the central part, on the first floor is the Great Chamber, the most richly decorated and furnished part of the house, complete with an elaborate 'Italian' fireplace and boldly decorated plaster ceiling. **(97)** Other rooms, such as

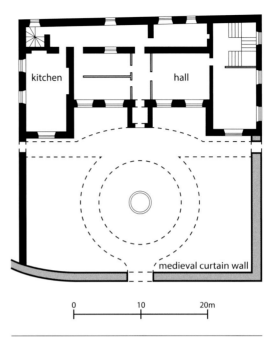

93 St Fagans Castle, Cardiff.

94 St Fagans Castle, Cardiff, entrance front.

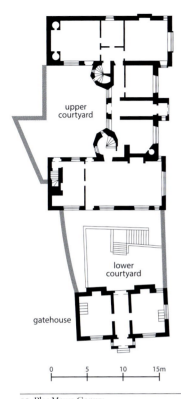

95 Plas Mawr, Conwy.

97 Plas Mawr, Conwy, Great Chamber showing fireplace and ceiling decoration.

98 Powys Castle, Montgomery, the Long Gallery.

96 Plas Mawr, Conwy, the gatehouse.

the hall, also have fine fireplaces and decorative ceilings.

The Tudor period heralded the beginning of formal planning, when comfort was of more concern than defence and dignified appearance was often considered even more important than comfort. Inside the emphasis was on greater comfort and privacy. Flat ceilings, panelled or plaster-covered with decorative patterns, as at Plas Mawr, replaced open roofs. The hall became a dining room and other rooms were added to cater for new amenities. Most of the rooms were panelled in wood, and handsome fireplaces were installed. In many of the larger houses, a long gallery, reached by an impressive oak staircase, was built over the hall to serve as a passage to upper rooms and as an area to display paintings and decorations. Powis Castle, Welshpool, for instance, was gradually transformed from the fourteenth century into a grand country house, and by 1592 had acquired a superbly decorated Long Gallery with tall windows overlooking the inner court. (98) In Pembrokeshire, Carew Castle had been similarly transformed, this time by Sir John Perrot between 1588 and 1592, with the addition of a major new three-storey wing with a bull-nosed end that overlooked the river. The two upper floors, of which the topmost was a 45 m Long Gallery, had ten bays of high, transom and mullioned windows (each of twelve lights), including two semicircular projections. Apparently never quite finished – although some windows had been glazed – it was nevertheless a brave and confident attempt to raise the level of architecture in Wales, much as had been done by Robert Smythson at Longleat and Wollaton Hall in England.

Renaissance and Baroque Houses

Almost the first intimation of Renaissance ideas in Wales is to be found at Trevalyn Hall, Denbighshire, a brick-built house (later rendered) of 1576 with stone pediments above the windows and a strong feeling for symmetry. A decade later Old Beaupre, Glamorgan, was enlarged by adding an outer court with a castellated wall-walk, entered through a large three-storey gatehouse with a mixture of late medieval windows and early Renaissance surrounds to its archway. (99)

As though this lavishness were not enough, an extraordinary porch designed in the 'Italian' manner with three tiers of superimposed columns of different orders was added to the house's main front as a showpiece in 1600. **(100)** Although the first 'swallows' of the Renaissance summer had arrived, there were comparatively few followers.

In fact, Wales has a disappointing number of good seventeenth-century Renaissance houses. Many of those that were built have been either destroyed or altered to a degree that makes it impossible to get a clear impression of what they looked like when first built. One of the reasons for the poor representation, however, stems from the inevitable sinking of national fortunes following the temporary euphoria of the Tudors and the death of Elizabeth, last of the dynasty. Losing the pace-setters of patronage, Wales started to decline architecturally for, as Dr Peate pointed out in *The Welsh House*, 'a nation bereft of its sovereignty cannot promote the growth of fine arts except by indirect and generally innocuous means.'[5] Typical of the *boneddigion* who became estranged from their Welsh background were the Cecils and the Herberts. William Cecil, famous descendent of the Sitsyllt (Seisyll) family, became Elizabeth's chief secretary of state and harped with pride on his Welsh ancestry, and corresponded with Morys Clynnog in Welsh; but the great houses of the family, Burghley and Hatfield, were built in England. Similarly, the Herberts of Raglan Castle as Earls of Pembroke became completely anglicized and moved to Wiltshire, where they commissioned Inigo Jones to design one of his best houses, Wilton.

Multiple-gable elevations continued to be used for houses of the gentry and lesser gentry well into the seventeenth century irrespective of layout, whether an E-plan, as at Old Gwernyfed (1600-13), Breconshire; a centralized plan as at Moynes Court (built for the bishop of Llandaf in 1609) and Treowen (1625), both Monmouthshire; a T-plan as at Nottage Court (early seventeenth century), Glamorgan; H-plan, as at Plas-yn-y-pentre (1634, half-timber), Denbighshire; or an L-plan as at Henblas (1645), Flintshire. The multiple gables at Rhual (1634) and Nerquis Hall (1637), both in Flintshire, feature windows with stepped lights.

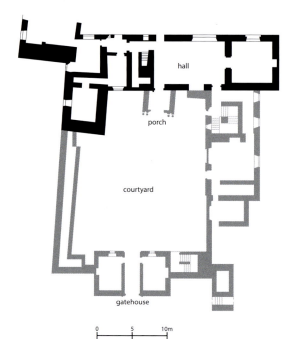

99 Old Beaupre, Vale of Glamorgan. The original house (c.1300) is shown black; additions (c.1540–1600), are shown grey.

100 Old Beaupre, Vale of Glamorgan, Renaissance Porch, 1600.

The most unusual collection of multiple gables can be seen on the main front of Plas Teg, Flintshire. Here, the overall severity of the building is relieved by three whimsical Dutch gables (rebuilt when the top floor was heightened during the eighteenth or nineteenth century). It is the first major house to be built in Wales that followed Renaissance ideals in centralized planning and emulation of the past. It is an impressive three-storey building that echoes the plan of Smythson's Wollaton Hall, Nottinghamshire (which in turn seems to have been based on Sebastiano Serlio's recording of the Poggio Reale, Naples, in his *Treatise of Architecture*, *Book III* (1540) and the corner turrets of Francisco de Mora's Ducal Palace of Lerma, Spain, which was being built at much the same time (c.1601–17) as PlasTeg.[7] The house, completed in 1610, has a compact, squarish central block with square towers and ogee cupolas topped by lanterns at each corner, presenting a castle-like appearance. **(101)** Inside,

the great hall runs from a recessed entrance right through to the back, and at the side an elaborate staircase leads to the great chamber above the great hall.

Ruperra Castle, Glamorgan, has a similar square plan to Plas Teg but with circular, castellated towers – presumably meant to evoke an ancestral castle – at each corner. **(102)** Built in 1626, it is closely related to Lulworth Castle (c.1608) in southern England in appearance. The elevations have a mixture of two-light and curious three-light windows, the latter with the centre lights taller than the rest. Ruperra Castle was built with an attic floor and dormer gables, as at St Fagans Castle, but these were replaced by a castellated parapet after a fire destroyed the originals in 1785. A projecting, two-storey entrance porch follows the tradition of Old Beaupre in its mixture of late Gothic and early Renaissance. The entrance leads directly into the great hall as at Plas Teg, but the hall itself is located in the south-east

101 Plas Teg, Denbighshire.

102 Ruperra Castle, Rudry, Glamorgan, aerial view.

corner of the house instead of at the centre. The interior was built in brick, the earliest large-scale use of brick in southern Wales. Following a fire in December 1941 that gutted the building, Ruperra Castle has been allowed to fall into ruins and one of the corner towers has collapsed, leaving a sad shell of a building.

There are few gentry houses of interest from the middle years of the seventeenth century. Three of the more attractive are in Flintshire. Rhual, near Mold, was built in brick (now unfortunately rendered) in 1634, as a double-pile house. The main front is in five bays, with slightly projecting outer bays, all beneath three coped gables (with stepped windows) that look somewhat heavy given the precise verticality of the windows on the ground and first floors. Nerquis Hall, also near Mold, was built 1637–8 to a traditional H-plan with bays (and also gables) of different widths and massive slablike chimneys at either end. It was designed, according to an early contract document, by Evan Joins, a carpenter in the capacity of master builder.[7] Henblas, Llanasa, dated 1645, has a slightly asymmetric three-bay, multi-gabled main front faced in ashlared limestone (possibly added in the eighteenth century) that gives it a distinguished appearance. The projecting centre bay has decorative panels between the doorway and a cantilevered oriel. There is a long gallery on the top floor.

By the later decades of the seventeenth century houses of distinction were also being erected in the south-east. Pride of place for fine proportions and urbanity must go to the Great Castle House, built for the first Duke of Beaufort in 1673 as a free-standing building within the grounds of Monmouth Castle. Additional blocks were added c.1900 on either side. The dignified main facade is faced in pink ashlar (probably reused from the castle) and has three storeys (marked by heavy string courses) over a semi-basement, and is divided into three bays and covered by a steep hipped roof with curving eaves and dormer windows. **(103)** The central bay, which is recessed, contains a two-storey feature incorporating superimposed classical pilasters around the doorway and window. Internally, the planning reflects Renaissance formality, with a very large entrance hall

103 Great House, Monmouth.

occupying a central position. The rooms themselves are of particular interest, with excellent woodwork and elaborately decorated plaster ceilings. More sober in appearance, Troy House, another house built for the first Duke of Beaufort – barely three kilometres (two miles) from Monmouth Castle House – in the same county, feels austere and bleak in comparison. Built in 1681–4, it is thirteen bays long by three bays wide and comprises three tall storeys with a hipped roof (with attic dormers) and a five-bay-wide pediment in the centre. The main entrance is on the first floor and approached by a double flight of steps.

Erddig, near Wrexham, was, if anything, even plainer than Troy House. The original house, built between 1683 and c.1687 to the designs of Thomas Webb of Middlewich, Cheshire, comprised a nine-bay, three-storey warm-red brick structure with regimented lines of windows, the tallest on the first floor, a continuous parapet and a hipped roof. The house's appearance was drastically changed in the

104   Tredegar House, Newport.

eighteenth century, when Mellor, the new owner, added wings at either end, each of five bays, giving a total length of nineteen bays. On the garden side the extensions are marked by two slightly projecting bays and three bays with a mixture of round-headed and square-headed windows. Even more drastic alterations were made in 1721–4 to the entrance front, when it was clad in ashlared stone and a three-bay pediment added to the designs of James Wyatt. The Doric doorway and the curving double flight of steps up to the entrance may also be from this date.

Already, however with the building of Tredegar House, near Newport, in the early 1670s, gentry houses had moved to a development of Renaissance architecture into something more decorative and showy – in other words the Baroque style. The house was largely a rebuilding by Sir William Morgan of two sides of a courtyard house that belonged to an earlier, mid-sixteenth-century, Tudor house. The master builder appears to have been either Roger or

William Hurlbutt, of Warwickshire.[8] Each of the new two-storey wings has been built in warm red brick with Bath stone dressings, and has slightly projecting corner pavilions. **(104)** An attic floor with dormer windows under curved roofs is contained within a fairly low hipped roof. Superimposed on each front are floridly designed central porches with twisted columns, lavishly decorated pediments and apron swags to the windows. Inside, the entrance hall is comparatively plain, but this leads to a splendidly carved staircase and a series of stately rooms that still retain most of their original decoration. The Gilt Room was lavishly decorated at the end of the seventeenth century with carvings, paintings and sculptures copied from continental examples, while the Brown Room with its elaborate carved wall panelling was probably decorated in the early years of the eighteenth century. A large stable block, also in red brick and lavishly ornamented, was built at right angles to the house at the same time.

Town Houses

The towns in Tudor times, though still small, were relatively prosperous. Most of them still retained their protective walls intact. The largest town was probably Denbigh with a population of about 3,000; few other towns had much more than 1,000 people. Within the town walls most houses were detached, and many stood in their own grounds. Altogether twenty-nine (possibly thirty-two) towns in Wales are known to have had half-timbered buildings.[9] Most of the half-timbered towns lay east of the main north/south watershed line, with only Bangor, Beaumaris, Caernarfon, Conwy, Dolgellau, and possibly Machynlleth to the west.

Tudor and Renaissance town houses are few and far between, whether built of timber or stone, as most have disappeared in successive rebuildings over the centuries. Ruthin, Denbighshire, has a number of timber-framed buildings surviving from the fifteenth to the seventeenth century (mostly altered later), of which Nantclwyd House, with its attractive, jettied porch, stands out as the most interesting.

In the south, the Murenger House, High Street, Newport, is the most rewarding. Probably dating from the early seventeenth century, and now used as a restaurant, it occupies a narrow plot, so that its gable end, with two upper storeys oversailing each other, faces the street. The first-floor room has contemporary decorated plastered ceiling. Monmouth, in addition to Great Castle House, has Agincourt House, Agincourt Square, an early-seventeenth century half-timbered building with a two-storey oriel window. Abergavenny has a single early town house, the Gunter Mansion, Cross Street, from the seventeenth century, barely distinguishable as such from the street, but more obviously so from the rear.

The ruins of Cardiff's last remaining Tudor mansion, the Herbert House, Greyfriars Road, were needlessly demolished in 1967 to make way for offices. Built in 1582, probably with stones from the old friary, the remains of the Herbert House included most of the south front wall with two deeply projecting, three-storey polygonal windows. A sketch by John Speed in 1610 shows what looks like a quadrangular building surrounding a court, with a tower on the west side,

105 Gwydr Uchaf Chapel, Llanrwst, decorated ceiling.

suggesting that the house may have incorporated parts of the friary's domestic buildings.

Religious Buildings

Few religious buildings of any kind survive from the period. After the dissolution of the monasteries (1536–40), there was less need for new churches, and it was not until the nineteenth century that there was much church building. Apart from rebuilding and repairs, most new religious building was confined to private chapels for the landed gentry, either as additions to existing parish churches or as free-standing chapels on their estates. The one important exception was Leicester's Church, an ambitious project in the outer ward of Denbigh Castle. It was begun by Robert Dudley, Earl of Leicester, in 1578, possibly as a replacement for St Asaph Cathedral, and would have been 'the only large new church in Britain'.[10] The new church, measuring 52 m by 22 m – slightly shorter but wider than the cathedral at St Asaph – was a ten-bay rectangle with alternating single and double columns separating the aisles from the nave and chancel. As it happened, work was abandoned in 1584 and never resumed. How far the church was completed is unclear, for John Speed's plan of 1610 shows it with a roof. However, by 1750 the church was roofless and partially ruined. What remains standing today are the windowless north and east walls and the foundations of the remaining walls.

A number of private chapels were built, particularly in the north, the earliest of which seems to been on the Vaynol estate at Felinheli, built in 1596. The most interesting architecturally are the private chapels at Rug (1637), near Corwen, and Gwydir Uchaf (1673), near Llanrwst. The Rug chapel is a simple rectangular building with a bellcote and debased Gothic windows (later replaced). The interior feels sumptuous with fine hammerbeam roof trusses carved with angels and decorated panels, a balustraded and painted gallery, wall paintings and profusely carved benches. **(105)**

The Gwydir Uchaf chapel is slightly smaller and was built for the Wynns of Gwydir Castle. It has a four-light Perpendicular window on the east wall, and a round-headed doorway on the north wall. The main points of interest inside are the painted gallery and the boarded ceiling, wonderfully painted in naive style inspired by the Italian Baroque.

The first appearance of Nonconformism in Wales is generally associated with the historic meeting held at Llanfaches, Monmouthshire, in 1639, when William Wroth organized his followers into a 'gathered' church. Yet even before this there seems to have been a *tŷ-cwrdd* (meeting place) converted from a barn at Blaencannaid, near Merthyr Tydfil. With the support of the Commonwealth Parliament, the Nonconformist movement continued to grow slowly, mainly in the early industrial centres of the south. In 1649 the first Baptist chapel was established at Ilston in the Gower peninsula. After the Restoration of the monarchy in 1660 the movement suffered something of a decline until the passing of the Toleration Act in 1689. Nevertheless, at the time of the Religious Census held in 1669 the Merthyr Tydfil

106 Maesyronnen Chapel, Glasbury, Radnorshire.

107 Maesyronnen Chapel, Glasbury, Radnorshire, interior.

district was estimated to have between 300 and 600 people attending secret conventicles. By the end of the seventeenth century a few other chapels had been established in different parts of Wales. Two of these still survive. The Baptist chapel at Govilon, Monmouthshire, was built in 1695, but enlarged during the eighteenth century and remodelled in the nineteenth. In mid-Powys the Independents erected a meeting-house at Maesyronnen, Glasbury, near Hay-on-Wye, in 1696/7. This was a new building that replaced the byre of a cruck-framed long-house. Despite its simplicity, the striving after symmetry and formality (and perhaps approval) can be detected in the main elevation – three tall windows centrally placed between two doorways, one of which was pedimented – heralding the shape of things to come in later chapels. (106) Astonishingly, Capel Maesyronnen has survived intact complete with its original furniture, and remains the oldest unaltered Nonconformist meeting place still in use in Wales. (107)

Educational Buildings

Educational buildings that have survived from the period are rare, although for much of the time there was considerable activity in founding and endowing new schools. Although several grammar schools were founded during the sixteenth century few of these were purpose-built. Usually they shared or occupied church buildings such as former Dominican friaries at both Bangor (Friars) and Brecon (Christ College). The grammar school at Ruthin was unusual in being a purpose-built school that has survived, albeit following considerable alterations in the seventeenth and nineteenth centuries. Refounded in 1574, it was built in rough limestone with sandstone dressings as a two-storey block with tall, mullioned windows – those on the upper floor as half-dormers. The ground floor was used as the schoolroom and the upper floor as sleeping areas for the master and boarders.

There was a marked increase in educational activity during the seventeenth century, when thirty-eight schools are known to have been endowed, mostly in the market towns, so that by the end of the century there was at least one new school in each of the old counties. Twenty of these schools were non-classical or elementary schools. The remaining eighteen were grammar schools. They varied considerably in size and accommodation. The former grammar school next to the churchyard at Botwnnog, in the Llŷn peninsula, still survives. It was originally erected about 1616 as a long, single-storey rubble-stone schoolroom, 9 m long by 5.5 m wide, before being altered at the beginning of the nineteenth century by raising the height of the school house to accommodate a bedroom.[11] It was later rendered and provided with new doors and windows, so that it is now barely recognizable. The four-bay grammar school at Northop, built about 1608, was on similar lines to that at Botwnnog, but somewhat larger with a schoolroom 14.5 m long by 5.8 m wide and lofty enough to provide space over the room at one end for the master's chamber. Llanrwst (founded about 1612) was deliberately built outside the town on a large plot of land that was not to be ploughed or enclosed but was to be for the benefit of the pupils who were 'to have liberty to play all over it'.[12] It comprised a T-shaped building with a large schoolroom (later used as the library) with arched trusses occupying the stem, 19.2 m long by 6 m, and the headmaster's house at right angles. The grammar school at Ruabon, Denbighshire, seems to have been an adaptation (in 1618) of an earlier house, and was altered to provide a complete set of rooms for the master on the first floor, above the schoolroom. At Hanmer, Flintshire, a school had been endowed since 1625, but not given a purpose-built home until 1676. This was built in brick with a door at one end and two splendid arch-braced trusses, each with a band of pierced balusters. The building was later incorporated in a primary school.

Few, if any, seventeenth-century school buildings seem to have survived in the south. Presumably this was because the rapid expansion of the towns during the Industrial Revolution and its aftermath, called for the rebuilding of old schools like the Free Grammar School in Monmouth (originally built, 1614–15). The appearance of some can be gleaned from old drawings. The elementary school at Hay-on-Wye (founded 1670), which once stood in the market square, was illustrated by Thomas Dingley in his account of the progress of first Duke of Beaufort through Wales in 1684.[13] From this it appeared to be a lofty, single-storey building built in rough stone with ashlar dressings and half-timbering to the upper part of the gable end, below which was a two-light pointed window, and below that a large pointed doorway.

Other Buildings

Public buildings were relatively few and far between in the sixteenth and seventeenth centuries, and fewer still have survived. Typical of these is the Courthouse (now the Town Hall) in Llantwit Major, Glamorgan, the basement of which was late medieval and the two upper floors late sixteenth century. The ground floor was divided into four units, perhaps as shops, with, on the first floor, the courtroom, lit by arched, two-light windows, and accessed by partly enclosed dual stairs. Denbigh's two-storey Town Hall (later Shire Hall) was built c.1571–5 under the patronage of Robert Dudley, Earl of Leicester.[14] Though remodelled with a heightened roof in the late eighteenth century, most of the original ground-floor market, with its Tuscan colonnades and stone end walls (the west with a round-headed entrance and blocked remains of two first-floor windows) can still be made out.

108 Market Hall, Llanidloes, Montgomeryshire.

Like many other communal halls of the period, it occupies an island site in the middle of the main thoroughfare. The Old Market Hall at Llanidloes, Powys, now the only timber-framed market hall in Wales, stands in the middle of a busy crossroads. Tree-ring dating confirms that the five-bay building was built about 1622. Its close-studded timber and plaster walls have survived well, apart from two end walls that were replaced later, one in stone and the other in brick. The upper floor (originally the courthouse) is carried over the mostly open ground floor on heavy oak arches. **(108)** Brecon Town Hall, built in 1624 by the famous carpenter John Abel, has long since disappeared; had it survived, it would have been a fascinating and bizarre example of the way Tudor and Renaissance elements were sometimes combined. Here classical-looking columns on both floors, together with elaborately carved bracketing, contrasted with the half-timber and multi-gabled roof of the building.

As for bridges, Pont Fawr (Great Bridge) in Llanrwst, Denbighshire, is one of the finest stone bridges in Wales and the first to break away from the medieval vernacular. Completed in 1636, it has long been associated with Inigo Jones, the first great professional architect in Britain. The bridge had been ordered in 1634 by the Privy Council when Jones was still Surveyor-General to the king (from 1613 to 1643), and in the circumstances it does not seem unreasonable therefore to credit Jones with the design of Pont Fawr. The bridge itself is beautifully proportioned and rises to a point, at the centre, marked by armorial tablets on the parapet walls. **(109)** The three spacious arches spanning the Afon Conwy, with their narrow hexagonal piers and low parapets, give the bridge an unusually slender appearance ∎

08 Tudor and Renaissance Architecture, 1536 to 1700
References

1   Griffiths and Thomas, *Making of the Tudor Dynasty*, p. 195.

2   P. Smith, *Houses of the Welsh Countryside* (first edn), p. 148.

3   Moelwyn I. Williams, 'A General View of Glamorgan Houses', *Glamorgan Historian*, 10 (1974), 162.

4   E. Hubbard, *Clwyd* (The Buildings of Wales), p. 42.

5   I. C. Peate, *The Welsh House*, p. 3

6   M. Baker and G. Stevenson, *50 Buildings that Built Wales*, p. 61.

7   P. Smith, *Houses of the Welsh Countryside*, p. 334.

8   H. Colvin, 'An Architect for Tredegar House?', *Architectural History*, 25 (1982), 7.

9   Smith, *Houses of the Welsh Countryside*, Map 11, 'Half-timbered towns'.

10   L. A. S. Butler, *Denbigh Castle* (Cadw Guide, 2007), p. 43.

11   C. A. Gresham, 'The Botwnnog Free Grammar School', *Arch. Camb.*, 116 (1967), 198–202.

12   M. Seaborne, *Schools in Wales, 1500–1900*, p. 31.

13   Seaborne, *Schools in Wales*, p. 40.

14   Susan Fielding, 'The Shire Hall, Denbigh', *Arch. Camb.*, 166 (2017), 304.

9

Vernacular Houses, Thirteenth to Eighteenth Century

Vernacular architecture is the term applied to buildings that were built without the guidance of a professional architect, i.e., buildings erected by local carpenters and builders working in the indigenous manner of the area. One of the features of vernacular architecture is the continuity of tradition over a long period. Unfortunately for us in Wales, very few genuinely vernacular houses have survived without either alteration or addition.

The earliest existing houses, other than the castles of the *boneddigion* (nobility), are generally the houses of the *uchelwyr* (gentry), and these were built in the vernacular tradition. As building methods improved and the gentry became more prosperous, they built bigger and better homes, leaving the older houses to be lived in by those lower in status. Thus the original houses of the gentry became the homes of the smaller landowners, and these were eventually transferred down the scale to the *crefftwyr* (craftsmen) and *tyddynwyr* (smallholders). So the farmhouse we see today may once have been the most important dwelling in its district. Small houses erected later would be built in the same vernacular tradition, perhaps even with the same plan and layout as the prototype. The later houses were often in effect merely copies of the earlier houses belonging to the *uchelwyr*.

The new houses of the *uchelwyr*, whether or not designed by architects, were still largely based on traditional methods of construction and layouts, so that new architectural styles evolved only gradually, or were hesitatingly borrowed from England or further afield. Before looking at later, professionally designed mansions, it makes sense to consider the characteristics of vernacular architecture, the materials with which buildings were constructed and the different layouts that were adopted and developed.

Building Materials

The appearance of vernacular buildings owes much to the materials that were used, not only for their colour and texture, but also for the different ways in which the buildings were constructed. The materials used were those that were most readily available and close at hand, and differed from one part of the country to another. **(110)**

Stone was the most easily available material for wall construction in many parts of Wales. The stones mostly used in building were generally the softer ones, such as limestone and sandstone, which were easier to use and shape. Of these, limestone was the most useful as it was easily worked in blocks and was fairly weather resistant. Limestone could also be converted to mortar, or made into lime-wash for external decoration and weather-proofing. The harder stones, such as the Precambrian, Cambrian and igneous rocks of Gwynedd, Pembrokeshire and close to the Shropshire border were difficult to shape. Consequently, these stones were often used as random boulders to give a very coarse, texture effect, or used for dry walling.

Stone tiles that might be used for flooring and roofing were thick slabs generally split from limestone or sandstone. The stone was usually quarried in blocks during the autumn and left to freeze in winter and then thawed out so that it would cleave more easily. The main types of stone used for tiles are Pennant sandstone in the Valleys and Old Red Sandstone in Breconshire and parts of Carmarthenshire and Monmouthshire.

Clay or earth, made plastic with water, and reinforced with stones, straw or rushes, and finished with coats of lime-wash, was a common building material in the past in the Llŷn peninsula and parts of the south-west. An alternative to mud or clay was turf, which was easier to use for building and more durable in the upland areas with their heavy rain, but could not be protected by lime-wash.

Slate comes in various colours from dark grey, through grey-blue to purple and green, and can be split into thin sheets and easily trimmed to size, making it an ideal roofing material. It is usually associated with the quarries of Gwynedd, although it was also found in Denbighshire, Montgomeryshire and northern Pembrokeshire. Slate has been used in parts of Wales since Roman times, and from the early nineteenth century was exported to the rest of the country, as well as England and places around the world.

Thatch is the common name for a material comprising vegetable matter. It was probably the commonest roofing material in the past and used for farmhouses and cottages throughout Wales. It was probably used for larger houses as well, at least in some parts of the country. Today, thatched roofs are rare, except in the Vale of Glamorgan. A number of different techniques were used for making thatch and these varied from district to district.

Bricks were introduced by the Romans, but after their departure were not used again in Wales until the late sixteenth century, and even then only exceptionally. Bricks were reintroduced in 1567, by Sir Richard Clough, probably

110 The distribution of Building Materials in Wales.

The Architecture of Wales

111 Cosmeston medieval village, Penarth, Glamorgan.

using bricks imported from the Netherlands. The production of bricks was a lengthy process, and as a result bricks were not employed in house building in many parts of Wales (apart from those areas near brickworks in the north-east and Bridgwater, England) until the coming of railways in the late nineteenth century, and the advent of the lorry in the twentieth century. Manufactured clay tiles for flooring or roofing were rarely used until the coming of the railways.

The most adaptable material for construction purposes was timber, as it was easy to shape, and could be cut to size and jointed. Wood is also strong in tension and comparatively easy to carry. The western areas, apart from some sheltered valleys, were generally more exposed and less heavily wooded than the eastern parts of Wales. The best timber for construction, especially oak, was more easily available in the east, where the trees grew more quickly and to greater lengths. However, wood was used whenever possible for the basic framework of houses in most parts of the country. Wood, especially oak, was also split and cut into short lengths as shingles for roofing.

Wood can be dated more easily than most other materials by a technique known as dendro-chronology or tree-ring dating. In this technique a core is taken of the wood (preferably a hard-wood) and the ring pattern is cross-matched by computer with known tree-ring chronologies. The pattern of tree rings varies according to climatic conditions, resulting in sequences of narrow or widely spaced rings. Studying the number of tree rings can give close approximations of the date when the timber was felled and hence the earliest possible date when the timber could be used in a building.

Late Medieval Houses

Although none of the houses built before the fifteenth century have, as far as is known, survived above ground in Wales other than those of a military character, archaeological excavations have provided us with a wealth of information about earlier houses. Following excavation at Cosmeston, Penarth, for example, it was possible to reconstruct part of a deserted, early fourteenth-century village. **(111)** A farmstead, three cottages and a tithe barn were reconstructed on their original foundations, showing that these buildings were well organized and surprisingly well built, with walls made of two leaves of limestone blocks filled with rubble, and thatched roofs laid on timber A-frames.

The earliest standing remains appear to be Hafodygarreg, near Builth Wells, built from timber felled in 1402, according to tree-ring dating[1], and Llwyn Celyn in the Black Mountains from timber felled in 1407-28. Tree-ring dating carried out on behalf of the Royal Commission on Ancient and Historic Monuments in Wales since 1996 shows that high-status houses tend to be the earliest that have survived, and that it was not until the early sixteenth century that ordinary farmers began building smaller versions of the gentry houses. For a century and a half the timber, single-storey lineal house, known as a hall-house, became the norm throughout the country, except in Pembrokeshire.

Hall-houses were generally cruck-framed, and, in their simplest form, were based on simple three-unit layouts that incorporated a hall, or living area, in the centre with a cross-passage at one end and the dais area at the other. The outer unit next to the cross-passage was used for service rooms, while the outer unit at the opposite end (next to the dais) was for sleeping or use as a parlour. Originally, the central hall would have been heated by an open hearth in the middle of the floor, and smoke found its way out through gaps in the thatched roof or open windows. The room was open to the roof, and in time the oak roof trusses became important features, elaborately carved for effect. Between the hall and the service rooms there would be a lightweight timber screen, or spere, to hide the cross-passage from the hall. The cross-passage provided access to the service rooms and served as an entrance hall with a door at both ends.

Hall-houses were usually constructed with cruck frames set apart at regular intervals, so dividing the building into a number of bays. **(112)** From the number of bays and the size of the hall it was possible to gauge the importance of the owners; thus great houses had halls of three or more bays, the local gentry had halls of two bays and ordinary peasant farmers had single-bay halls.[2] Further bays could be added to the length of the house to provide additional rooms for animals or storage. Hendre'rywydd Uchaf, from Dyffryn Clwyd (now re-erected at the St Fagans National Museum of History), a cruck-framed peasant hall-house, was constructed with crucks felled in the early sixteenth or early seventeenth century, giving five bays, only one of which was used for the hall and two for housing cattle. The crucks rest on a low stone sill, the walls are panelled with wattle-and-daub, the windows are unglazed, and the roof is thatched; inside, the original open hearth has been reconstructed on an earthen floor.

The basic three-unit hall-house was developed into increasingly complex layouts according to the needs of the owner, and, as time went on, the open hearth would be replaced by a fireplace with a chimney at the back or side of the hall. The original building could be extended lengthways by adding on extra bays, or at right angles to produce either T-shaped or, more rarely in Wales, H-shaped layouts. A further development was to add floors above the end rooms, accessed by stairs.

Status in the more important gentry houses was sometimes emphasized by replacing the spere screening

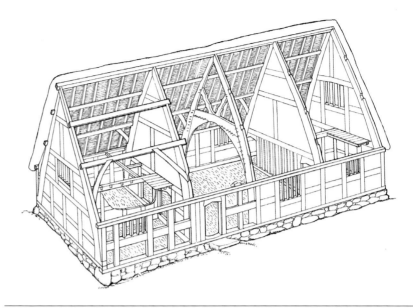

112 Cutaway drawing of late medieval cruck-built hall-house, based in Leeswood Green Farm, Flintshire (from *Houses of the Welsh Countryside*).

the cross-passage with a spere-truss that comprised an elaborately carved roof truss supported on aisle-posts at either side of the hall, such as those at Plas Ucha (c.1435), near Corwen, Tŷ-Mawr (c.1460), Castell Caereinion (see **264**), and Penarth-fawr (c.1476), near Pwllheli. **(113)** In theory aisle-posts would allow greater roof spans to be achieved, but this could not be done if, as normally happened in Wales, they were only used as spere-trusses and not at regular intervals along the length of the hall.

The growing need for wider spans in England led to the development of the hammer-beam, a projecting timber bracket with short vertical posts to support a roof truss without the need for aisle-posts. It was originally devised during the early fourteenth century for places such as the

113 Penarth-fawr, Caernarfonshire, interior showing spere-truss.

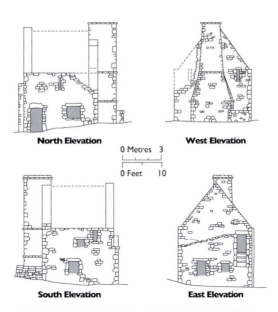

North Elevation   **West Elevation**

0 Metres 3

0 Feet 10

South Elevation   **East Elevation**

114 Carswell, near Tenby, Pembrokeshire.

Cruck-frame Construction

The cruck-frame method of timber construction was the dominant form during the late medieval period. A cruck frame was made from a pair of crucks (curved blades of wood fashioned out of a trunk and main branch of a tree by splitting it down the middle) that were joined together near the apex by a collar beam to form an 'A'-shaped frame. The feet of a full cruck-frame rest on the ground or sill beams, while the feet of a 'raised' or 'upper cruck frame' are set on top of solid walls. The whole weight of the roof was carried on the cruck frames by timber purlins so that the non-structural walls between each frame could be filled with panels of wattle-and-daub, clay or stone. Cruck frames were also commonly used in farm buildings such as barns, where they are often more visible than in houses.

Pilgrims' Hall, Winchester. In Wales hammer-beam roofs were used in a number of gentry houses in the north, but mostly in churches. Two of the best examples of medieval halls that retain their ornate hammer-beam roofs (late fifteenth or early sixteenth century) are in Caernarfonshire, at Cochwillan, near Bangor, and Gloddaeth (St David's College), Llandudno.

First-floor halls in Pembrokeshire were upper-class houses built in stone, above vaulted undercrofts, during the late Middle Ages. This localized house type developed for a number of reasons, of which the availability of suitable stone is one, and the early colonization of the area by the Anglo-Normans is probably another. It may be that the Anglo-Normans brought with them a tradition of building first-floor halls such as those depicted on the Bayeux Tapestry. Whatever their origin, similar kinds of construction were used not only for the great bishops' palaces at St David's and Lamphey, but also for the rural gentry and town-dwellers alike. It was used even for very small yeomen's houses, such as that at Carswell, near Tenby, which consists of a single first-floor room over a single vaulted ground-floor room complete with a massive stone chimney built in the Pembrokeshire fashion. **(114)** It probably dates from the end of the fifteenth century, as does a similar house at nearby West Tarr.

The ground-floor farmhouses of the area were also stone-built. Although few have survived intact, they appear to have been built to a similar three-unit layout as the hall-houses elsewhere, but without the need for full-length crucks, the roof trusses resting instead on the tops of the stone walls and stone partitions. The farmhouses are also notable for the various side projections that they have under outshut roofs, and side-wall fireplaces with round chimneys constructed at the same time as the rest of the building.

The tower-houses found in areas that came under Anglo-Norman control, were also built in stone. In these the main rooms were assembled above each other at first- and second-floor levels for defensive purposes. Surprisingly, when one considers the intermittent wars and feuds that took place before the sixteenth century, very few examples of tower-houses are known to have been built in Wales, compared with the hundreds built in Ireland and Scotland. (115) As with first-floor halls over vaulted undercrofts, the majority were in Pembrokeshire, of which the best surviving example is the Old Rectory, at Angle. (116) Here, the late fourteenth- or fifteenth-century building comprises a stout tower of three rooms, each roughly 3.2 m square, raised one above the other over a stone-vaulted undercroft. Access to the first floor appears to have been by a wooden drawbridge, and to the remaining rooms by spiral stairs within a round corner turret. The walls of the tower are more than a metre thick and flare outwards towards the bottom.

Remnants of a few tower-houses have survived in Glamorgan and Monmouthshire, with a couple of more or less complete examples in Breconshire. The most complete of the latter is Tower House, Talgarth, a possibly fourteenth-century three-storey tower similar in size to the Old Rectory, Angle, but with an unvaulted semi-basement built partly into the sloping ground. Less than a handful of tower-houses have survived in the north. Here, the best is the much restored example at Tower, near Mold, with two stone-vaulted lower floors and a single upper floor.

Platform Houses and Long-houses

The growth in population during the twelfth and thirteenth centuries – partly natural due to a warmer climate, and partly due to considerable alien (i.e., Anglo-Norman) immigration – led to a land shortage and land hunger that resulted in 'a

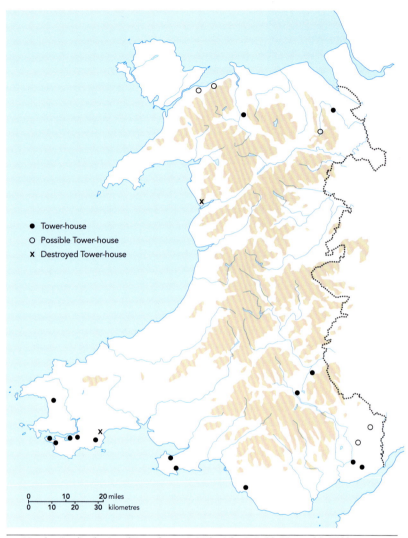

115 Map showing distribution of Tower-houses in Wales (after P. Smith, *Houses of the Welsh Countryside*, with amendments).

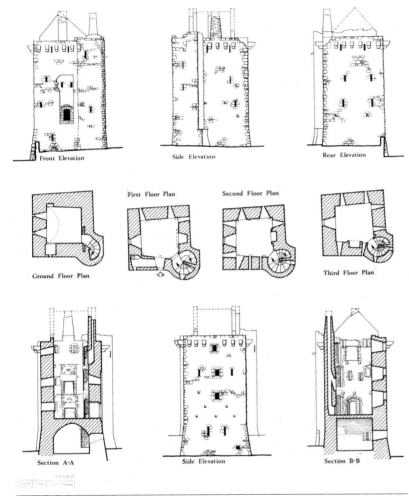

Front Elevation   Side Elevation   Rear Elevation

First Floor Plan   Second Floor Plan

Ground Floor Plan   Third Floor Plan

Section A-A   Side Elevation   Section B-B

116 Old Rectory tower-house, Angle, Pembrokeshire.

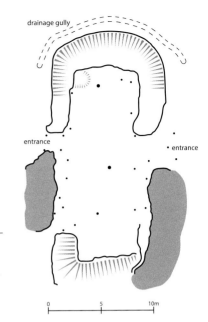

drainage gully

entrance   • entrance

117 Dinas Noddfa
Platform-House,
Gelli-gaer Common,
Glamorgan (plan based
on archaeological
excavation, 1936).

0   5   10m

profound impact on the settlement pattern of the country'.[3]
As a consequence of the pressures arising from this situation
there was an expansion of peasant farming and settlement
into the upland areas.

The platform-houses that emerged out of this
development were built on artificially levelled platforms
– located at right angles to the contours (probably to aid
drainage) – that had been dug into the ground at one end and
raised above the ground at the lower end. The distribution of
platform-houses, either in pairs or singly, was widespread
over much of Wales, but mostly in the upland districts
between about 220 m and 330 m above sea level. Generally
speaking the remains of platform-houses are so scanty that
accurate dating is extremely difficult.

A number of platforms were excavated at two
separate sites on Gelli-gaer Common, Glamorgan, during
the 1930s by Sir Cyril and Dr Aileen Fox.[4] The main platform
at the Dinas Noddfa site (1936) was a 'classic' of its type,
and would have supported a roughly rectangular building
17 m long by 8 m (maximum) wide internally, with drystone
walling and post-holes for poles to support a central ridge
piece and thatched roof. (117) There were opposed entrances

at natural ground level serving to divide the building into two halves, as in a cross-passage. The upper part, with its hearth, was a living or working area, while the well-drained lower part may have been used for storage or, in similar platform houses, as a byre for animals. Finds of pottery in the nearby Graig Spyddyd site were dated to the thirteenth or early fourteenth century.

The long-house, with accommodation for both humans and cattle, appears to have developed as a result of climate reversion to a colder period during the fourteenth century and its adverse effect on upland settlement, and with it a decline in the population. With their generally upland settings, they seem to be, despite a lack of dating evidence, a natural successor to the platform-house. However, it now seems clear that most, if not all, long-houses were derived from hall-houses. and were comparable to 'several cruck-framed medieval houses [that] have been excavated' and found to have 'the remains of animal stalls in the lower-end bays'.[5]

The term 'long-house', now commonly used for the type of rectangular house where people and cattle were housed under the same roof, was coined by Dr Iorwerth Peate in the 1940s as the English equivalent of the Welsh term *ty-hir* (literally 'long-house').[6] Since then the term, and the house type it denoted, have caused considerable controversy, some resolutely opposing its long ancestry, stating that 'the long-house is a product of the Industrial Revolution'.[7] Certainly, such houses were far more widespread in the past, for buildings that once housed both humans and animals (as well as hay or corn) can be seen in many open-air museums across northern Europe. The long-house as envisaged by Peate was essentially a long, rectangular structure of a single-build split by a cross-passage (which could also be used as a feeding walk) with, on the upper side (*pen uchaf*), the living quarters, and, on the lower side (*pen isaf*), the cow shed, both of which were accessed from the same cross-passage (*pen-llaw*), as at Nannerth–ganol, in Radnorshire. **(118)**

The long-house according to this definition seems to have begun in the late medieval period, sometimes as an integral part of a cruck-framed hall-house, as at Ty-draw (c.1480), Denbighshire.[8] Many, however, appear to have been converted later from existing hall-houses., while still later

118 Cutaway drawing of Nannerth-ganol long-house (from *Houses & History in the March of Wales: Radnorshire 1400–1800*).

119 Cilewent long-house, National Museum of History, St Fagans.

ones would have been purpose-built in stone. In theory, a three-bayed peasant hall-house could be easily converted to a long-house just by using an outer bay as a byre for cows. In practice, however, the change probably came about when the open hearth in the centre of the hall was replaced by an enclosed stone fireplace and chimney that backed onto the cross-passage at the end of the hall. Presumably a ceiling would be inserted into the upper part of the hall at the same time to create an upper room, or *croglofft*. This left the outer, or lower bay(s), on the further side of the cross-passage, free to be used for storage or as a cow shed. The final alteration would be the rebuilding of all, or part of, the outer walls in stone.

Such farmhouses became relatively common in the upland areas of southern and central areas of Wales, but not, apparently, in the north-west or south-west. In fact the distribution of long-houses largely covers the same areas as those that had become, by the late sixteenth century, prone to 'stealinge of Catell'. They were known as 'disturbed areas', and their distribution was specified in a report by the Queen's Surveyor about 1570.[9] This might suggest that long-houses had developed not so much for economic reasons or for the cattle's benefit, but rather 'as a prudent response to the need to safeguard cattle where cattle-rustling was endemic'.[10] Whatever their purpose, it is clear that by now hall-houses were already giving way to long-houses in these areas, and 'new houses of long-house plan continued to be built in the seventeenth and eighteenth centuries.'[11]

Cilewent, originally from a moorland site near Rhayader, Radnorshire, is an example of the long-house process. It began life in the late 1470s as a cruck-framed hall-house and was later (1734) rebuilt in stone. **(119)** At some time it had been converted to a long-house, and this may have occurred between the two dates mentioned, for the 1734 rebuilding gave it an unusual L-shaped layout by adding on a parlour or dairy at right angles to the original building. At the same time the cross-passage seems to have been moved uphill to make a larger byre and the fireplace, instead of backing onto the cross-passage as in the 'classic' long-house, has been moved to the upper gable end.

Another long-house rescued from dereliction, this time by the Elan Valley Trust, is Llanerch-y-cawr from the neighbouring parish of Llanwrthwl. It began life as a cruck-framed hall-house before being rebuilt in stone in 1588. The byre was rebuilt in the eighteenth century – reusing the cruck trusses – when a separate door for the cows was added.[12] This suggests that the cross-passage must originally have been used by people and animals.

Post-medieval Houses

The development of houses and farmhouses during the sixteenth century led to storeyed cellular buildings, with layouts that came to be based on the position of the main fireplace and its relationship to the entrance, as well as the need to incorporate stairs. These relationships differed in various parts of the country, resulting in a variety of house types, usually referred to as regional houses **(120)** Although each type was dominant in a certain area, they were often found more sparsely distributed in other areas as well. The house types in Glamorgan and the north-east were, however, more mixed than in other parts of Wales. Most regional houses, except those in the eastern borderlands and the Severn valley, were stone-built.

A house type that was common in the north-east and fairly well distributed in the rest of the country, apart from Ceredigion, Carmarthenshre and Montgomeryshire, has a plan based on the earlier three-unit hall-house. It differs from the hall-house in that it was stone-built, and the main fireplace was on a lateral wall of the hall. The cross-passage was not usually separated from the hall by a screen or spere. Sometimes the house was based on only two units, with a parlour next to the cross-passage and a secondary fireplace on the gable-wall.

In the north-west, the predominant house type was also related to the hall-house, but based on two units rather than three. The cross-passage, undivided from the hall, usually has two opposed entrances. A service room and parlour were placed next to the cross-passage and were, as a result, near the entrances. The main fireplace was on the gable-wall of the hall at the dais end, furthest from the cross-passage, while any secondary fireplace was usually on the gable wall of the service rooms. Winding stone stairs are commonly squeezed between the main fireplace and a lateral wall, and lead to two bedrooms. Often the houses with chimneys at both ends were gentry houses, such as two Gwynedd houses, Y Garreg Fawr (1540–54), **(121)** and Tŷ-mawr-Wybrnant (c.1565), famous as the home of Bishop William Morgan, translator of the Bible into Welsh. In 1988 Tŷ-mawr was restored by the National Trust to celebrate the fourth century of the Welsh Bible. Houses with only a single chimney and attached farm buildings were usually of lower status.

In southern and central Wales the dominant house type usually has the entry into the hall from a cross-passage behind an internal fireplace as in many long-houses. In the late sixteenth-century two-unit Old Rectory at St Mary Church, Glamorgan, the hall was originally open to the roof and the stairs from the hall led to a loft over the outer room which was unheated until the insertion of a fireplace in the outer wall in the eighteenth century. In a three-unit house the kitchen was next to the cross-passage and might have its own secondary fireplace and chimney on a gable wall, while the parlour was next to the dais end of the hall. In a single-unit house, the hall served as an all-purpose room with an end entrance next to the fireplace on the gable wall, as at Kennixton (1610), Llangennith, Glamorgan, before it was enlarged about 1680. The upper floor was probably reached by stairs between the main fireplace and the side wall.

Over much of the eastern borderland and Glamorgan a two-storey house plan developed with an internal fireplace and an entrance lobby (instead of the cross-passage) backing onto the side of the fireplace. In Glamorgan these houses were all stone-built, and sometimes had a secondary fireplace and chimney on a gable wall. In Montgomeryshire most houses were half-timbered, i.e., of box-framed construction (see box feature) such as Abernodwydd (1608), which was built as a single-storey hall-house before becoming a storeyed house by the insertion (about 1708) of a loft. **(122)** Often the larger houses had back-to-back fireplaces (like the letter 'H' on plan) behind a lobby, and later a porch as well. These houses would have been built from the start as two-storey houses.

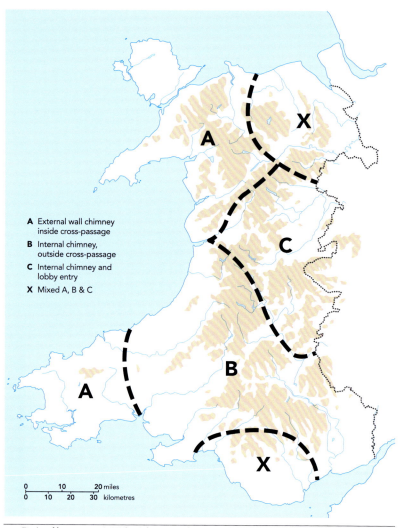

A External wall chimney
inside cross-passage

B Internal chimney,
outside cross-passage

C Internal chimney and
lobby entry

X Mixed A, B & C

120 Regional house types in Wales (after P. Smith, *Houses of the Welsh Countryside*, with amendments).

121 Y Garreg Fawr, National Museum of History, St Fagans.

122 Abernodwydd, National Museum of History, St Fagans.

Box-frame construction

The box-frame form of timber construction first appeared in eastern Wales during the fifteenth century, presumably as a westward extension of a system previously used in the west Midlands of England. Its use gained ground during the sixteenth century, and by the seventeenth century it had superseded the use of cruck frames, at least in the eastern counties. In box-frame construction the walls are built up as frames with a grid of vertical and horizontal timber pieces, and these frames support separate (triangular) roof trusses. Diagonal timber braces were added for structural stability or simply for decorative purposes. The intermediate panels within the grid were filled with wattle-and-daub or brick, often lime-washed white, while the timber frames were treated with tar to give the houses their characteristic black-and-white or half-timbered appearance. Many storeyed box-frame houses have the upper floor jettied out beyond the face of the lower floor.

As houses became larger and more sophisticated there was a conscious interest in their exterior appearance. This was made easier where the house had a lobby entrance or an entrance porch, as these could be elaborated as a central feature, leading to symmetrical or near-symmetrical front elevations. Half-timbered houses were suitable for consciously designed exteriors as the materials used could be decorated and arranged imaginatively, as at The Vicarage (1616), Berriew, or Maesmawr Hall (c.1690), near Caersws, where storeyed porches together with cusped and quatrefoil bracing have been used to dramatic effect. (123)

The emphasis was on symmetry of plan as well as elevations. Gradually the layout of lobby-entrance houses

124 Llainfadyn croglofft cottage, National Museum of History, St Fagans.

Cottages

In its simplest form, the cottage or *bwthyn* is a single-storey, one-roomed or two-roomed building and was the most widespread house type of the Welsh countryside up to the twentieth century. They were the homes of poorer people who had insufficient land to live off, such as craftsmen, servants, and workers in early industry. Despite their humbleness, many famous men and women were nurtured on their hearths. Sir Owen Morgan Edwards, for instance, a man of letters and pioneer educationist, was born in 1858 in a cottage at the foot of Aran Benllyn in the heart of Meirioneth, while the novelist Kate Roberts spent her childhood in a quarryman's cottage in Snowdonia.

The one-roomed cottage was usually divided into two areas – one for living and one for sleeping – at first by furniture and later by a screen of lath and plaster or simply by a curtain. When more accommodation was required, the room could be augmented by a loft in the roof space that had been built over the sleeping area and was reached by a ladder. This method, very commonly employed in small cottages, resulted in a type of dwelling known as a *croglofft* cottage.

The kind of material that was locally available could have a considerable effect on the character and stability of a cottage. In the north-west, for instance, many cottages were solidly built with large boulders and had slate roofs, such as Llainfadyn (1762), a *croglofft* cottage from Caernarfonshire. **(124)** It was basically little more than a single room that had been subdivided with furniture according to use. Somewhat later, and from the same area, is Cae'r Gors (c.1827), built in similar materials as a quarry worker's cottage. Originally it comprised a small hall and even smaller parlour with a loft above, before a service room and small bedroom were later added at the rear, and a byre at the side. At the other end of the scale was the *tŷ-clom* (clay-house), such as Nantwallter (c.1770) from Carmarthenshire. **(125)** The clay was dug locally and, mixed with straw, was laid in layers, each course left to dry out before laying the next course. The walls of a clay-house were finished with successive layers of lime-wash and were usually very thick and had rounded corners.

Even less substantial than the clay-house was the *tŷ-*

developed into a T-shaped or a cruciform plan, with either a central fireplace and tall chimney or fireplaces and chimneys at both gables. Instead of linear layouts, as in the hall-house and long-house, the rooms are grouped around a centralized stair and entrance hall, with the living rooms and parlour at the front and the kitchen and dairy at the rear. A further development of the symmetrical house plan produced 'U'- or 'H'-shaped layouts with a glorified entrance hall and grand staircase in the centre, and large rooms on either side with projecting wings. Alternatively, a house could have a roughly square plan with a long, narrow entrance hall and stairs in the centre, and rooms two deep on either side. This, the double-pile layout, was the most economical plan, as the house could be covered with two parallel roofs (without awkward diagonal valleys), had a ratio of external walls to rooms less than in other layouts and, because each room had less external wall, was easier to heat. At the same time as all this was going on, classical Renaissance ideas were slowly introduced to houses belonging to the gentry.

123 Maesmawr Hall, Llandinam, Montgomeryshire. (left)

unnos (one-night house) that needed, according to custom, to be built during one night and have smoke rising from the hearth by the following morning before a patch of common land could be claimed. The one-night cottage was usually constructed with prepared turf and had a thatched roof, and was often rebuilt later in a more substantial way. Many of these cottages were built during the eighteenth and nineteenth centuries, before the common lands in the uplands had been enclosed by the local gentry ∎

125 Nantwallter clay-built cottage, National Museum of History, St Fagans.

09 Vernacular Houses, Thirteenth to Eighteenth Century
References

1   R. Suggett, *Houses and History in the March of Wales*, p. 277.

2   R. Suggett and G. Stevenson, *Introducing Houses*, pp. 35–6.

3   R. R. Davies, *The Age of Conquest*, pp. 147–8.

4   A. Fox, 'Early Welsh Homesteads on Gelligaer Common, Glamorgan', *Arch. Camb.*, 94 (1939), 163–99.

5   Suggett and Stevenson, *Introducing Houses*, p. 87.

6   I. C. Peate, *The Welsh House*, p. 52.

7   Ffrangcon Lloyd, *Liverpool Daily Post*, 15 January 1963; the writer made similar comments in the *North Wales Society of Architects' Year Book* for 1963.

8   W. J. Britnell et al., 'Tŷ-Draw, a late-medieval cruck-framed hallhouse-longhouse', *Arch. Camb.*, 157 (2008), 174 and 178.

9   Suggett, *Houses and History in the March of Wales*, p. 188.

10 Suggett and Stevenson, *Introducing Houses*, p. 89.

11 Suggett and Stevenson, *Introducing Houses*, p. 92.

12 R. Scourfield and R. Haslam, *Powys*, p. 542.

Eng. & Pub. by Newman & Co. 48, Watling St.

10

Neoclassicism, Gothick and the Picturesque, 1700 to 1799

The eighteenth century was a period of educational and religious revival, literary renaissance and economic revolution in Wales. Much of the architecture was characterized, here as in the rest of Britain, by the intellectual appeal of classical architecture or by romantic excursions into historicism and irregularity. For much of the century many of the more important buildings were again domestic in character. In this field it was a period of great activity, partly as a result of increased prosperity after the introduction of scientific methods of agriculture on the more important estates, and in consequence many country houses were built, enlarged or rebuilt in the fashionable style of the period. Unfortunately, many were later demolished for one reason or another, the sad scale of which can be seen from Thomas Lloyd's *The Lost Houses of Wales*. The architects employed to design these houses were more often than not from England, for the gentry was becoming more and more estranged from their Welsh background and now organized their way of life on English patterns.

Despite the lead given by Tredegar House in the previous century, there were few excursions in Wales into the florid style of baroque classicism in the early eighteenth century. More usual in the early years of the century were houses like Abercamlais, in the far reaches of the upper Usk valley, which was rebuilt about 1710 in a style more like that of Troy House or Erddig than Tredegar House. Three storeys high, with a steeply pitched, hipped roof (the dormer windows being nineteenth century additions) and simple details, its only concession to baroque showiness was a timber roof cornice with curved brackets.

Nevertheless, there were two notable exceptions, namely Llanelly House, near Crickhowell and Pickhill Hall, near Wrexham. The latter is distinguished by a quite dramatic facade of red brick and white stone, attributed to Richard Trubshaw, that was added in about 1720 to a late seventeenth-century building. Seven bays wide and three storeys high, with a balustraded parapet, the central bays are separated from the outer bays by two giant fluted pilasters of Composite design. **(126)** The outer corners of the facade are marked by ashlar quoins, while the central windows are segmental-headed with the window above the porch emphasized by sided volutes. The house was badly damaged by fire in 1985 and subsequently converted to flats.

Further examples of baroque art in the early eighteenth century were with the marvellously fashioned wrought-iron gates and screens that ornamented the entrances to a number of parks and churches in different parts of the country. In the north-east the works of Robert Davies of Bersham and his brother John, stand out. Robert Davies (1675–1748) is reputed to have been a pupil of Tijou, the famous French wrought-iron smith. The art of the Davies brothers is seen at its most magnificent at Chirk Castle and at Leeswood Park, near Mold. The superb gates at Chirk Castle, begun in 1712 and finished eight years later, are full of exuberantly elaborate and flowing patterns, with hollow boxlike piers topped by dogs and simpler palisaded side screens. They were originally set up in front of the castle but were removed to their present site at the entrance to the park in 1888. Slightly later (c.1726), the brothers provided two sets of gates at Leeswood Hall. The White Gates, with two bays on either side of tall screens separated by piers similar to those at Chirk Castle, form a 30 m-long divider of astonishing delicacy. The Black Gates are similarly complex and flowing in detail, but somewhat flatter; they originally stood at the forecourt to the house but were later moved to the Mold road. Other gates and screens attributed to the Davies brothers can be seen at St Giles's church (1720), Wrexham, St. Peter's church (1727), Ruthin, and Erddig Park, Wrexham. In the south-east, the splendid wrought-iron gates at Tredegar House, Newport, are equally fine, but less flowing and baroque in character. They were made by William and Simon Edney of Bristol in 1714–18.

Neoclassicism

Neoclassicism entailed a return to the principles of Italian classical architecture as expounded by Andrea Palladio (1508–80) and put into practice by Inigo Jones in the early seventeenth century. The principles were revived in 1715 by the Scottish architect Colen Campbell with the publication of the first volume of his *Vitruvius Britannicus* in which he advocated the 'Antique Simplicity' of Vitruvius. The style, now dubbed 'Palladian', made an appearance in Wales with the erection of Leeswood Hall, near Mold, in about 1724–6, a massive house built from wealth provided by a lead mine on Halkyn Mountain. Designed by Francis Smith and built in brick, the centre block was eleven bays long with fluted Corinthian corner pilasters and a third floor above the main cornice, while, at either end, there were thirteen-bay wings with three-bay pediments and cupolas. Subsequently, when the lead had been exhausted, the house lost its wings and

126 Pickhill Hall, Denbighshire.

127 Nanteos, Ceredigion.

upper floor and was later rendered. A few years later, in 1736–8, Smith was employed to enlarge Wynnstay, an ancient half-timbered house near Ruabon. Apparently the new work was only part of a larger scheme which was never fully carried out and was, in any case, lost in a fire 1838.

Another mansion very much in the Palladian spirit is Nanteos, home for a time of the *Cwpan* – a broken wooden bowl once thought to be the Holy Grail, but later proved to be medieval in origin. Built in 1738–9 near Aberystwyth, the house is a dignified and subtly austere stone building, seven bays wide and three storeys high, with a simple band of ashlar stone between tall ground- and first-floor windows and a simple cornice below the parapet. **(127)** The outer wings were given a slightly rustic effect by the use of squared local thin quoin stones and slightly baroque pediments (possibly reused) to the first-floor windows. The three-bay central section is faced in smooth ashlar and has tall, round-headed first-floor windows (lighting a salon within) with blank roundels above and a balustraded parapet above those. The main entrance is marked by a colonnaded porch of Doric columns that was added by Edward Haycock in the 1840s.

Llandaff Court, Cardiff, was built in 1744–6 not far from the cathedral temple designed by John Wood (the elder) of Bath. Despite the Court's use of similar classical details, it is unlikely to have been designed by Wood, according to the author of the Royal Commission volume on Glamorgan's greater houses, while John Newman has suggested that it is 'surely a craftsmen-designed house'.[1] Even plainer than Nanteos, the ashlar-faced, three-storey main front of Llandaff Court has an absolutely regular pattern of windows, all equal in size except for the slightly shorter windows on the upper floor, and rusticated quoins. The original parapet was taken down when a new hipped roof was added (although the cornice survives), and the Doric porch was added after 1850. The remaining walls are all rendered.

Meanwhile, the character of many older houses, such as Plas Taliaris, a seventeenth-century mansion near Llandeilo, was altered by remodelling or refronting, more to keep up with the current fashion than for any practical purpose. Plas Taliaris was gracefully refronted in ashlared

128 Taliaris, Carmarthenshire.

limestone in about 1725, giving the cubelike, three-storey house a nine-bay facade with extremely narrow windows bold cornice and simple parapet. **(128)** The ground floor has rusticated stonework and a central doorway with a later Roman Doric porch. The first-floor windows have surrounds and curved and triangular pediments, while that in the wide, slightly projecting centre bay is set back and emphasized by Ionic pilasters. The east front is similar in general style but plainer. A two-storey wing with Venetian windows was added in the nineteenth century, but has since been demolished.

Peniarth, near Tywyn, a stone-walled, double-pile house mentioned in fifteenth-century poetry, was altered in 1730 when it was given a seven-bay red-brick front. The central section is defined by subtle, red-brick pilasters, with a three-bay pediment over, and a timber cornice was added to unify the whole composition. In the nineteenth century the ground floor was concealed from view by a continuous red-brick extension with a heavy cornice. Another fine house is Trevor Hall, near Llangollen, which was remodelled by Thomas Lloyd in 1742. It has a red-brick front, three storeys by nine bays long including two-bay wings projecting a bay, all with stone quoins, string courses, window dressings and a deep cornice. **(129)** The central doorway is pedimented. After damage by fire in 1960, the house was beautifully restored by David Mansfield-Thomas and Michael Tree, c.1990–2. Also worth a mention is Plas Gwyn, Pentraeth, Anglesey, a similar-sized house of c.1756, all in red brick with a hipped roof, but with few classical embellishments, merely a simple, three-bay pediment to the main front and a neoclassical doorway.

A number of other houses between Hay and Talgarth in the middle Wye valley were fashionably refronted, such as Trefithel in the early eighteenth century, or rebuilt, like Aberllynfi (c.1760), both modest houses with eye-catching central bays to their main elevations. Perhaps the most interesting house was Pen-yr-wrlodd which, if the date of 1707 is correct, was a very early example of enlargement by adding a dignified and almost free-standing two-storey block at right angles to the original house. It is five bays wide, with a slightly projecting centre bay and a high, hipped roof with sprocketed cornice and centre pediment. Unfortunately the house was destroyed by fire in 2002.

Some of the most interesting work during the middle years of the century was concerned with interior decoration. The finest example in the south is at Fonmon Castle in the Vale of Glamorgan, where the first floor of the twelfth-century keep was remodelled as a large library, subdivided by depressed segmental arches, and the thirteenth-century hall was remodelled as a stair hall with an elegant staircase and gallery by Thomas Paty of Bristol, c.1766–7. Here, the ceilings of the stair hall and the ceilings and arches of the new library were superbly decorated in elegant rococo style by Thomas Stocking.

Further north, at Chirk Castle, the State Dining Room, Saloon and Drawing Room of the north range, with their fine stucco ceilings, and the Grand Staircase Hall, with its Ionic columns, were all remodelled by Joseph Turner (of

129 Trevor Hall, Denbighshire.

130 Chirk Castle, Denbighshire, the long gallery.

Denbighshire) between 1766 and 1778, resulting in a series of interiors totally at variance with the exterior character of the drum-towered castle. The magnificent ceilings are either coffered or coved and are elaborately, but delicately, decorated with shallow carved floral mouldings and painted panels, while the walls have carved timber panels and richly moulded door casings. **(130)** Occasionally, as at Plas Newydd in Anglesey (1793–9), it was a fusion of classical order and symmetry with Gothic details, as though the architects, James Wyatt and Joseph Potter of Lichfield, were unconvinced of what the final outcome ought to be.

Romantic Gothick

The rococo decorations at Fonmon and Chirk were harbingers of the early 'Gothick' phase of the Gothic Revival, when domestic architecture experienced an extraordinary volte-face. During this phase – which may have begun as a flickering flame in the south, but was to become a forest fire in the nineteenth century – many architects retreated, at first somewhat lightheartedly, to medieval buildings for their inspiration. The earliest of these buildings in Wales was Coleg Trefeca (1752–60), Breconshire, inspired by the whimsical Gothick of Horace Walpole's Strawberry Hill in London (begun by Walpole and John Chute in 1750).

The first major Gothick building was Wenvoe Castle, near Cardiff, where an earlier house was rebuilt in 1776–7 in castle style to designs of Robert Adam, modified 'possibly by Thomas Roberts who supervised the construction'.[2] The battlemented main building comprised a long two-storey block with engaged octagonal towers at either end and a square entrance tower in the centre, each a storey higher than the remainder. Battlemented screen walls linked the house to square, storeyed pavilions. Malkin, writing in 1803, criticized the building, saying that 'the towers … seem rather to aim at the convenience of a bow-window, than at any of those purposes for which such structures [i.e., castles] were intended.'[3] The house was burnt down in 1910, but the carefully detailed, neoclassical stable court – apparently designed by Henry Holland who was working at Cardiff

Castle at the time – has fortunately survived. Malkin would have been pleased! The stable court, a two-storeyed, three-winged, building around a rectangular court was built on the east side of the house. Its north and south wings have pedimented archways in the centre of each, while the east wing (formerly containing a coach-house) has a central, three-storey archway with a hipped roof surmounted by a square clock-cupola.

At Cardiff Castle Holland was to add, from about 1777 for the first Marquess of Bute, a square tower (Bute Tower) on the outer face of the west wing to balance the sixteenth-century Herbert Tower, and a two-storey block next to the fifteenth-century Library and Banqueting Hall on the courtyard side. The additions were battlemented to blend with the medieval and later remains, though the profusion of large windows (albeit some with pointed heads) looked anything but medieval. The upper floor of the Bute Tower was rebuilt in a different stone during the nineteenth century.

In the last decade of the eighteenth century Hensol Castle, near Llantrisant, was also given the Gothick treatment, but not for the first time. Earlier William Talbot had 'added two wings with the towers … between the years 1730 and 1740, which gave it its present castellated appearance'.[4] Its Gothic character was extended by further additions between 1790 and 1815, when a three-storey tower and *porte cochère*, each with angle turrets, arrow loops and machicolations, were added to the south front.

An important adjunct to the country mansions was their parks which, during the latter half of the eighteenth century, were landscaped in as naturalistic a manners as possible. This new style of landscape gardening was in direct contrast to the formally laid out and French-inspired gardens that had previously characterized the surroundings of large houses in Britain. In their desire to persuade nature to imitate romantic art – for this is really what it amounted to – landscape gardeners like 'Capability' Brown (Lancelot Brown) contrived sinuous lakes and artificial grottoes, adding 'follies' (often in the form of 'Gothick' ruins) to aid the 'naturalistic' appearance of the parks. Brown was responsible for laying out the park at Wynnstay, near Ruabon, where he

131 Penrice Castle, Gower, old and new.

132 Penrice Castle, Gower, the new house.

introduced a lake, plantations and an artificial waterfall. At Clytha Park, near Abergavenny, the grounds were laid out in 1790 by John Davenport (of Shropshire) to include a tall, Gothic gateway (by John Nash) at the entrance, a small lake and a folly in the form of a sham castle erected as a memorial to the owner's wife. The sham castle (by Davenport), known as Clytha Castle, is laid out to an L-shaped plan with a square tower at the corner and round towers at either end, linked by machicolated screen walls that curve up and down.

Late Classicism

For much of the later part of the eighteenth century neoclassicism remained in vogue. Cresselly House (1769–71) and Brownslade (1792) – both possibly designed by William Thomas of Pembroke – were two south Pembrokeshire houses of a new villa type. Brownslade was demolished in 1976, but Cresselly House, a sober five-bay, three-storey structure, fortunately survives. The central three bays project on both the entrance and garden fronts: that on the entrance side only slightly, while that facing the garden forms a bold, angular half-tower. The ground-floor windows

in the outer bays are recessed within simple, blind arcades on both fronts, and the drawing room ceiling is decorated with delicate rococo plasterwork.

Penrice Castle, in Gower, is another restrained, but somewhat larger villa type, built 1773–7 in Bath stone ashlar for Thomas Mansel Talbot of Margam, to designs by Anthony Keck, as a replacement for the long-ruined twelfth-century castle, nearby. (131) Three storeys high on the entrance front, and five bays wide – with a pedimented porch with Tuscan columns – the three central bays project slightly under a wide pediment. The garden front is four storeys, owing to a fall in the ground, with the central bays projecting in a semicircular bow under a continuous cornice. (132) When he moved into Penrice Castle, Mansel Talbot had retained his collection of citrus trees at Margam Abbey and in 1780 he employed Keck to design an orangery to protect the trees. When erected in 1787, Keck's elegant and disciplined Margam Orangery became one of the finest of its type anywhere in Britain. (133) The great length of the Orangery (at 100 m, reputed to be one of the largest in the world) is punctuated with floral carvings over the centre bays, and is terminated by a pedimented pavilion at either end. The numerous tall, round-headed windows are neatly linked by rusticated piers that contrast with the simple frieze and cornice running along the length of the building.

Stouthall, also in the Gower, was built a few years later (1787–9) than Penrice Castle to a similar design, but on a smaller scale and in rubble stone, by the local architect William Jernegan. Perhaps the most interesting of Jernegan's villas was Marino, a three-storey, octagonal house built in 1784 on rising ground overlooking Swansea Bay. Early nineteenth- century paintings and drawings show that it was like an octagonal pepper pot, with a conical, hipped roof surmounted by a giant urn that acted as a central chimney for numerous fireplaces.[5] Externally, the faces had tall, round-headed panels – partly glazed and partly blank – alternating with rectangular cartouches on the first floor, while the ground floor had alternating doors and rectangular windows, and the second floor had small, square windows on each face. In 1818 Jernegan was called in again to add two wings to the house, and later (1823–35) Marino was almost completely subsumed in further extensive additions and alterations (by Peter Frederick Robinson) in what was to become Singleton Abbey.

The first of the ironmasters' involvments with great houses was Penydarren House, Merthyr Tydfil, which was built in 1784 for the Homfray brothers. It was a two-storey building and largely unostentatious except on the garden side, where a five-bay block was set between two large, round, fenestrated 'pepper pot' towers. According to Benjamin Malkin, writing in 1804, the house 'is large and elegant ... but the splendours of Merthyr Tydfil begin and end with this mansion.'[6] Thomas Lloyd suggested that the house might have 'a possible connection with Anthony Keck', the front elevation being like Keck's Longworth, in Herefordshire.[7]

The most outlandish house of the period was Llewenni Hall, near Denbigh, where Thomas Fitzmaurice, another industrialist, added (c.1780) to the existing, partly medieval, L-shaped house 'two arms of roughly thirteen bays each, bedecked in part with Gothic towers and turrets and built around one of the greatest of the medieval halls'.[8] (**134**) With its mixture of windows, pediments, chimneys, towers and spires, it must have been not only one of the strangest sights but also one of the largest buildings in Wales, vying in size, if not in architectural character, with Fitzmaurice's nearby Bleach Works. The house was bought by the Revd Edward Hughes in 1810, and later demolished.

Two historically important houses in the west that suffered severe declines in their fortunes, but managed to survive into the twenty-first century are Nannau, near

133 Margam Orangery, near Port Talbot.

Dolgellau, and Trawsgoed in Ceredigion. The earliest house at Nannau (1581) was rebuilt twice (c.1600 and c.1690) before the present house was built, probably to designs by Joseph Bromfield of Shrewsbury, in 1792. Three storeys high and five bays wide, with a cornice, parapet and hipped roof, the house was mostly built of squared stones with its centre bay emphasized in a dark, slatey stone. It has a recessed entrance behind Ionic columns. Trawsgoed was rebuilt c. 1650 as a three-sided court, before being rebuilt again, c.1795, as a long, nine-bay wide two-storey house with a rusticated lower floor and a heavy, raised pediment above the three centre bays. The porch, with paired Ionic columns, was added later.

Middleton Hall (1793-5), near Llandeilo, was one house that did not survive, being destroyed by fire in 1931. Designed by Samuel P. Cockerell, it was one of the finest houses in the south, with three sets of Venetian windows on the lower floor of the balustraded garden front and a wide pedimented portico with giant Ionic columns. The seven-bay entrance front had a partly recessed and pedimented Venetian porch lushly decorated with cornucopias around the central arch and bronze statues in wall niches. The surrounding park became home to the National Botanic Garden of Wales in 2000.

One of the worst losses was at Piercefield Park, near Chepstow, where 'Mr Morris's improvements … are generally thought [in 1770] as much worth a traveller's notice as anything on the banks of the Wye.'[9] John Soane was commissioned to design a new house in 1785, but as nothing came of this, he drew up a designs in 1792 for a three-storey neoclassical villa, which was built. The precisely detailed entrance front was divided at ground and first floors into five bays by giant Ionic pilasters which finished under a frieze and cornice, all surmounted by a plain upper floor under a further, full-length cornice. Alternate bays on the ground floor have wide, tripartite windows under semicircular blank panels, and the intervening bays decorative niches. The owner went bankrupt before completion, and a new owner commissioned Joseph Bonomi in 1795 to finish the interior and add a semicircular Tuscan porch to the entrance. In addition, a couple of two-storey pavilions with three-quarter Doric columns and heavily detailed friezes were built on

either side of the main block and linked back to it by single-storey colonnades. The house was abandoned in 1923, after being stripped of its fittings, and was used for target practice during the Second World War and then left to slowly decay.

Hafod Uchtryd and the Picturesque Movement

Eventually, the latent anachronism in the relationship of a 'formal' neoclassical house with an 'informal' park setting was appreciated. It now seemed necessary that the house too should form an integral and informal element within the whole scene. One way of doing this was to avoid symmetry in the design of houses, just as such regularity was to be shunned in landscape gardening. The artistic attitudes which brought about this merger of architectural and gardening ideals had been developing for some time but were not clearly defined until theories relating to the *picturesque* were formulated at the end of the century. Although the picturesque movement was not a strictly architectural one, it had a profound effect on architectural thinking and is of especial interest here because three of the principal figures concerned with it were of Welsh stock and were intimately connected with the pictureque in Wales and the Welsh Marches. They were the Herefordshire landowner Sir Uvedale

134 Llewenni Hall, near Denbigh.

135 Hafod Uchtryd, post 1853. Etching showing Campanile (left) and Baldwin's pavilion (right), but without Nash's octagonal library.

inherited Hafod Uchtryd, in the beautiful and secluded valley of the Ystwyth, in north Ceredigion. Johnes, though born in Ludlow, was of Welsh stock through his father (also Thomas), a native of Llanfair Clydogau, near Tregaron. At Hafod, Johnes was able to develop the ideas of Price and Knight in a remarkable way by building an exotic new house. The completed house was romantic almost to the point of being bizarre; for though the details were 'Gothic' the building as a whole had a distinctly oriental flavour. This was partly because different architects worked on the house at various times. The first was Thomas Baldwin of Bath, who erected a Gothick pavilion in 1786, complete with pointed windows, embattled parapets and weird pinnacles. Behind this an octagonal library – with a coffered dome and columns – and a long, glass conservatory with minarets was added in 1793 by John Nash, then a comparatively unknown architect. Malkin (writing ten years later) described the library as

> an octagon, with the light admitted from the dome. It is surrounded by a gallery, supported on pillars of variegated marble. These pillars are very magnificent, of the Doric order ... It opens into a conservatory, one hundred and sixty feet in length ... the view from the end of the conservatory, through the library, into a seeming second conservatory, almost realizes the fictitious descriptions of enchantment.[10]

Malkin claimed that Johnes was 'his own architect', though, according to Suggett, 'there can be no doubt that the principal feature of the design was owed to Nash.'[11] In 1807, a fire destroyed most of the interior, including the library with its priceless and irreplaceable collection of Welsh and French manuscripts. Stunned but unbeaten, Johnes commissioned Baldwin to rebuild the house as before.

On the landscaping side, Johnes drained bogs to improve the land and planted three million trees between 1796 and 1813 to provide shelter for his estate. In 1853 a later owner added an Italianate campanile and terrace were added to the house by Nash's pupil Anthony Salvin. (135) A year later George Borrow described Hafod in 1862 as 'a truly fairy place ... beautiful but fantastic, in the building of which three styles of

Price (1747–1829), Thomas Johnes (1748–1816), of Hafod Uchtryd, and John Nash (1752–1835), then working from Carmarthen. Between them they crystallised the aesthetic theory of the picturesque and put it into practice. It was Price who gave deeper meaning to the word 'picturesque' and, together with Johnes's cousin Richard Payne Knight, he is generally regarded as the originator of the cult. In 1794 Price published *An Essay on the Picturesque, as compared with the Sublime and the Beuatiful*, and in the same year Knight published his didactic poem, *The Landscape*. In his essay Price had extolled the virtues of an emotionally romantic approach to landscape, and considered Gothic architecture to be better fitted than Grecian on the grounds that a rough and rugged ruin is more naturally 'picturesque' than an artificially neat and smooth new building.

Knight had already built in 1772–8 – with the help of Thomas Farnolls Pritchard – a neo-Gothic castle at Downton in Herefordshire. A few years later the ideals of the picturesque were manifested in Wales when Thomas Johnes architecture seemed to have been employed ... the walls were of resplendent whiteness, and the windows which were numerous shone with beautiful gilding.'[12] By the 1940s the house was empty and dilapidated, and in 1958 it was demolished, a tragic loss. The grounds, now owned by the Forestry Commission, are, with the help of the Hafod Trust gradually being brought back to something like they were in Johnes's time.

Another house that was given the 'picturesque' treatment, but not until the early nineteenth century, was Stanage Park, near Knighton, at the eastern tip of Radnorshire. Coincidentally, the house had also (during the late eighteenth century) belonged to a branch of the Johnes family (of Croft, Herefordshire). Following the advice of Humphry Repton, the landscape gardener, the new owner, Charles Rogers, had a range designed by Repton's son, John Adey Repton, to include a battlemented tower and cloister added to the existing building in 1807. Further extensions with more turrets and towers and Gothick windows were added between 1822 and 1867.

John Nash in Wales

John Nash considered himself Welsh, for though his father was from a Shropshire family, his mother had connections with a Glamorgan family (Edwards), and he himself was probably born in Neath in 1752.[13] By the time that he was fourteen or fifteen he was living in London and apprenticed to the architect Sir Robert Taylor. Later Nash set up on his own account as a surveyor and builder, before becoming bankrupt when a building speculation went wrong. After an acrimonious divorce he left London and returned to Wales in 1785. Here he set up in practice in Carmarthen, employing as a draughtsman Auguste Charles Pugin, a refugee from revolutionary France and future author of various books on Gothic architecture. Nash's architectural talents were many-sided, and during his lifetime he found that he could turn his hand to any style required of him, whether 'Gothic', 'picturesque', 'Italianate', or even 'Hindoo'. He had also tried his hand at 'Grecian' when he designed, with Payne Knight, 'a Pantheon-like dining room for Downton Castle in 1782

complete with coffered ceiling'.[14] The Welsh years (1785 to 1796) were especially important to Nash as it was during this period that his inimitable genius first flowered and he became involved in the picturesque movement.

Most of Nash's work in Wales was of a domestic character and, apart from a couple of notable exceptions, followed a clear trend. The earlier, mostly rectangular houses from 1788 to 1790 were generally straightforward in layout with wide, canted bays and entrances leading directly into stair halls, all in neoclassical dress, apart from Priory House (1788–9), Cardigan, which had Gothic windows. After that, from 1791 to 1795, Nash produced a series of boxlike villas, starting with Whitson Court (1791), near Newport, that often had centralized entrances with vaulted inner halls and top-lit staircases, and ground-floor windows set in recessed arches. **(136, 137)** Whereas Whitson Court was parapeted, three storeys high and rectangular in plan, other villas by Nash, such as Ffynone, Pembrokeshire, and Llanerchaeron, Ceredigion, had low, hipped roofs, were two storeys and square in plan. The latter has an interesting, well-proportioned main elevation that is split by a columned entrance porch to suggest a double-pile house. **(138)**

The exceptions to the general run were Castle House (1791–4), Aberystwyth, built for Uvedale Price, and extensions to Hafod Uchtryd, both designed in a 'picturesque' manner. Castle House was a strange pseudo-Gothic affair, based on a triangular plan with a three-storey, octagonal tower at each corner, so arranged as to make the most of the views, including that of the ruins of the genuine castle behind it. There were entrances under two of the towers, a top-lit semicircular staircase, a dining room with a large bow window overlooking the sea, and tiny flanking 'watch-towers'. The house was demolished in 1897. Only one other house is known that is remotely like Castle House, and that is Moor Park, near Crickhowell, an equally strange affair that consists of four circular towers (with conical roofs) arranged as a rough square. **(139)** The areas between the towers are occupied by entrances at the front and back and by tall chimneystacks at the sides. At the centre is a square hall with a swirling, spiral staircase. Said to have been 'built about 1760 by John Powel',[15]

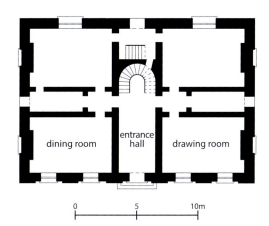

dining room   entrance
                    hall   drawing room

0   5   10m

it looks later, and one cannot help wondering if there was a connection with Nash, whose Llanwysg was built just three kilometres (two miles) away at Llangattock in c. 1792.

Nash returned to London in 1796 to set up a large and fashionable practice, becoming a successful architect to the Prince Regent (afterwards George IV). Though he eventually closed his Carmarthen office, he kept his property in Carmarthen until the end of the century, being 'listed in 1796, 1797, and 1799 ... for rates for a property described as a house in the Wilderness ... and also listed in 1796, 1797, and 1799, as being assessed for rates for The Playhouse'.[16] He also visited Wales from time to time to see to his contracts, which included designs for a few minor buildings at the Nanteos estate in 1814 and the enlargement of Rheola, Glamorgan, in 1814–18 to an asymmetrically planned country house with a top-lit stair hall. (140) In London, as chief exponent of 'picturesque' attitudes, he became one of the great virtuoso architects of his day, renowned for his asymmetrical villas, replanning Regent's Park and Regent Street, London (1811–18) and remodelling the Royal Pavilion, Brighton, in oriental style (1815–21).

Town Houses

This was also an important period for urban building. Again, there is nothing to compare with the fine terraces and crescents of the planned parts of London, Bath and Edinburgh, but many Welsh market towns owe much of their urbane character to the elegant neoclassic houses that were built then. The essence of these houses' appearance was in their simplicity and fine sense of proportion matched by tall sash windows and pedimented doorways set in stuccoed facades. Abergavenny, Monmouth and Cowbridge in the south-east; Carmarthen, Laugharne, Haverfordwest, Tenby and the earlier parts of Swansea in the south-west; Montgomery and Welshpool in mid-Wales — all these contain good examples of domestic street architecture of the time. Montgomery is perhaps the best, unspoilt example, for it has seen comparatively little change. It still retains its well-proportioned houses – some with early iron-framed windows noted in 1754 by the Swedish industrial spy Angerstein – built around a central square with cobbled pavements and its Town Hall. At Aberystwyth and Beaumaris the best domestic architecture belongs to the nineteenth rather than the eighteenth century, but it is still in a style derived from and similar to that of the earlier period.

Of individual buildings, Llanelly House, Llanelli, stands out as an excellent example of an early eighteenth-century town house. The house, parts of which go back to Tudor times as a two-unit, two-storey building, was largely rebuilt early in the century and completed in 1714 as a three-storey, seven bay house with tall sash windows and a central doorway. **(141)** The outer and centre bays project slightly, with a timber cornice above the first-floor windows. There are sunk panels above all the second-floor windows and eight decorative urns on the parapet. Internally the house retains much good-quality timber panelling with overmantel paintings in ground- and first-floor rooms – one a landscape and the other a seascape. The house was later divided into tenements and shops, and fell into poor repair, until carefully restored in 2011–13 ■

140　Rheola House, near Neath, Glamorgan.

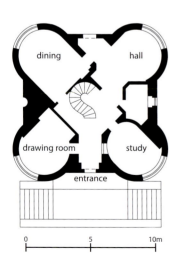

139　Moor Park House,
　　　near Crickhowell,
　　　Breconshire.

0　　　5　　　10m

141　Llanelly House, Llanelli.

10 Neoclassicism, Gothick and the Picturesque, 1700 to 1799
References

1   J. Newman, *Buildings of Wales: Glamorgan*, p. 259.

2   RCAHMW, Glamorgan: *The Greater Houses*, p. 346.

3   B. H. Malkin, *The Scenery, Antiquities and Biography of South Wales*, p. 135

4   Malkin, *The Scenery*, p.74.

5   B. Morris, *The Houses of Singleton*, pp. 7–10.

6   Malkin, *The Scenery*, p. 177.

7   T. Lloyd, *The Lost Houses of Wales*, p. 91.

8   Lloyd, *Lost Houses of Wales*, p. 24.

9   W. Gilpin, *Observations on the River Wye*, p. 46

10 Malkin, *The Scenery*, p. 359.

11 R. Suggett, *John Nash*, p. 80.

12 G. Borrow, *Wild Wales: Its People, Language and Scenery*, p. 433.

13 R. Suggett, 'The Early Life of John Nash, Architect: Family, Marriage and Divorce; Speculation, Bankruptcy and Litigation', in *Cymmrodorion Society Transactions* 15 (2009).

14 J. S. Curl, *Georgian Architecture in the British Isles*, p. 189.

15 S. R. Jones and J. T. Smith, 'The Houses of Breconshire, Part iv: The Crickhowell District', *Brycheiniog*, 12 (1966–7), 60–1.

16 'John Nash's Properties in Carmarthen', *Society of Architectural Historians of Great Britain: Newsletter 53* (Autumn 1994), 5-6.

11

Non-domestic Architecture in the Eighteenth Century

Religious Buildings

The Church in Wales – Anglican and organized from Canterbury, and largely ruled by absentee English bishops – saw comparatively little in the way of new church building during the eighteenth century. By then, Gothic architecture had generally ceased to be the prevalent style used for churches in Britain as a whole. Nevertheless, a trickle of churches in the Gothic tradition continued to be built in a few places in Wales, on the comparatively rare occasions when new edifices were required. At St Mary's, Cardigan,

for example, a bold new tower in Gothic style was erected after the old tower collapsed in 1705. The new tower, with its diagonal, stepped buttresses, battlemented parapets and slightly pointed openings could, at first glance, easily be taken for a medieval tower, though the first phase was not built until 1711 and the second phase in 1745.

A revived Romanesque seems to have been more popular than Gothic, possibly because it appeared, with its round-headed windows, more in keeping with neoclassical architecture. The church of St Myllin, Llanfyllin (Powys), built 1711–14 with local red bricks and stone dressings, has round-headed windows with chevron ornament and shafts, plain, unconvincing battlements and a curiously out of place pedimented doorway. **(142)** A few years later, St Mary, Dolgellau, was rebuilt (c.1716–23) in the hard local stone, more or less in traditional style, again with large, round-headed windows and an apse. **(143)** Inside, it had a cambered ceiling supported on eight timber columns. Together, these two churches represent a watershed between the old and the new; a survival in the long line of Romanesque and Gothic tradition, yet something clearly different.

Of the neoclassical churches, the most interesting is St Deiniol, Worthenbury, built 1736–9 to designs by Richard Trubshaw. Built in red brick and stone, it has a three-storey tower and an apse, both with balustraded parapets, and stone clasping buttresses to all the corners. The windows and doorways are mostly round-headed, although there are also some circular windows. Inside there is a coved ceiling, with rococo plasterwork in the chancel. Trubshaw was also responsible for the three-storey west tower (1726) at Bangor-is-coed, also in brick and stone.

More interesting still would have been the rebuilding of Llandaf Cathedral (1734–52), had it survived. By the beginning of the century the cathedral had become a ruin, picturesque and open to the sky, with only the Lady Chapel fit for use. Rather than abandon the building, it was decided to repair it, and John Wood of Bath was brought in to make a survey and prepare estimates. Instead of a conservative restoration, Wood proposed a radical rebuilding in the form of a much smaller neoclassical temple within the nave's

142 St Myllin's Church, Llanfyllin, Montgomeryshire.

143 St Mary's Church, Dolgellau, Meirionnydd.

outer walls, using wherever possible the existing structure to save money. The aisle walls were bricked up and plastered over, the clerestory was lowered and filled with semi-circular windows and roofed with a simple groined plaster vault ceiling, while the aisles themselves appear to have been covered with flat roofs. Wood had intended building a central, domed tower over the nave and a Tuscan portico surmounted by a Venetian window on the west front, but due to cost these were never carried out. In the end, it was a hotch-potch affair, which made it look, from the outside at least, more like an assembly room or town hall than a place of worship. It was disliked by contemporary critics and eventually, more than a century later, was replaced.

Three other churches in the south were partly rebuilt in neoclassical dress at about the same time with varying degrees of success. At St Mary, Monmouth, the medieval nave was taken down and a new aisled nave built in a slightly different position in 1736–7 (by Francis Smith), only to be largely rebuilt, apart from the north and south walls, by G. E. Street in 1881–3. The four-bay nave of St Mary, Nash (Newport), was rebuilt (probably in the 1730s or 1740s) with a baroque porch and round-headed windows, and the interior was fitted out with box pews, gallery, three-decker pulpit and an almost semicircular boarded ceiling at the end of the century. St Thomas, Neath, was enlarged in 1730 by the addition of aisles with round-headed windows and pedimented doorways, while the chancel was given a Venetian window.

Later in the century there were more rebuildings further north. St Michael and All Angels, Criggion, in the Severn valley, survives from 1774 as a red-brick building with stone dressings and a little tower with round-headed openings. The nave of St Marcellus, Marchwiel, near Wrexham, was rebuilt in stone ashlar in 1788, with a pedimented doorway and some round-headed windows. Its west tower – complete with balustraded parapets and corner pilasters – was added by James Wyatt in 1789. Wyatt was also responsible for designing St Eleth, Amlwch, in 1787, although it was not actually rebuilt until 1800. Constructed in rough, local stone, it again has a prominent west tower with balustraded parapets and corner pilasters in ashlar, as well as circular and round-headed windows. The original windows of the pedimented nave were later replaced with Gothick versions.

In the west John Nash was responsible for designing a curious neo-Gothic west front to St David's Cathedral, some of the drawings being by Auguste Charles Pugin (father of the indefatigable Augustus Welby Pugin), who was then working for Nash at his Carmarthen office. The cathedral had been suffering from settlement and structural problems, and the new front, built 1790–3, had huge buttresses to conceal the shoring needed to support the wall and internal arcades, as well as a large west window in stylized Perpendicular. It was not a success, aesthetically or structurally, and was replaced in the 1880s. Nash was probably also responsible for the little estate church (St Non) at Llanerchaeron, near Aberaeron, 'attributed to Nash on stylistic grounds'.[1] Built in 1798, and originally stuccoed, it had a battlemented nave and a tower with pinnacles and a dome. It was radically altered in 1878, but the dome was later restored.

144 Capel Pen-rhiw, National History Museum, St Fagans.

Roman Catholicism still kept a precarious hold in some parts of Wales, notably at Holywell, Flintshire, and northern Monmouthshire. St Winefride's Well, in Holywell, was to remain a centre of pilgrimage long after the Protestant Reformation. In Monmouthshire the Jones family of Treowen and Llanarth Court were known to have harboured Roman Catholic priests in the seventeenth century. Late in the eighteenth century, John Jones of Llanarth Court had the Chapel of St Mary and St Michael built next to his house (itself rebuilt in the early 1790s). The long, rendered building with six tall, round-headed windows looks more like an orangery, which was probably the intention.

The Roman Catholics also built (1793) St Mary's Church in Monmouth, originally hidden behind a row of cottages in St Mary Street (subsequently demolished), and now largely hidden by later extensions in 1837 and 1871.

While the Church in Wales remained ailing and dispirited, certain native clerics flashed like meteors through this spiritual gloom. Among these were Griffith Jones of Llanddowror (the great pioneer of Welsh education), Daniel Rowland (the most eloquent and popular of Welsh preachers), William Williams Pantycelyn (celebrated hymn-writer and poet) and Thomas Charles of Bala (organizer of Sunday Schools). Throughout much of the eighteenth century these 'methodists' in the Church attempted to reform official indolence from within, although it was not until the next century that the inevitable schism took place and they began ordaining their own ministers. Nevertheless, the Nonconformist movement continued to gather strength and momentum.

During the early part of the eighteenth century a number of small chapels were erected in the industrial parts of the south-east culminating in 1742 with the erection of Capel Groes Wen, near Caerphilly, the first Calvinistic Methodist chapel in Wales. During the second half of the century new chapels, albeit small in size, were being erected in all parts of the country. Some, such as Capel Pen-rhiw (1777) from Felindre in Dyffryn Teifi – now re-erected at the National Museum of History – were simply conversions of farmyard barns. (144) Most appear to have been new buildings, but rarely were they professionally designed – except in special cases such as William Edwards's Capel Libanus (1782) at Morriston. Generally the early chapels were built to a similar plan as the Maesyronnen meeting-house – that is with the pulpit placed in the middle of one of the long walls, either between or facing the twin entrance doorways.

Probably well over a hundred new chapels had been built in Wales by the end of the eighteenth century. Many of these were in the industrial south. In the Merthyr Tydfil district alone five *capeli* had been established before 1797 when the first English-language chapel was opened there. Almost all of the early chapels were later enlarged, remodelled or totally rebuilt, and only the occasional building in the more isolated districts has survived unaltered. Typical of these Dissenting forerunners were Capel Pen-rhiw already mentioned, and Capel Newydd (1769) at Nanhoron (Gwynedd), a simple but singularly moving monument to a past religious fervour. The latter edifice is again a barn-like structure with entrances on either side of the pulpit, an earthen floor and box pews. **(145)** Pentre Llifior Wesleyan Methodist chapel (1798), Betws Cedewain (northern Powys) is comparatively sophisticated with a gable-end entrance, round-headed windows with pointed tracery, and panelled and painted pulpit, box pews and gallery. The Pales Quaker meeting house has also survived at Llandegley (mid-Powys). Dated 1745, it has a very domestic appearance with a thatched roof, large windows and central entrance porch.

145 Capel Nanhoron, near Pwllheli, Caernarfonshire.

146 Coleg Trefeca, Talgarth, Breconshire.

Educational Buildings

The eighteenth century was a time when there was 'a good deal of activity in education', with many elementary schools being established for the poor.[2] Much of this activity, especially during the earlier part of the century, was related to short-term schools, like the circulating schools associated with Griffith Jones of Llanddowror and the charity schools established by the Society for Promoting Christian Knowledge (SPCK), where existing buildings such as churches and houses were used. When existing buildings were not available, one-room buildings might be built in a corner of a churchyard or even two-storey schools no larger

than a modest house. Outstanding amongst these early schools, and a model for the layout of many later schools, was that built as early as 1724 at Caerleon, under the will of Charles Williams, a native of the town who had made his fortune in London. The school – still in use as a primary school – is a flattened H in plan, two storeys high, with round-headed windows and a hipped roof. The lofty boys' classroom occupies the centre of the ground floor, with a master's and mistress's house at either end, and a girls' classroom, lit by dormer windows, above the boys' classroom.

In addition to the earlier grammar schools, eight more endowed grammar schools were built between 1712

own architect, influenced, no doubt, by his supporter Selina, Countess of Huntingdon, a friend of Walpole. Unfortunately the building suffered drastic alterations in the early twentieth century, making it a mere shadow of its former self. Following the completion of Coleg Trefeca, Lady Huntingdon leased a nearby sixteenth-century farm (Trefeca Isaf, later College Farm) to convert (1767–8) into 'a seminary for the preparation of earnest and devout young men' to provide preachers for the chapels she was building throughout England and Wales.[3] During the alterations a wing was added at the rear, the hall was transformed to a chapel and many of the windows were gothicized to Venetian or ogee windows.

Civic Buildings

The most important civic building of the earlier part of the eighteenth century is the Shire Hall in Monmouth, a bold structure built in 1724 to a late baroque design by a certain Fisher of Bristol. In its urbanity, scale and unity of design it stands alone among Welsh public buildings of the period. Built to the traditional town hall pattern, it has an open ground-floor market with an assembly room above, reached, in this case, by a noble staircase at the rear. The main, six-bay facade has tall, paired full-height windows, over a continuous arcade with wide, flattened arches. (147) The bays are divided by giant Ionic pilasters, with coupled pilasters at either end, the two central bays being united under a wide pediment. Later (1792), a statue of Henry V (born in Monmouth) was inserted between the two central bays.

During the latter part of the century a number of new town halls – beginning with Cardiff's Guild Hall (erected 1747; demolished c.1851) – were erected in various market towns. One such is the plain, stuccoed Town Hall at Laugharne, built in 1747 with a charming tapered clock tower of whitewashed rubble topped by a slate pyramid and bellcote. (148) Montgomery's attractive red-brick Town Hall, facing the square, was designed (William Baker, 1748–51) on a similar plan to that at Monmouth, but on an altogether more modest scale. Five bays long, with a slightly projecting wider central bay, it was originally built with an open arcade of round-

and 1762. Not all flourished, and there is little architectural evidence now of those that did, as most were rebuilt in later centuries. Most grammar school building in the eighteenth century was in fact devoted to schools that had been founded in the seventeenth century, such as at Bangor, Beaumaris and Ruthin in the north, and Carmarthen, Cowbridge and Swansea in the south.

There were also a number of private Dissenting academies, most of which met in houses or chapel buildings. Architecturally the most unusual was Coleg Trefeca, near Talgarth (Powys), where Howel Harris, one of the founders of Calvinistic Methodism in Wales, converted Trefeca Fach (his family home) between 1752 and c.1760 into a college for his 'family' of followers. Three parallel wings were added to the house, all in the Gothick style of Strawberry Hill near London. The central three-storey wing and the outer two-storey wings had battlemented gables, slim, circular turrets and gothicized Venetian windows. (146) Harris was said to have been his

148 Town Hall, Laugharne, Carmarthenshire.

149 Town Hall, Montgomery.

headed arches to the ground floor market and windowless walls – save for a lunette in the centre – to the courtroom above, plus a low, hipped roof, central pediment and cupola. **(149)** The upper floor was raised in height in 1828, windows were inserted and the ground-floor arches filled in.

Carmarthen's Guildhall (Sir Robert Taylor, 1765–77) was originally built, as at Monmouth and Montgomery, with an open ground-floor market, and a tall stuccoed upper floor with three large Venetian windows, each with a central round-headed light. The ground floor was later enclosed and

fronted (1860–2) by rusticated Bath stone walls and a wide but shallow porch with paired Tuscan columns. At the same time the stucco was removed from the upper floor and a clock turret added to the hipped roof.

Other small-scale town halls were erected at Bala (late eighteenth century), Meirionnydd, and Beaumaris (1785), Anglesey, in the north; and at Llantrisant (1773), in Glamorgan, the first two probably following the traditional design of an open, arcaded ground floor.

Ruthin has a modestly scaled Denbigh County Hall (now a library) designed by Joseph Turner, a Hawarden architect who practised from Chester. Begun in 1785 as a place to house the records of the Court of Great Sessions, it was later extended to contain the courthouse, and completed in 1790. Its outstanding feature is a monumental portico with Greek Doric columns and pediment, to which were added, on either side, screen walls containing arches with segmental pediments.

Towards the end of the eighteenth century a number of new prisons were built, implementing proposals left by the prison reformer John Howard. One of these, the old Gaol,

Ruthin, was designed (1755) by Joseph Turner. Its five-bay front has a broad three-bay pediment above a central arched recess. In the south, John Nash was responsible for designing new gaols at Carmarthen (1789–92), within the grounds of the castle, and at Cardigan (1791–7) to a radial plan. According to Richard Suggett, 'Nash's prisons made a considerable impact because of their scale, ingenuity, and architectural sophistication.'[4] All three were later closed or replaced.

Industrial Buildings

From early in the eighteenth century Wales was involved in an extraordinary period of industrial change that was to transform much of its landscape and townscape. The first major industry was that of copper smelting, which was initially established in 1584 at Aberdulais in the Neath valley.

150 Dyfi Furnace, Ceredigion.

By the early eighteenth century, the industry had moved to the Swansea area, primarily because of the town's superior harbour and its nearness to Cornwall, the main source of copper ore until the rediscovery of the ore in Anglesey in 1764. The establishment of the Fforest Copperworks in 1748, the fourth to be sited alongside the Tawe river, had an innovative design and layout, thanks to the employment of William Edwards of Groes-wen – chapel minister, self-made mason and bridge builder – as the architect. Here, instead of the furnaces being in a long, shedlike building, they were located in four circular pavilions with truncated conical roofs, arranged at the corners of a square with an octagonal refinery in the centre of the group. The two pavilions nearest the river were connected to each other by a low, single-storey building with, in the middle, a pedimented gatehouse surmounted by a cupola. A three-arched bridge (also designed by Edwards, 1747–52) in front of the gatehouse gave access to the copper-rolling mills on the other side of the river.

The ironmaking industry had from the latter part of the sixteenth century used small charcoal-burning blast furnaces scattered around the countryside. Typical of these early plants was the old-fashioned Dyfi Furnace in northern Ceredigion, dating from 1755. It was built on two floors cut into the steep river bank, with water from the river used to turn a water-wheel at the side of the building. **(150)** Raw materials were carried to the charging platform on the upper floor and tipped into the bottle-shaped furnace at the end of the building, where a pair of bellows (driven by the water wheel) on the ground floor provided a continuous blast of air to raise the furnace temperature sufficiently to liquefy the materials into iron.

At about the same time as the Dyfi Furnace was being built the ironmaking process was radically improved by using coke instead of charcoal as a fuel for smelting the ore. There is some doubt about the earliest use of coke in Wales, although Charles Lloyd is known to have experimented with it at the Bersham furnace near Wrexham as early as 1721. But when Isaac Wilkinson took over the ironworks in 1753, it still seems to have been 'operating as a charcoal furnace, or with charcoal and coke alternately'.[5] It was here, too, that the earliest known railway – an eighteenth-century wooden wagonway built to take coal and iron ore to the furnace – was discovered. The first coke furnace to be built in the southern coalfield – with its plentiful supply of carbon-rich coal, limestone and water power – was at Hirwaun, near Aberdare, in 1757. This was soon followed by new ironworks in the Merthyr Tydfil area, at Dowlais (1759), Plymouth (1763) and Cyfarthfa (1765). As a result of the new industry Merthyr Tydfil rapidly developed from a small village to become the largest and most important town by the mid-nineteenth century. Other ironworks were built further east at Sirhowy (1778), Blaenafon (1789) and Clydach (1793), each of which has still visible remains of early blast furnaces. The Blaenafon Ironworks was designed as a multi-furnace site from the beginning, and by 1792 had three furnaces encased by tall, tapering towers of masonry together with their casting houses. In order to attract key workers from the English Midlands, three terraces of spacious (by the standards of the day), two-bedroom cottages were built around an open yard on the site in about 1788. **(151)**

The woollen industry was next to agriculture in the economy of the country districts, but as a rural craft it has left little in the way of dedicated buildings, apart from fulling mills. These gradually became larger towards the end of the century as spinning machines and dye houses were added to the looms, and the industry gradually developed on factory

151 Stack Square, Blaenafon Ironworks, Blaenafon.

lines, particularly in the Severn valley where flannel was prepared for English markets in Shrewsbury.

In fact the earliest textile mills had nothing to do with wool but were for the cotton trade, first established in the north by John Smalley and John Chambers in 1777 in an old paper mill at Holywell, Flintshire. Two years later, and using stones from the ruins of nearby Basingwerk Abbey, they erected a three-storey cotton mill with a large water wheel. When Smalley died in 1782, his son Christopher took over the enterprise and erected two new six-storey mills, along the banks of the Greenfield valley, completely dominating their rural surroundings. The Upper Mills, 'which had nearly

152 Lleweni Bleach Works, near Denbigh.

200 windows – was completed within six weeks' in 1783, followed by the Lower Mills two years later.[6] A fourth, similar mill, the Crescent Mill, was built in 1790.

Even more impressive than the Holywell mills was the Bleach Works near Denbigh, where Thomas Fitzmaurice of Lleweni Hall had a factory built in 1785 for treating linen brought over from his Irish estates. Designed by Thomas Sandby (brother of artist Paul Sandby), it was built on a vast scale in the form of a two-storey crescent, 122 m wide, with a projecting three-bay loggia with cupola in the centre and majestic, sixteen-bay curving colonnades on either side. (152) The upper floor was set back from the colonnades and punctuated by semicircular drum towers. In front were five fountains in circular pools. Pennant described it as being 'without parallel, whether the magnitude, the ingenuity of the machinery, or the size of the bleaching ground is to be considered'.[7] Fitzmaurice was succeeded in 1793 by Viscount Kirkwall, who sixteen years later went bankrupt and put his estate and the Bleach Works up for sale.

Bridges and Viaducts

For most of the eighteenth century Wales was inadequately provided with reasonable roads. Partly this was due to a lack of any perceived need for better communications, but most importantly because of the mountainous nature of much of the country, the difficulty of building roads and the numerous bridges that were required. Gradually attitudes changed and attempts were made to improve the situation by building new bridges.

The finest by far of these early bridges was Pont-y-ty-pridd (Bridge by the earth house), or the Old Bridge as it is now known, which was built in the middle of the century across the Taff river at Pontypridd by William Edwards of Groes-wen. His first attempts to span the river, in 1746 and 1751, ended in failure, but at his third attempt in 1756 he successfully constructed an elegant, single-arched bridge with an unprecedented span of 43 m. (153) It was a significant event on three counts: 'the span, at the date of construction, was longer by at least 30 ft (9 m) than that of

The Architecture of Wales

any other arch in Britain, the arch was recklessly slender and the spandrils pierced by open cylindrical voids never seen in Britain before.'[8] To reduce the bridge's self-weight – and also to allow the passage of flood water – Edwards had pierced the spandrils with three large cylindrical holes, descending in size, at each end, thus contributing to the structure's extraordinary grace. Later, Edwards built other bridges to a similar design, including those at Pontardawe (c.1770), Dolauhirion (1773), near Llandovery, and two at Morriston (c.1780 and 1778), near Swansea, but none was as wide a span or as daring as the one at Pontypridd.

To transport the materials from where many of the major industries were located to other parts of Britain, it was necessary to improve the existing communications and this resulted in some magnificent works of engineering. The first major improvement was achieved during the latter part of the eighteenth century through the construction of canals from the manufacturing centres to the ports. More often than not, these involved expensive cutting and embanking along narrow twisting valleys, as in the case of the Glamorganshire Canal, which was constructed from Merthyr Tydfil to Cardiff between 1790 and 1794. In its comparatively short distance of 40 km it traversed a landfall of 150 m and incorporated forty locks.

In the north, William Jessop and Thomas Telford constructed a canal (now a World Heritage Site) from Llangollen to join the Shropshire Union Canal at Ellesmere, that included building two dramatically situated aqueducts in addition to tunnels and embankments. The canal is carried across the aqueducts in troughs of cast-iron plates bolted together. At Chirk (1796–1801) they are supported 21 m above the Afon Ceiriog by ten round-headed stone arches, and at Pont Cysyllte (1795–1805) they are supported 38 m above the Afon Eglwyseg on eighteen slender, tapering (and partly hollow) stone piers of exceptional elegance. (154)

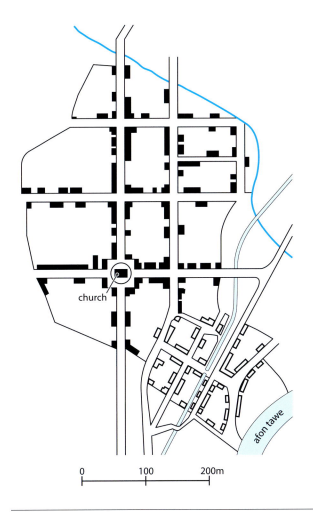

church

afon tawe

0   100   200m

155 Morriston, Swansea, begun 1779.

Planned Towns

There were few attempts to build towns according to preconceived plans until the end of the century. In the fast-growing industrial areas planning was, with a single exception, non-existent, or at best only limited to small housing estates. The exception was Morriston, near Swansea, which was founded by Sir John Morris to attract and house labour for his copper works. Morris employed William Edwards to design the new town, which was laid out in two phases occupying four fields. The earlier phase, beginning in 1779, occupied the field nearest to the river where four short streets were laid out in straight lines roughly parallel to the Tawe. (155) In the main phase that followed, and occupied the remaining three fields, the streets were laid out on spacious lines to a gridiron plan at an angle to the first phase, and plots of land were leased on condition that the lessees built their houses according to prescribed plans. The development was bisected by a long, straight street (Woodville Street) that was originally intended to have two squares, one for an Anglican church (built in 1787) and the other possibly for an open-air market. In the end the second square was not constructed, and a market hall – 'a communal structure of some pretension', with arched ground-floor openings and battlemented walls 'flanked by two small towers with gothic windows'[9]– was built close to the junction where the two road layouts met. Once started, Morriston flourished and grew, so that by 1796 there were already 141 houses with a population of over 600. By 1815 the size of the community had almost doubled.

Away from the industrial areas the clearest example of forward planning was at Milford, in Pembrokeshire. The town came into being in 1790, when an Act of Parliament was obtained 'to make and provide Quays, Docks and Piers and other erections and to establish a Market with proper Roads and Avenues thereto'. Little seems to have been done however until 1797 when a French architect, Jean-Louis Barallier, was employed to design the new town. The layout that Barallier devised was a simple grid pattern of three parallel streets crossed at right angles by shorter streets. This has survived, giving the centre of Milford its distinctive character, although the buildings themselves were only developed slowly and haphazardly. The larger houses were in the lower street, shops in the middle street and smaller houses in the upper street. At the end of the lower street a plain Gothick church (1802–8), probably designed by Barallier, was built to terminate the vista. A quay, custom house, market hall and chapels were also built. In addition it was hoped to found a naval and engineering college, but of this only an octagonal observatory appears to have been completed ∎

11 Non-domestic Architecture in the Eighteenth Century
References

1   R. Suggett, *John Nash*, p. 114.

2   M. Seaborne, *Schools in Wales, 1500–1900*, p. 44.

3   G. Davies, 'Trevecka (1706–1964)', *Brycheiniog*, 15 (1971), 45.

4   Suggett, *John Nash*, p. 29.

5   P. Riden, *A Gazetteer of Charcoal-fired Blast Furnaces in Great Britain*, p. 65.

6   A. H. Dodd, *The Industrial Revolution in North Wales*, p. 284.

7   Quoted by Celina Fox, *The Arts of Industry in the Age of Enlightenment*, p. 418.

8   E. C. Ruddock, 'William Edward's Bridge at Pontypridd', in *Industrial Archaeology*, 11/3 (1974), 194.

9   S. Hughes, *Copperopolis*, p. 202.

12

Industry and Transport, 1800 to 1915

The full impact of the Industrial Revolution was felt in the nineteenth century when the old pattern of building development was often overlaid and largely obliterated. In Glamorgan, Monmouthshire and parts of Carmarthenshire, beautiful secluded valleys were transformed into monotonous sprawls of ironworks, coal mines and terraced houses. To a lesser extent, parts of the north-east, and north-west were also radically changed by iron-making, coal mining or quarrying. With the coming of new industry went the need for improved communications, and these

also left their mark on the countryside in the form of canals, turnpike roads, railways, bridges and tunnels. Change was not limited, however, to the industrialized areas. In the rural parts of Wales the landscape was permanently affected by innovations brought about by the Agricultural Revolution and by the enclosure of common land.

Building activity was vastly affected by these changes. Not only was there more urgent building activity than ever before, but new types of buildings were required and new forms of construction were evolved. Within the wide range of buildings that were erected during this period some of the most exciting were those concerned with industry and transport. Indeed, as Elisabeth Beazley has commented, 'Wales, by chance of time and geography, saw structures that were to amaze the world. A history of industrial revolution building might be written using Welsh examples only.'[1]

Metallic Industry

By the beginning of the nineteenth century ironmaking had established itself as the major industry in Wales, initiating a massive change from agricultural to industrial work, and with it an extraordinary increase in population. With the exception of ironworks at Bersham and Brymbo near Wrexham, the iron industry was predominantly sited in the south, mostly in a series of ironworks along the northern outcrop of the coalfield. The distribution of these ironworks led, in turn, to the creation of a string of new towns, such as Aberdare, Blaenafon, Ebbw Vale, Nant-y-glo, Pontypool, Rhymney and Tredegar, with Merthyr Tydfil as the main centre of the iron industry and the largest town in Wales. The largest ironworks – Dowlais and Cyfarthfa (with sixteen and seven furnaces respectively in 1881) – were both in Merthyr Tydfil, and covered vast areas of ground. Already in 1796 there were sixteen ironworks in the south with twenty-four furnaces. By 1823 this had increased to twenty-two ironworks with seventy-two furnaces, and by 1839 to 40 ironworks with more than a 120 furnaces. In 1796 the ironworks in the south produced 27 per cent of the total amount of pig iron in Britain; by 1830 the south had become the leading iron-producing area in Britain, accounting for 41 per cent of all production (figures based on L. Ince, *The South Wales Iron Industry 1750–1885*). In their heyday, the ironworks would have been awe-inspiring sights, especially at night when the sky was lit up by rows of monumental blast furnaces billowing clouds of glowing smoke from the fires below.

All of the Welsh ironworks were closed long ago, and little remains to be seen now except for the derelict ruins of furnace towers and engine houses at some of the sites. The buildings of the ironworks were solidly constructed and functional in design, and though rarely pretentious, they were often of a high standard of design when compared with the workers' housing built close by. Perhaps the most characteristic feature of an ironworks was the bank of monumental, tapered masonry towers that enclosed the furnaces. The furnace towers were usually set against a bank of cliff for charging (i.e., loading the raw materials) from the top, solidly built and up to 18 m high, with arches on two or three sides for the tuyères that took the blast into the furnace, and for tapping the molten iron. Good examples of furnace towers can still be seen at Cyfarthfa, Blaenafon and Neath Abbey ironwork sites. Other important buildings

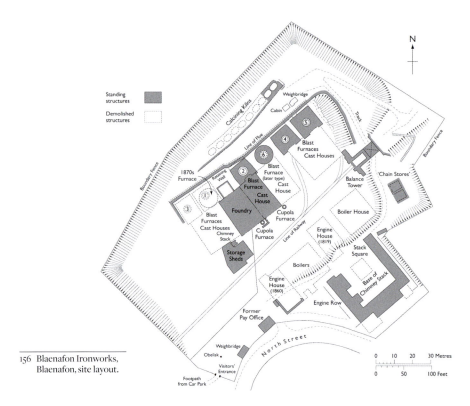

156 Blaenafon Ironworks, Blaenafon, site layout.

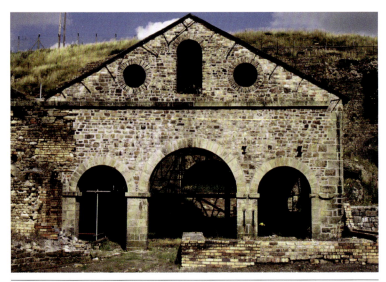

157 Blaenafon Ironworks, Blaenafon, Cast House.

158 Blaenafon Ironworks, Blaenafon, Water Balance Tower.

159 Dowlais Ironworks, Merthyr Tydfil, stables.

were the blowing engine houses needed to provide blast for the furnaces. The engine house (1836) of the Ynysfach Ironworks (a subsidiary of the Cyfarthfa company), Merthyr Tydfil, still retains something of the dignity of these early industrial buildings where a simply repeated pattern of arched openings is outlined in ashlar limestone against a background of Pennant Sandstone rubble.

The Blaenafon Ironworks is now the most rewarding site to visit, for here numerous relics of the industry can still be seen. **(156)** At the back of the site, below the cliff, are the remains of five tapering, masonry furnace towers, built from the late eighteenth century to 1861. In front of these are remains of the Cast Houses where molten iron from the furnaces was run into pig iron beds. **(157)** They, like many ironworks buildings were recognizable by the large circular openings for ventilation. At the furthest end of the site is the elegantly designed Water Balance Tower, built about 1839 to lift (by balancing tanks of water) loaded trucks to a tramroad at the upper works level. **(158)** To the right are the house terraces built in the late eighteenth century to house key workers. At Dowlais near Merthyr Tydfil – once the largest ironworks in the world, employing 7,300 men, women and children – all

160 Bute Ironworks, Rhymney. *A South Wales Industrial Landscape*, attributed to Penry Williams, c.1825.

161 Hetty Shaft Colliery engine-house, Hopkinstown, near Pontypridd.

162 Lewis Merthyr Colliery, near Pontypridd, headframe.

remains have been swept away save for a red-brick engine house with a lofty porch carried on cast iron columns and a grandiose stable block that still dominates the town. **(159)** Twenty-one bays long and two storeys, high with pedimented end bays and a tall, pedimented entrance arch in the centre, the stables were built in 1820 to house the ironworks' horses.

Almost certainly the most architecturally ambitious of all the ironworks was the Bute Ironworks in Rhymney, which David Stewart (surveyor to the Bute estate) hoped in 1824 'may become the first works in Wales and consequently in the world'.[2] The buildings were designed in supposedly Egyptian style (based on the ruins of Dendera) by the physician, geologist and amateur architect John MacCulloch. **(160)** In 1828 the designs were exhibited at the Royal Academy in London, where, together with articles in the engineering press, they caused much publicity.

Allied to ironmaking was the tinplate industry. This came to be concentrated in parts of Glamorgan and Carmarthenshire. The remains of a number of early tinplate buildings still stand, though, as they were later adapted for use by other industries, they are often difficult to recognize. The famous tinplate works established in 1815 by the Crawshays

of Cyfarthfa at Trefforest, in the Taff valley, survive and are of interest for their spidery wrought-iron roof trusses and the disciplined architectural treatment of their external walls. Five long, narrow, whitewashed stone buildings remain, each punctuated by a pattern of very tall round-headed openings and smaller circular ventilation openings in the Cyfarthfa manner. Tinplate manufacture began at Kidwelly in 1737 on the site of an earlier forge, and was only the second works of its kind in Britain. It is now an industrial museum, and among its relics are a water-powered mill, rebuilt in 1801, and the Assorting Room and Boxing Room, both dating from c.1880.

Extractive Industry

Until the 1970s coal mines, with their easily recognizable winding towers, engine houses and tall, free-standing chimneys, were familiar feature of the Glamorgan and Monmouthshire valleys, as well as parts of Carmarthenshire and Pembrokeshire and in Flintshire and Denbighshire in the north-east. Now, apart from a handful of iconic relics at a few mining museums, they have, together with the enormous coal tips, nearly all gone. Until the 1840s the coal industry

163 Crumlin Navigation Colliery, Crumlin, Monmouthshire.

was mainly a secondary adjunct to the ironworks, and was concerned almost entirely with providing fuel for the furnaces of the ironworks and other metallic industries. As early as 1828, however, Robert Thomas had opened a level at Abercanaid, near Merthyr Tydfil, and begun selling coal for general use, thus pioneering the steam coal trade in southern Wales. The earliest collieries were mostly established along the northern rim of the coalfield and were consequently fairly shallow. Later in the century, as the demand for coal increased and as more elaborate methods were evolved for sinking shafts, deeper pits were opened up further down the valleys.

The winding-houses that accommodated the huge engines and winding drums – often the largest surface building of a colliery – were usually simple, straightforward masonry structures built on valley side sites, and often raised high on masonry podiums, like that at the Hetty Shaft, built for the Great Western Colliery in 1875 and still standing, complete with its original machinery. **(161)** Usually they had round-headed windows and doorways – sometimes picked out in ashlar or red or yellow brickwork – and were often reminiscent of local Nonconformist chapels, being in many cases designed and built by the same architects and builders. In some of the later

winding houses, a large semicircular arch adorned the main front, as at National Colliery (1890), Rhondda, giving them a resemblance to many Nonconformist chapels of the period.

The most distinctive feature of any colliery, however, was the headframe (usually in pairs) used for hauling the cages (for men and coal) up from the coal face to the surface. Originally headframes were constructed in timber, with many surviving into the early twentieth century. But by the middle of the nineteenth century as the pit shafts became deeper and deeper, taller and stronger frames were needed, up to 18 m high and made of either iron or steel, first with complex lattice girders, as at the Bertie (1880) and Trefor (1890) shafts of the Lewis Merthyr Colliery (now Rhondda Heritage Park), Trehafod, **(162)** and later with rolled-steel joists. Many of the coal companies had their own distinctive type of headframe, of which Nixon's were amongst the most complex, as at the Merthyr Vale Colliery (1864) in the Taff valley. The main part of the headframe normally comprised four vertical legs to form a straight or tapered tower, supported by diagonal backstays that were stiffened by additional struts, or by curved struts, as at the Deep Navigation Colliery (1878), Treharris.

For most of the coal era, rubble stone was the usual material for constructing the buildings of a colliery. Brick appears to have been used in conjunction with stone at the Plas Power Colliery near Wrexham as far back as 1875, and by the 1890s all-brick colliery buildings were being erected in the north-eastern coalfield. The most dramatic use of brick, however, was at the new Crumlin Navigation Colliery in the southern coalfield, where the whole array of buildings was erected in polychromatic brick between 1907 and 1911. **(163)** The colliery closed in 1967, but the red and cream buildings – including two winding engine houses, a pumping house, offices, pithead baths (from the 1930s) and a splendid chimney – have been saved for possible community and commercial use.

In mid-Wales the most important extractive industry was lead mining. Although the Ystwyth valley at Cwmystwyth is scarred with the waste heaps and workings dating from as far back as the sixteenth century (and possibly earlier), there is little to see of nineteenth-century lead-mining structures of any real architectural interest. Similarly in Montgomeryshire, where the principal site of lead working was at the Bryntail mine, near Llanidloes. Here the most productive period was in the mid-nineteenth century. The low-wall ruins of a number of mining buildings have been conserved, but nothing sufficient to give a clear impression of what the buildings once looked like.

The main extractive industry in Gwynedd has long been slate – reputedly 'the most Welsh of Welsh industries' – which was once quarried on a limited scale by the Romans, and also on a small scale during the Middle Ages and later for local use. It was not until the late 1780s onwards that slate quarrying became a substantial industry and slate had a major influence on the building industry as a cheap and weatherproof form of roof covering. The result could be seen in industrial towns everywhere, in the rows of terrace houses roofed with the thin grey-blue slates of Gwynedd. The industry was mainly concentrated in four areas, around Bethesda, Llanberis, Blaenau Ffestiniog and the Nantlle Valley. Slates were also exported in immense quantities from specially built docks, such as Porthmadog, Port Penrhyn and Y Felinheli.

Port Penrhyn has a collection of interesting buildings, including the Port House, a neoclassical villa-type office block with a Doric porch, designed by James Wyatt, son of Benjamin Wyatt, in 1832, a single-storey Italianate style Estate Office, c. 1860, and a circular, twelve-seater, tide-flushed privy with a conical roof. Occasionally the buildings at the slate quarries themselves were designed with some concern for appearance. The Dinorwig Quarry Workshops (now a museum), Llanberis, built in 1870, were planned as a quadrangle around an open yard. It has a symmetrical, two-storey main front with a tall round-headed arch to the central gatehouse, and corner towers topped by pyramidal steeples, all built with local granite. On the hillside nearby are the remains of two, long single-storey barrack terraces, built between 1869 and 1873 in slate, for quarry workers from Anglesey. Perhaps the most evocative and impressive monument of the slate industry is the Ynysypandy Slate Mill, near Porthmadog. Built in 1856–7 and probably designed by James Brunlees, it now stands roofless in the valley of Cwm

164 Ynys-y-pandy Slate Mill, Dolbenmaen, Caernarfonshire.

Ystradlyn, surrounded by gaunt mountains. **(164)** Built into the natural slope of the site to aid the manufacturing process, it has three floors of rhythmic rows of closely spaced, tall and round-headed window openings reminiscent of a cathedral building. A curving railway on a high embankment brought the raw slate in at the top floor level, where it was sawn; the slate was then dressed on the middle floor before being carried out to another railway running parallel with the upper one. A giant water wheel at ground-floor level drove the machinery.

Limestone has long been used in building, either as masonry or as lime used in mortar and cement, and as a soil-improving agent in agriculture. Limestone is burnt to form lime, either at the quarry where it is worked or in limekilns nearer to where the lime is to be used. Consequently, limekilns are found all over the country, making it one of the commonest forms of industry. Generally speaking limekilns are a small-scale type of industry, often in the form of single

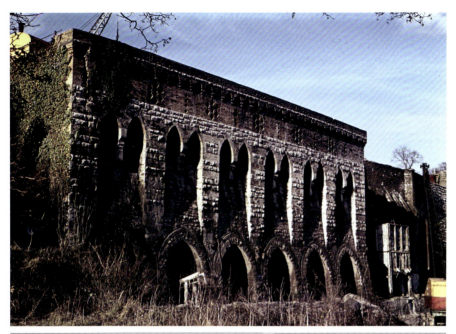

165 Lime-kilns, Llandybie, Carmarthenshire.

the eighteenth century the leading place of manufacture of bright-red Ruabon bricks, and from about 1870 of the hard, pressed terracotta that was usually used as floor tiles but also (as in Cardiff's Pierhead Building) as a facing material. Clay was also used in the short-lived china and porcelain industry, based at the Cambrian Pottery in Swansea and the partly restored Nantgarw Pottery near Cardiff. The potteries were instantly recognizable in their time by the distinctive, bottle-shaped kilns that were used for firing the clay.

Textile Industry

During the eighteenth century the manufacture of woollen flannel had become the main textile industry, mostly located in the Severn valley. Initially carried on in scattered farmsteads, flannel making was becoming increasingly centralized by the 1790s, especially in Llanidloes and Newtown. With the construction of the Montgomeryshire Canal in 1821 and the erection of a Flannel Exchange in 1832, Newtown became the main centre of the flannel trade, with eighty-two cottage-factories and thirty-five spinning mills. The two-storey Flannel Exchange was designed by Thomas Penson in neoclassical style with a Doric portico and paired pilasters, large windows on the ground floor and small square windows to the upper floor. After conversion – first to public rooms, then a post office, and latterly to a cinema and leisure centre – it lost some of its detail but still stands in Broad Street. The cottage-factories were built in three- or four-storey (mostly brick) terraces, with pairs of back-to-back cottages on the lower floors and weaving rooms on the two upper floors accessed by external stairs. The weaving rooms were open from end to end and were lit by large and wide casement windows between which stood the handlooms. Most of the cottage-factories have now gone, although a few remain on the Penygloddfa side of the river. Numbers 5 to 7 Commercial Street, originally with six tiny back-to-back cottages, were restored and opened in 1967 as the Newtown Textile Museum.

Further south, a growing demand for flannel from the thriving towns of the coalfield led to the development of many new woollen mills, mainly in the Teifi Valley and northern

kilns built into a bank for ease of loading from the top, or as rows. The limekilns at Llandybie, in Carmarthenshire, were something different in that here the making of lime was treated on an industrial scale in a bank of six giant limekilns. **(165)** They were built in 1856–7 to a pseudo-Gothic design by the Welshpool architect R. K. Penson, who exhibited a perspective of the kilns at the Royal Academy in 1858. The draw-holes at the base had large pointed arches set in a slightly inclined wall, out of which emerged stone and brick buttresses with pairs of smaller, sharply pointed arches between each, all surmounted by a perforated frieze of coloured brickwork and a corbelled parapet.

The clay industry provided opportunities for building brickworks – sometimes as a subsidiary of ironworks or coal mines – in many parts of the country, but especially in the Buckley area of Flintshire and Ruabon in Denbighshire. The Penybont Works at Cefn Mawr was from the middle of

Breconshire. Although some were built on the pattern of the Yorkshire mills, they were generally much smaller, up to three storeys high and mostly built in stone with red-brick trimmings. Some of the woollen mills had been converted from older corn mills or fulling mills. The Cambrian Woollen Mill at Llanwrtyd, for instance, had been a corn mill (built c. 1820) before it was converted to wool produce in about 1850. The stone-built Esgair Moel Woollen Mill, from the same area, had also started, c.1760, as a corn mill before being converted during the 1830s to wool. The original two-storey building was too small, however, and had to be greatly extended for adaptation to weaving. Once converted, it continued in use until 1947, before being transferred, stone by stone, and re-erected at the National Museum of History.

After a decline in sales, the woollen industry in the Severn valley revived with the arrival of the railway in 1862, when three steam-driven factories were built. At about the same time, Pryce Jones began selling woollen goods, first to local gentry by sending out textile patterns and later by catalogues throughout Britain, thereby establishing the world's first mail order business. In 1879 Jones had the Royal Welsh Warehouse built at a cost of £13,000 for his mail order business and department store. Designed by David Walker in Italian Renaissance style, the four-storey, red-brick building is divided into seven bays by brick pilasters and has a projecting, pedimented doorway in the centre. **(166)** The building was later extended to the right and a six-storey factory (Agriculture House, designed by George Hornblower) was built in 1895 on the opposite side of the road and linked to the original Warehouse by a bridge (now gone).

Transport: Bridges and Viaducts

The continued rapid increase of industry, often in remote and almost inaccessible places, required further improvements in transport facilities, and this inevitably led to the building of many new bridges and viaducts. The most substantial long-distance road improvement was the Holyhead Turnpike Road built in 1815–29 to Thomas Telford's design to improve the stage coach route from London to Dublin. The first important

166 Royal Welsh Warehouse, Newtown, Montgomeryshire.

167 Menai suspension bridge.

structure along this route is the beautiful Waterloo Bridge (1815) across the Afon Conwy at Betws-y-Coed. The cast-iron spandrels of this bridge are elaborately decorated with giant leeks, roses, thistle and clover, and bear the inscription that *This arch was constructed in the same year the battle of Waterloo was fought*. Telford's masterpiece was Pont-y-Borth (1819–26), joining the Welsh mainland to the Isle of Anglesey by crossing the Menai Strait in what was at the time one of the world's largest iron suspension bridges. **(167)** The centre span, 176 m long, carries the road 30 m above the water – as demanded by the Admiralty – and is suspended from towers faced with Penmon limestone at each end by massive chains (originally wrought-iron). It is approached by arched stone viaducts from both sides of the Strait. The last crossing, between Valley and Holy Island was achieved by building an embankment 1189 m long. Of the original octagonal toll-houses that lined the route, only one remains, that built at Llanfairpwllgwyn in 1823. While the trunk road was being built, Telford also designed the suspension bridge (with a centre span of 100 m) that crossed the Afon Conwy just below Conwy Castle. Opened in 1826, it has castellated round towers to blend with the castle.

At the opposite end of the country the most striking iron road bridge is the gently curving Wye Bridge at Chepstow. Designed by John Rennie and opened in 1816, it has five graduated spans (the longest being 34 m) with cast-iron, radially patterned spandrels resting on stone piers. At first glance, the three-arched Long Bridge at Newtown in mid-Wales, looks outwardly similar to the Chepstow bridge. In fact it was built as a stone bridge in 1826 and the iron spandrels (designed by Thomas Penson) were only attached after pavements were added following a road accident. The elegant single-arch bridges crossing the Severn river at Llandinam (1846) and Aber-miwl (1852) were also designed by Penson. Both are braced cast-iron structures, the former with a 27.5-m span, and the latter with 33 m span.

While the world's first load-carrying steam locomotive had made its pioneering run as early as 1804 at Penydarren, near Merthyr Tydfil, the railway mania proper did not arrive until much later. Because of the mountainous nature of the country, railway construction, when it commenced, required the building of many bridges and viaducts. These were mainly in the south, but two of the most notable railway bridges were built in the north, both by the engineer Robert Stephenson in association with the architect Francis Thompson. Both bridges were built alongside Telford's earlier road bridges across the Afon Conwy and the difficult Menai Strait. In each case, Stephenson's answer to the engineering problem was in the form of continuous rectangular tubes through which the trains pass, representing a new landmark in the world development of bridge building. Like Telford, Francis Thompson designed castellated towers (but rectangular instead of round) at each end of the Conwy Tubular Bridge (completed 1848) in deference to both the earlier bridge and the medieval castle. The Britannia Tubular Bridge over the Menai Strait, was built (completed 1850) with two separate metal tubes, one for each track, and is in four spans divided by great stone pylons 'superbly detailed by Thompson'.[3] The entrances at either end of the bridge are flanked by enormous stone lions sculpted by John Thomas. The bridge has a total length of 460 m and is 30 m above water, a stipulation that necessitated building the long centre spans (each 140 m) on land and floating them out on pontoons to the required positions and then slowly hauling them up by hydraulic pumps. In 1970 the great wrought-iron tubes were badly damaged by fire. This led to rebuilding the bridge on two levels (road above railway) with the centre spans supported on steel arches with spandrels braced with N-trusses and the end spans supported on concrete piers.

Many railway viaducts were built in stone with round-headed arches, as at Cefn Mawr and Chirk, where Telford's aqueducts were paralleled by masonry railway viaducts designed by Henry Robertson in 1846–8 for the Shrewsbury and Chester Railway. The Cefn Mawr viaduct over the Dee river has nineteen arches, is 459 m long and stands 43 m high, making it the highest viaduct in Britain. The Chirk viaduct, over the Afon Ceiriog, has sixteen arches and is 259 m long. Robertson was also responsible for the remotely sited masonry viaducts at Cynghordy (1858) and Cnwclas (1862) in mid-Wales for the Central Wales Railway.

168 Hengoed railway viaduct, near Caerphilly.

The former has eighteen arches and the latter has thirteen, with castellated towers at either end. Stone-arched viaducts are difficult to dismantle economically, and consequently they have tended to last longer than iron or steel viaducts. A number of fine examples, Roman in scale, still exist in the mining valleys of the south. The longest, the sixteen-arch Hengoed viaduct at Ystrad Mynach, was built in 1857 to designs by Liddel and Gordon and strides majestically across the Rhymni valley for 260 m at a height of 39 m. **(168)** The graceful viaduct at Cefncoedycwmer, Merthyr Tydfil, a slim fifteen-arch structure laid out to a bold curve, was erected in 1866 to the designs of Conybeare and Sutherland.

During the middle years of the century Isambard Brunel – one of the greatest railway engineers – built the South Wales Railway from Gloucester to Swansea, as well as the Vale of Neath Railway and the Taff Vale Railway, though

little of architectural interest remains. His tubular bridge at Chepstow (1852) has been replaced, and his wooden 'fan' viaducts at Neath (1851) and Aberdare (1854) have been demolished, as well as his long, twenty-seven-span wooden viaduct (1850) over the Tawe at Swansea. Fortunately, one of Brunel's stone viaducts is still in use at Quakers Yard, near Merthyr Tydfil. Built as a single-track viaduct for the Taff Vale Railway in 1840–1 (and later widened for two tracks), it spans the Afon Taf and the track of the old Penydarren Tramroad in a fine sweeping curve of six arches across one of the most attractive stretches of the valley. The Bute Street Station, terminus of the Taff Vale Railway in Cardiff, was built (possibly to a design by Brunel) in 1841, making it the oldest surviving station in Wales. **(169)**

The most dramatic of all British viaducts, was that across the deep valley of the Ebbw river at Crumlin for the

169 Bute Street Railway Station, Cardiff.

170 Transporter Bridge, Newport.

Newport, Abergavenny and Hereford Railway. It was built in 1853–7 to the design of T. W. Kennard, and was constructed in two sections on either side of a rocky knoll: one section 325 m long in seven equal spans, at a hair-raising 64 m height above the valley floor, and the other 178 m long of three spans. The tapering piers each comprised twelve cast-iron columns with wrought-iron bracing, and supported spans comprising Warren truss girders, the whole affair looking deceptively slim and fragile from a distance. Unfortunately this fine viaduct was demolished in 1965, although remnants of the end abutments remain.

An unusual kind of bridge that still survives is the Transporter Bridge at Newport. Designed by the French engineer, Ferdinand Arnodin (who had previously built similar bridges at Marseilles and Rouen), and completed in 1906, it is really a suspension bridge with the main span – in the form of a continuous truss – supported at a high level on deceptively slender latticed pylons to allow clearance of shipping. **(170)** The legs of the lattice pylons, tapered to points at the base, are delicately balanced on top of stone piers. Hovering over the water and suspended from the main span 54 m above is a travelling carriage that transports vehicles and people across the Usk river.

Ports and Maritime Buildings

Ports, as the name implies, are clearly related to transport. This was certainly the case with Holyhead, which, after the union with Ireland in 1800, became the major transport link between mainland Britain and Ireland, and the official Irish packet port in 1801. The Old Harbour (John Rennie, engineer) was constructed in 1810–17; Thomas Telford's road link between London and Ireland eventually reached Holyhead in 1824 via the 1180 m long Stanley embankment; the railway followed in 1848, and a new station and hotel were erected in 1879–80. Marking the end of Telford's road is a Memorial Arch (Thomas Harrison, 1824) to commemrotae George IV's landing here in 1821; it is in marble from Benllech and has two Doric columns. Next to the arch is a Customs House and the Harbour Office, the latter with a clock tower and octagonal belfry. The station was built to a V-shaped plan with glass-roofed platforms on either side of the Inner Harbour, with the four-storey, red-brick hotel (since demolished) at the point where the platforms meet. In order to provide shelter for the packet boats as well as for Liverpool shipping an enormous 2.5 km long breakwater, engineered by J. M. Rendel, was constructed between 1847 and 1873.

A number of Glamorgan ports have (or had) interesting examples of buildings illustrating technological progress made during the nineteenth century. The well-preserved Jennings Warehouse dating from the 1830s on the quayside at Porthcawl, is the earliest of note. Used for storing iron, it is a two-storey stone building, fifteen bays long with double-light windows with brick arches. The Bute Warehouse (by W. S. Clark, 1861) at the north end of Cardiff's Bute East Dock (by John Rennie, 1852–9) is a neat four-storey building faced in red brick, the elevation punctuated by rows of small round-headed windows and two vertical series of haulage doors (now glazed). **(171)** The brick-vaulted floors are carried on parallel iron beams that are supported by an internal framework of round, cast-iron columns.

The former Coast Lines' twenty-one-bay banana

171 Bute Warehouse, Cardiff.

172 Weaver's Flour Mill, Swansea.

173 Pierhead Building, Cardiff.

174 Docks Office, Barry.

At much the same time two notable port buildings were being erected in what can only be termed architectural 'fancy-dress'. The Pierhead Building, in Cardiff, designed by William Frame (former assistant to William Burges) for the Bute Dock Company, was built 1896–7 as a spiky 'French Gothic' landmark, with pinnacled turrets and a castellated tower over the entrance, all faced in florid red terracotta. (173) Inside, and behind the majolica tiled vestibule, is an aisled hall with three bays of round-headed arches resting on square panelled columns. The Docks Office, Barry, designed by Arthur E. Bell for the Barry Railway Company, was built 1897–1900 in Portland stone and red brick as an elaborate and grand neo-baroque 'temple' of commerce with Corinthian columns and pilasters and a domed clock tower. (174) The two buildings make a strange pair: built a few miles from each other to serve precisely the same function, they epitomize the double-faced nature of much nineteenth-century architecture while at the same time reflecting the clients' personalities – the church-like Pierhead Building for the third Marquess of Bute, who was a multi-millionaire aristocrat, High Tory and Roman Catholic convert, and the civic-looking Docks Office for David Davies, self-made industrialist, Liberal and fervent Calvinistic Methodist.

The Royal Dockyard, Pembroke Dock, at the western end of the country, symbolizes not so much commerce and transport as shipbuilding and defence. The Royal Navy Dockyard was established in 1814 at the height of the Napoleonic wars to build ships for the Royal Navy. Construction of the 32 ha dockyard began the following year to plans by Edward Holl, which were probably based on an earlier report by John Rennie. The dockyard is surrounded by a high wall, with the main entrance and lodges roughly halfway along the southern wall. To the left of the entrance are offices, surgery and guard house, and on the right three blocks of limestone houses, mostly three storeys high with arcaded ground floors, and some with innovative iron roofs, largely completed by 1825. Parallel to the houses is The Avenue, with oval-shaped flower beds and, at the end, a plain chapel (1830–1) by G. L. Taylor in neo-Greek dress with a tall portico under a domed tower. The Defensible Barracks

warehouse (now part of the National Waterfront Museum) at Swansea's South Dock is an interesting, but less adventurous building. Completed in 1901, it is a vast red-brick, twenty-one bay, two-storey 'shed' with an exceptionally wide-span roof, stepped corbels and large round-headed and segmental windows to the gables. More exciting was the huge, six-storey granary and flour mill built for Weaver and Co. in 1897–8 to the designs of the French engineers, Hennebique and Le Brun. This was the first multi-storey, reinforced concrete-framed building to be erected in Britain, and the materials for constructing it had to be imported from France. Even at this early date in the story of modern concrete, the structural possibilities of the new material were exploited by cantilevering the five-storey end bays three metres out on concrete brackets. (172) The building was demolished in 1984 to make way for a supermarket, outside which one of the concrete columns has been preserved.

175 Defensible Barracks, Pembroke Dock, aerial view.

176 Martello Tower, Pembroke Dock.

were built in 1841–6 as a fort on the hill overlooking the dockyard to accommodate Royal Marines and protect the dockyard from naval bombardment. Roughly square in plan with angled bastions at the four corners, and surrounded by a deep, dry-moat, it looks strangely out of date, as though belonging to an earlier century. **(175)** The two-storey barracks are built around a square yard in the centre of the fort.

As relations with France deteriorated, further fortifications were erected to protect the dockyard and the seaward end of the Milford Haven. Two Martello gun-towers were built (1848–51) off opposing corners of the dockyard at Pembroke Dock to deter seaborne attacks. Constructed in ashlar limestone, they have battered sides with small rectangular windows, recessed arches and parapets. **(176)** Six large forts were built to safeguard the Haven from naval attack, beginning with Stack Rock (1852 and 1870) in mid-channel, followed by South Hook (1859–65), near Herbrandston, Popton (1859–72), Hubberston (1860–5),

Scoveston (1861–8) and Chapel Bay (1890), near Angle. While each had a different (often geometric) layout to suit requirements and the terrain, they were all built to the highest standards of masonry, creating a spectacular collection of buildings. A further fort was built 1868–70 on St Catherine's Island to protect Tenby and its harbour. It was disarmed in 1906, sold a few years later and converted into a house.

Fortifications were also erected further up the Severn Sea to protect the ports of Bristol, Cardiff and Swansea. They were on a much smaller scale than those in Pembrokeshire. The island of Flat Holm had a small fort and three separate sets of gun batteries (all erected 1866–71), while Lavernock Point (1866–71) and Mumbles (1859–60) each had a single set of gun batteries. It was from Lavernock Point in May 1897 that Guglielmo Marconi and George Kemp transmitted the first-ever wireless message across water to Flat Holm ∎

12   Industry and Transport, 1800 to 1915
References

1   E. D. Beasley, 'A Tour of Wales', *The Architect's Journal*, 129 (1959), pp. 860–3.

2   Quoted by J. Davies, *Cardiff and the Marquesses of Bute*, p. 223.

3   H.-R. Hitchcock: *Architecture: Nineteenth and Twentieth Centuries*, p. 180.

13

Country Houses and Planned Towns, 1800 to 1915

Castellated Mansions

In the early part of the nineteenth century revived medieval styles took on a new lease of life in the castellated mansions of the great estate owners and the newly rich industrialists. These vast houses were built to impress. They implied a pedigree, even if none existed. They also represented the attainment of a romantic ideal, and in this their picturesque outlines were admirably suited to the often wild and beautiful surroundings in which they were set.

The pattern which had been started by Nash at Castle House, Aberystwyth, in 1788, the rebuilding of Kentchurch Court, Herefordshire, in Gothic style between 1795 and 1807, and his transmutation of Broadlane Hall into Hawarden Castle in 1807 ('work subsequently carried out, with some departure from the original', by Thomas Cundy, 1809–10), [1] was followed by the fanciful creation of Gwrych Castle, Abergele, for Lloyd Bamford Hesketh. Though initially designed by C. A. Busby in 1814 (who became bankrupt in the same year and left for the USA), it seems to have been redesigned by Thomas Rickman, of Liverpool, in 1817 in collaboration with Hesketh, a noted amateur architect, and built between 1819 and 1822. Sited at the base of a hill, the 'castle' looks out towards the sea as an extravagant make-believe. It comprises a main block, with several other buildings at different levels together with long battlemented curtain-walls and frowning towers (eighteen in all) strung out along a wooded hillside with an eccentric disregard either for cost or for military logic. Inscribed tablets listed genuine and legendary historical events connected with the locality in an attempt to give the baronial lair an air of respectable authenticity. By 1985 the buildings had been vandalized and fallen into disrepair. Gwrych Castle was partly reopened in 2015 after the establishment of a preservation trust. Other notable 'castellated mansions' in the north-east are Bodelwyddan Castle, remodelled by Edward Welch in the 1830s with many turrets and towers, and Talacre Abbey, a new house by Thomas Jones built (1824–9) in Tudor Gothic style.

A few years after Gwrych Castle, the London-based Robert Lugar designed Cyfarthfa Castle for William Crawshay, the notorious 'Iron King' of Merthyr Tydfil. Built in 1825 in a curious mixture of 'Norman' and 'Late Gothic', its near-symmetrical and overfenestrated main facade looks unconvincing close up, despite its battlemented walls and square, octagonal and round towers. (177) Nevertheless, the general massing gives the hillside building a striking appearance from a distance. Lugar was also responsible for Glanusk Park (1825–30), in the middle Usk valley, and Maesllwch Castle (1829–c.1840) in the middle Wye valley. Both were squarish buildings with symmetrical wings built around atrium-like halls, and both in Tudor Gothic style, the former with twin, spindly turrets and the latter with six

177 Cyfarthfa Castle, Merthyr Tydfil.

178 Penrhyn Castle, Bangor, the Great Hall.

dissimilar towers. Glanusk Park was demolished in 1954, and Maesllwch Castle was partly demolished in 1951, but leaving some impressive remains. Hensol Castle, near Llantrisant, was remodelled by Thomas Henry Wyatt from about 1838. Erected in 1835, it is outwardly evocative of Cyfarthfa Castle, and again the impression of medieval authenticity was spoiled by an overprovision of too many large and out-of-character windows. Ironically, though the client wanted a medieval fortress, he also wanted more light than his ancestors, or, for that matter, more than his tenant farmers or ironworkers.

For George Pennant, the inheritor of a vast fortune from slave-worked sugar plantations in Jamaica and an extensive, slate-rich estate, Thomas Hopper of Essex designed a more convincing 'Norman fortress' at Penrhyn Castle near Bangor. It was built around the great hall of an earlier 'castle' (designed by Samuel Wyatt, c.1782) which in turn incorporated the remains of a medieval mansion built by the Tudors of Penmynydd in the early fourteenth century (and enlarged by Gwilym ap Gruffydd in the fifteenth) on the site of the palace of Rhodri Molwynog, the eighth-century Prince of Gwynedd. An immense structure by any standard, Hopper's Penrhyn Castle took thirteen years (1827–40) to complete. It was built to an irregular layout that included a panoply of rectangular, round and octagonal towers with a monumental neo-Norman 'keep-tower' (based on that of Hedingham in Essex) tagged on at one end. The general massing and handling shows Hopper at his best, though where a more picturesque skyline was required he was happy to mix Romanesque with Gothic crenellations. Inside, the Great Hall was built on a vast scale with high cross-vaulting – with curious windows of stained glass interspersed between the ribs – elaborately decorated with deeply-cut Norman chevron, billet and double-cone ornament; it is, however, nightmarishly oppressive, and must have been a most uninviting place in which to live. **(178)**

Hopper's other works in Wales in the south, at Llanover, near Abergavenny, and Margam (Glamorgan), were inspired by the Tudor style. Llanover Court (1828) took almost as long to build as Penrhyn Castle but was unfortunately demolished in 1935. The Tudor-style Margam Abbey (begun in 1830 alongside the ruined Cistercian

carried out by Henry Pope in the 1880s, while Aston Webb added an Arts and Crafts-style library at a forty-five-degree angle to the rest of the house in 1896.

At Chirk Castle Augustus Welby Pugin was commissioned to make various alterations to the castle in the 1840s and give it a neo-Gothic touch. He was one of the leaders of the Gothic Revival and son of Auguste Charles Pugin who, as a refugee from France, had begun his career in Carmarthen as John Nash's draughtsman. Pugin replaced part of the east range beneath the Long Gallery with a fine suite of rooms, and, in collaboration with J. G. Crace, redecorated much of the castle and revamped the entrance hall with oak-panelled walls, a panelled ceiling and an ornate stone chimneypiece.

Late Neoclassicism

The castellated mansions of the nineteenth century tend to get more attention than the 'classically' designed mansions of the same period, although the latter often expressed more clearly the functional requirements of the age. The earliest of these classically designed houses is Rug, near Corwen, where Lord Newborough had his mansion rebuilt in a neo-Grec manner to designs by the Shrewsbury architect Joseph Bromfield. It was a rectangular, seven-bay, two-storey block built in buff-coloured Cefn ashlar sandstone and completed in 1801. A high portico with four giant Ionic columns supporting a flat entablature (without a pediment) masks the entrance on the north front. The garden front, with nine closely spaced bays has a projecting semicircular bow with Ionic three-quarter columns. A later five-bay extension, added in the 1880s by Henry Kennedy, with a three-bay pediment on the north front and a five-bay Corinthian arcade facing the garden, gave both fronts oddly asymmetrical appearances.

Glansevern, at Berriew near Montgomery, also by Bromfield, was completed in 1807 and is smaller and more elegant. **(179)** The excellent main facade – five bays with four giant Ionic pilasters and a shallow architrave – is reminiscent of the Petit Trianon at Versailles (but without the balustraded parapet), built forty years earlier. The somewhat heavy porch

Abbey) is dominated by a great octagonal tower in the centre. The main part of the house is infinitely varied in appearance, with pinnacles and chimneys of all shapes, bay windows, oriel windows, hooded windows and arched windows, gables, crenellations, buttresses and setbacks, all designed to give the venerable impression of a building which is the fortuitous result of the accumulation of centuries. The irony of Hopper's work at Margam is that it should have replaced the enormous residence of the Mansels, which, started about 1537, was the genuine result of additions and stylistic alterations over many generations.

Almost as large as Penrhyn Castle, but less overpowering, is the Hendre, near Monmouth, the home of the Rolls family. The house was begun in neo-Norman style to a cruciform layout in the late 1820s, and was later enlarged to the sides and rear by T. H. Wyatt in various stages from 1837 to 1872 in a mixture of neo-Norman and neo-Tudor modes. The work included a tiny chapel at the corner that rises up above the general roof line as a square tower capped with a curved roof. Further additions were was added in 1909. A neat and purely Greek entrance lodge, begun in 1808, was demolished to make way for roadworks. Orielton, in south Pemrokeshire, is plain and austere in conparison. Originaly a fortified manor, it was rebuilt in 1743 and further extended and remodelled in 1810, ending up as a three-storey, thirteen-bay-long house. It was later reduced in size and survives now as an almost featureless house with corner pilasters and simplified cornice with camber-headed upper windows and a Doric porch.

The most robust and gracious example of the neo-Grec movement in Wales must be Clytha House, Gwent, designed by another Shrewsbury architect, Edward Haycock, completed in 1828 and built in Bath stone. **(180)** Four-square in plan, the house's splendid main (south-east) front has a notable portico with four giant Ionic columns and pediment and wide bays on either side with pedimented ground-floor windows. The adjoining south-west front is divided into seven bays, the centre three bays forming a semicircular bow through two storeys with an encircling arcade of Doric columns to the ground floor only. The entrance leads into a circular vestibule with shallow domed ceiling and marble Doric columns, and beyond that a spacious, top-lit hall with a cantilevered grand staircase. This was probably the last 'Greek' house in Wales and a worthy swan-song of the movement inspired, largely, by the arrival of the Elgin Marbles in Britain at the beginning of the century. Haycock was probably also responsible in 1820 for Coedrhiglan (or Coedarhydyglyn), west of Cardiff, a neat two-storey, seven-bay villa with a central three-bay portico with Doric columns, flanked by slightly projecting, pedimented bays.

Haycock's other great mansion, Glynllifon, near Caernarfon, erected for Lord Newborough in 1836–46, is vast and rendered, and less pleasing to the eye than Clytha; it is now an educational institution of the Gwynedd authority. The main front is thirteen bays by three storeys with a five-bay portico with giant Ionic columns rising from the first floor under a wide pediment. The first-floor windows to the outer bays are pedimented. A long, ten-bay, two-storey wing was added at the west side of the original in about 1890, increasing the appearance of vastness. Standing in the park,

180 Clytha House, near Abergavenny.

a kilometre or so south-east, are the remains of a Mausoleum begun in 1826 by the second Lord Newborough. It comprises a circular tower standing on a podium, with cruciform rooms on the lower two floors and an octagonal room above that was intended as a chapel but never completed.

Penoyre, near Brecon, by Anthony Salvin in 1846–8, is a medium-size three-storey, five-bay Italianate mansion that looks large and strangely urban. A balustraded arcade with Tuscan columns partly surrounds the ground floor, the *piano nobile* is emphasized by precise pediments over the windows, and there is a bold and heavily detailed cornice to act as lid to the house. The entrance is on the east side, under a four-storey tower with an open loggia on the uppermost floor.

181 Wynnstay, near Ruabon, Denbighshire.

182 Kinmel Park, near Abergele, Denbighshire.

Continental Influences

Pure 'classical' architecture was altogether too restrained, too intellectual and ascetic, for the grand and fustian tastes of most Victorian empire builders. They wanted something more showy, something more extravagant. The seductive châteaux of the French Renaissance – with their high curving, almost Gothic, roofs – were ideal exemplars of pomp. Wynnstay, near Ruabon, was rebuilt for Sir Watkin Williams Wynn in 1858–65 by Benjamin Ferrey on the foundations of the house designed by James Wyatt in 1789, which in turn had replaced a house designed by Francis Smith in 1736. Ferrey's design was a basically symmetrical, two-storey building with a three-storey tower at one end, a smaller three storey tower at the other, and in the middle, projecting well forward like the prow of a galleon, a four-storey tower. **(181)** What united the ensemble are the exceptionally steep and slightly curving slate roofs of the towers, the stratification of floors by intermediate cornices and superimposed pilasters, all in the style of the sixteenth-century château of Gallion in Normandy.

Hafodunus, Conwy, was an important country house by Sir George Gilbert Scott. Built in 1861–6, it has brick walling with diaper work and generous stone dressings in a Venetian Gothic-inspired style, but was largely destroyed by fire in 2014 and is now undergoing restoration. The near-symmetrical garden front had a rich variety of windows, including pointed windows separated by slim shafts, and some with 'thirteenth-century' plate tracery, as well as an octagonal, monastic-looking kitchen, at one end of which was a top-lit billiard room.

William Eden Nesfield was responsible for at least two country houses in north-eastern Wales. His Kinmel Park (c.1868–74), Abergele, was, despite its French overtones, 'one of the earliest manifestations of the "Queen Anne" style in country-house architecture'[2] and greatly influenced Richard Norman Shaw – one of the most successful of Victorian architects in England – and consequently much of late nineteenth-century domestic work. **(182)** Built in red brick with stone dressings, its symmetrical and palatial entrance facade, proud, high-roofed with dormers and dominated by a central pavilion, echoes François Mansart's

183 Gregynog, Tregynon,
Montgomeryshire.

Château de Balleroi, but the more loosely composed garden facade is reminiscent of the Dutch-influenced 'William and Mary' style of late seventeenth-century England. It was damaged by fire in 1975, and after restorations used as a conference centre. It has been derelict since 2011. More Dutch than French also is Nesfield's delightful and richly carved, single-storey gate lodge (the Golden Lodge), with its frieze of medallions, high roof, tall dormers and chimney, at the entrance to Kinmel Park. Bodrhyddan Hall (an ancient Welsh seat near Rhuddlan), was remodelled and enlarged, 1872–5, by Nesfield in red brick at roughly the same time as Kinmel Park. More *petite* and prettier than Kinmel, its small-paned sash windows, high pitched roof, coy dormers and curving gable show more Dutch than French influence.

Nesfield was apparently also involved at Gregynog in Montgomeryshire, having prepared designs for a new house for Henry Hanbury-Tracy in 1877 (though they were not in the end adopted). Gregynog as built was extraordinary by any standards, for at first glance it appears to be a stately, E-plan half-timbered house from the seventeenth century. (183) In fact, the house was constructed during the 1870s in mass concrete, carefully profiled so that the imitation wood strips (painted in black) stood proud of the surface. Three storeys high with dormers, and seven bays long, the central, full-height bay forms an entrance porch on the garden front. The designer is unknown, although the most likely person

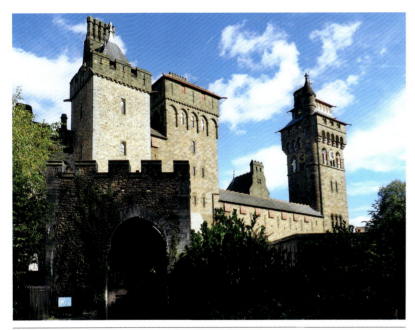

184 Cardiff Castle, Cardiff, the west range from Bute Park.

seems to have been the estate agent, William Scott Owen, or possibly the owner, Henry Hanbury-Tracy. The house was acquired by the Misses Gwendoline and Margaret Davies (granddaughters of the coal and railway magnate David Davies) in 1920 as an art centre, and subsequently bequeathed to the University of Wales in 1960. Many other structures on the estate were also built in concrete.

For sheer ostentatious extravagance and sumptuous theatricality, Cardiff Castle and Castell Coch (8 km north) were easily the most remarkable domestic buildings to be resurrected during the nineteenth century. In their way they were symptomatic of their age, and illustrate perfectly one side of the dichotomy that existed between the arts and industry, resulting in a traumatic reaction of the wealthier classes to the brutal reality of the Industrial Revolution, the source of their expanding wealth. The transformation of the two castles by William Burges of London between 1868 and 1881 was the ultimate in nostalgic escapism from the industrial squalor that everywhere accompanied the sources of wealth. His romantic approach to the restoration of the castles was largely inspired by Viollet-le-Duc and his restorations of French castles. Ironically Viollet-le-Duc himself had been inspired by the popularization in French romance of the Arthururian legends of Celtic Britain. 'Romantic Military' architecture stemming from Arthurian attitudes reached its culmination on the Continent in Château de Pierrefonds (for Napoleon III in 1857–68) in France, and the even more fantastic Schloss Neuschwanstein (for Ludwig II in 1869–82) in the Bavarian Alps. Just a few years later the theme was transmitted back to Wales in the guise of Cardiff Castle and Castell Coch.

Both castles were partly altered and largely rebuilt in exotic restorations by Burges in conjunction with his excessively wealthy but highly cultured patron, the third Marquess of Bute. They were both 'hopelessly in love with the Middle Ages', and in these two castles they gave full vent to their passion. The internal restorations of the castles were on such a scale as to completely alter the character of the rooms. They became (in the words of Henry-Russell Hitchcock) 'more like settings for Wagnerian opera than anything the Middle Ages actually created'.[3] At Cardiff Castle – which had been tentatively gothicized and enlarged by Henry Holland ninety years previously – Burges revamped and heightened two existing towers, added an ornate spire to the octagonal Beauchamp Tower and built a new, 40 m high clock tower at the south-west angle, the result of which may be seen in today's magnificently romantic skyline. (184) Inside, he added new rooms and divided existing rooms, embellishing them with coffered and vaulted ceilings, massive and ornate fireplaces and walls decorated with rich carvings, stained glass, marble and inlaid precious stones. Burges opened up the original fifteenth-century hall to provide a Library on the lower floor and a two-storey

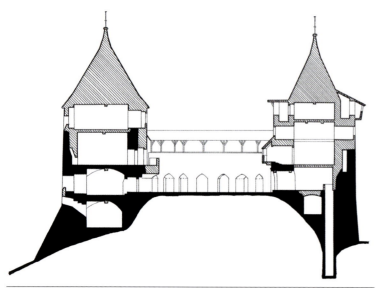

185 Castell Coch, near Cardiff, cross section, showing original work in black and 19th-century work shaded.

186 Castell Coch, near Cardiff.

Banqueting Hall complete with a lofty vaulted hammer-beam roof at the upper level, while the rooms in the Clock Tower were stacked, one above the other, culminating in an extraordinary Summer Smoking Room with an Upper Gallery and a magnificent gold chandelier hanging from the dome.

Castell Coch was in a completely ruinous state, with upstanding remains of two towers and the hall block, when Burges made his recommendations for restoration in 1872. Work began in 1875 and Burges made a serious attempt to reconstruct the triple towered castle externally as it might have been built in the twelfth century, complete with working portcullis and drawbridge. **(185, 186)** Nevertheless, the flamboyant design of the chimneys and conical roofs over the three round towers suggests that Burges was more influenced by continental examples, particularly French, than British in this case. Inside, Burges indulged in a sumptuous extravaganza of interior decoration, which in the case of rooms such as the Drawing Room had been directly prompted by Viollet-le-Duc's reconstruction of the Château de Pierrefonds. **(187)**

Burges was also the designer of Park House, in Park Place, Cardiff, built in 1874 for Bute's engineer Mr McConnochie. A fine two-and a-half-storey, asymmetrically planned neo-Gothic town house, with an arcade of three pointed arches to the front and a similar loggia at the side giving access to the entrance and lofty stair hall, it became the model for other houses in the area.

Llangoed Hall, in the sylvan Wye valley between Brecon and Builth, was originally built in 1632. Clough Williams-Ellis was commissioned to design an enlargement in 1913. This he did with a handsome and sympathetic stone-faced two-storey mansion – set at an angle to the smaller original – with wide mullioned windows, a steep hipped roof, tall brick chimneys and many dormers. At the centre of the main front is a three-storey entrance tower of Gwespyr stone, with an arched doorway and pyramidal roof. A comparatively early work of Williams-Ellis (1883–1978), it was the last great country house to be built in Wales, and was largely complete when the First World War brought everything to a stop. After a period of post-Second World War dereliction, it was converted into a country house hotel.

Planned Towns and Villages

The new ideas of urban design that were introduced into England and Scotland during the seventeenth century, and reached fulfilment in the planning of Bath and Edinburgh during the following century, did not have the opportunity of gaining acceptance in Wales until the late eighteenth and early nineteenth centuries. Since the Middle Ages there had been no urban development of any consequence in Wales until the late eighteenth century, and pre-planned layouts had hardly been necessary. Even when adopted, formal planning was but a faint echo of the ideals of Renaissance town planning which had been originally formulated in Italy and France, for despite the new layouts, the buildings themselves are generally small in scale and lacking in grandeur. Swansea was an early exception to this rule, using the reclaimed land at the Burrows near the river mouth to establish a fashionable resort with elegant terraces. One such terrace off Somerset Place, three storeys high and nearly thirty bays long with a slightly projecting three-bay gabled block at the centre, is shown on Thomas Rothwell's etching of 1792. Three decades later, a not dissimilar situation arose in Beaumaris, where 'Joseph Hansom and Edward Welch, of York, were responsible for all the major buildings erected there from the late 1820s to the early 1830s, working for both the Corporation and the Baron Hill estate.'[4] Their Victoria Terrace, for instance, on the sea front near the castle, was an opulent building completed in 1833. **(188)** Three storeys high, twenty-eight bays long and built on a curve, it has a projecting centre block embellished with flat pilasters and a wide, four-bay, pediment. Edward Welch,

187 Castell Coch, near Cardiff, the Octagonal Drawing Room.

188 Victoria Terrace, Beaumaris, Anglesey.

who had been born in Overton, Flintshire, parted company with Hansom in about 1836; Welch's younger brother John had a flourishing practice based in St Asaph. Tenby, too, had some handsome terraces, the best being Lexden Terrace, overlooking the sea front from a height. Three storeys high with tall, narrow windows, it had a rusticated ground floor with stuccoed upper floors divided by giant Ionic pilasters on the street side, and a wrought-iron balcony on the seaward side. It was apparently built in 1843 by John Smith, who was possibly the designer.

Tremadoc and Aberaeron, on the west coast, grew out of the eighteenth-century spirit of improvement and were built according to some of the basic principles of Renaissance formal planning. They were the work of enthusiastic individuals who wished to develop their estates and make them into outlets that served the surrounding districts. Tremadoc, however, remained tiny, without any concomitant development, because its purpose was immediately negated by the nearby town of Porthmadog, which grew rapidly as a result of slate exports. Small though it is, Tremadoc has a rugged and masculine character partly due to its dramatic setting at the foot of near-precipitous cliffs. It was the creation of W. A. Madocks of Dolmelynllyn, and apparently built from rough sketches contained in letters to his agent between 1800 and 1811, as part of a successful venture in reclaiming the Traeth Mawr estuary. In layout, Tremadoc is simply a 'T' plan with a rectangular market place in the form of a Renaissance *piazza* at the junction itself. **(189)** Enclosing the sides of the market place are continuous terraces of two-storey houses and shops. The north side of the market place is completed by an attractive Town Hall-cum-market-cum-theatre with an open arcade on the lower floor. On the outskirts of the town, Madocks built a Gothick church on one side of the road, and on the opposite side a neoclassical chapel. Here, apart from a four-storey woollen mill built further away on another road, the original development ended and very little was added until recently.

Some of the terraces of Aberaron have a Nash-like character and local tradition has it that the town was planned by John Nash, though there is nothing in writing to support this. Nevertheless, it is obvious that the layout of the town was the work of one man, and Edward Haycock, designer of the town's church in 1835, seems to be the probable author. In 1805 the Revd Alban Thomas Jones Gwynne, possessor of two local estates by marriage, inherited money and proceeded to obtain an Act of Parliament in 1807 to found the town, build piers and provide shipping facilities. Aberaeron's layout is based on two large open-ended squares, on either side of the main coast road, each partially enclosed by mainly two-storey house terraces. The harbour was the first part of the scheme to be constructed between 1807 and 1811, and this was followed by the open square around the harbour and an adjacent rectangular grid of terraces and a further terrace beyond the bridge. During this phase the sturdy Town Hall (1835) was erected in a prominent position facing Pwll Cam harbour, as well as a chapel. Finally, after 1840, three sides of Alban Square were laid out around a large public green with two-storey terraces, accented by larger houses at the ends and in the middle, but too small to give a realistic sense of urban enclosure.

189 Tremadoc, Caernarfonshire, the Market Place.

The latter part of the nineteenth century produced a new type of town – the planned seaside resort – which, if not grander in conception than some of the earlier ports and industrial estates, was at least better able to fulfil its expectations. The outstanding example is Llandudno, sited on a narrow neck of land between the Irish Sea and the Conwy estuary and between the limestone headlands of the Great Orme and the Little Orme. Llandudno, like nearby Colwyn Bay (begun in 1865), was made popular and brought within easy reach of the industrial towns of north-western England by the opening of the Chester and Holyhead Railway in 1849. Both towns were developed by local landowners from their country estates, and taken together they represent a unique attempt at creating planned resorts by the sea.

The layout of Llandudno is a grid of streets artfully adjusted to follow the long, crescent-shaped curve of the beach. Two main thoroughfares lie parallel with the sea and are intersected at one end by a broad boulevard that links the north shore, facing the sea, with the west shore facing the estuary. Development was controlled by an Enclosure Act (1848) obtained by Lord Mostyn, and the basic framework of Promenade and streets on his Gloddaeth estate was set out in 1849 in a sale plan that showed the layout of the 179 leasehold plots on offer. The development was controlled by an Act of Parliament (1854), and strict building regulations were laid down regarding the width of streets and pavements and the maximum size of houses, the intention being that 'the town that is to be, shall resemble, as far as is possible, the "country", securing at the same time in the laying out of the various plots of ground order and uniformity.'[5] This aim was largely achieved in the development, at least up to about 1918. On the Promenade a great crescent of mainly three-storey hotels and houses sweeps boldly along the front of the bay ending in a fine pier (by James Brunlees and McKerrow, 1876–8) at the foot of the Great Orme. Behind this is the main shopping street (Mostyn Street), with its four- and five-storey stucco-faced terrace blocks and iron-and-glass arcades. Later development has not robbed the town of its sense of spaciousness, its pleasant scale and consistent order. Though there are few buildings of particular interest,

Llandudno is still one of the most rewarding examples of a planned town in Wales.

Model estate villages in the more rural areas during the nineteenth century were sometimes given a 'vernacular' picturesqueness, as at Marford (near Wrexham), a fanciful hamlet of Gothick cottages, with ogee arches, cross 'arrow slits', curious eye-shaped windows, and an inn. The cottages were originally thatched, and some, constructed of pise and rendered, were built between 1803 and 1815 for George Boscawen with money inherited by his wife ten years earlier. The walled village at Llandygai, near Bangor, was built for the Penrhyn estate in the mid-nineteenth century, probably to designs by James Wyatt. It had rustic, Tudor-style cottages with steep roofs and brick chimneys, as well as a school. In the south, most attempts at creating estate villages resulted in little more than collections of scattered cottages treated in a 'picturesque' manner. Margam Groes, near Port Talbot, was a more substantial effort, laid out in the 1830s by Edward Haycock with semi-detached cottages with tall chimneys; unfortunately the village was demolished to make way for the M4 motorway, its unusual chapel being rebuilt at Port Talbot.

Not all model villages had, however, been designed in such a whimsical and wistful manner. The outstanding exception was Tregynon, Montgomeryshire, where in about 1870 Henry Hanbury-Tracy of Gregynog had a series of cottages and a school built entirely in concrete, then a daring and novel method of construction. Not only were the walls and floors of unreinforced concrete, but so also were the roof slabs (covered by slates), staircases and chimneys. Some of the detailing was based on traditional construction, such as the Victorian Gothic porches and occasional pseudo-black-and-white-timberwork, but generally the mouldings are simple and in keeping with the new material. Thomas Nicholas claimed that Mr Tracy had set 'the landowners of Wales an example in *cottage-building*, which it is to be hoped will be extensively followed'.[6] The Hanbury-Tracys were eventually forced to sell the estate after overextending themselves in various industrial and commercial experiments, including the concrete buildings.

Model villages of a different kind were those begun by

followers of Robert Owen, the Newtown (Montgomeryshire) social reformer, who, after reorganizing New Lanark, Scotland on utopian lines, set about establishing a cooperative settlement at New Harmony in the USA in 1825, and later at Queenswood, Hampshire. Both attempts at social planning were, however, short-lived, as were to be most attempts to set up 'Owenite' communities in Wales. At the remote, upland site of Pant Glas, near Dolgellau, it was claimed in 1840 that 'cottages for twenty families, and twelve single persons' had been erected as well as two buildings for use as a library, school and public meetings.[7] These claims may have been erroneous, for within a year the venture had fizzled out and all that remained was a farm. At Garnllwyd, set up in 1847 near Carmarthen, the project never got beyond that of a working farm.

Coed-duon in the Sirhowy valley turned out to be something more resilient. It was here that the industrialist John Hodder Moggeridge, of Plas Bedwellty, set up, after discussions with Robert Owen, his 'village system' plan in about 1820 for workers at a nearby colliery and local farms. The workers were to pay ground rent and build their own homes, repaying loans over a set period of time. Workshops for craft workers and tradesmen, shops, medical services, a school and a market hall (doubling as a chapel) were all to be provided, and within a decade a village of 250 houses had developed. Though the village continued to expand, eventually becoming Blackwood with a population of more than 8,000 people, little of the original development has survived.

Generally, the industrialists in the coalfields showed little interest or social concern in housing their workers. Early accommodation was usually in the form of rude collections of cottages near to the ironworks or pitheads, followed later by ribbons of terrace-housing built along the sides of the valleys and following as far as possible the contours. Gradually, the terraces coalesced to form continuous linear settlements, with little to break the monotony apart from the colliery winding-towers or the frequent chapels. The two-storey terrace houses of these districts, though unimaginative and stereotyped, were usually neat and reasonably well built, with entrances at back and front, avoiding the noisome

190 Y Drenewydd (Butetown), Rhymney, Monmouthshire.

back-to-back terraces and miserable tenement courts found elsewhere. In the south, most terraces are built in rust-brown sandstone, giving them a strongly idiosyncratic air that often had more character than many later council house estates. In Flintshire and the Wrexham area most of the industrial terrace houses were built in hard red brick.

An early example of a model industrial village was Y Drenewydd ('The new town') at the upper end of the Rhymney valley, erected in 1802–4 to house the workers of the nearby Union Iron Company, and reputedly designed by the ironworks' manager, R. Johnson. A simple layout of four parallel terraces was planned, but only three were erected. These were built in an impressive 'classical' manner with projecting end and middle sections and hipped roofs with wide overhanging eaves (190) The middle sections are a storey higher than the rest of the houses and may have been intended as barracks for single men. When the second

Marquess of Bute bought the ironworks in the 1820s, the estate's name was changed to Butetown. In contrast to the classical symmetry of Butetown is the stark simplicity of the early housing estates built for ironworkers at Blaenafon and at Pentre-bach, near Merthyr Tydfil. Both had an appearance of being planned. Stack Square (1788) at Blaenafon, comprises three sides of an open square overlooking the ironworks. The Triangle (demolished), at Pentre-bach, was started about 1810 for workers at the Plymouth Ironworks, and consisted of three similar two-storey terraces arranged around a large triangular court with a longer curved terrace at the rear.

In the Wrexham area the remains of the Plas Power estate village that served the Bersham Ironworks (closed 1820) are mostly of eighteenth-century buildings (including a workers' barracks from 1775), although two pairs of 1859 cottages by John Gibson survive. At the site of the nearby Brymbo, the only nineteenth-century residential building is a stone-built terrace of three cottages from 1815. Two interesting brick-built terraces at Panton Place (1816), Holywell (now converted to old people's homes) have survived. They have alternating rhythms of paired doorways under single, wide arches and single doorways under smaller arches, due to the original mixture of dwellings with workshops, and dual-access dwellings with single-access ones.

The earliest attempts to develop a new town that was complete in itself took place in Blaenau Gwent, where in 1819 it was reported that 'a new town was laid out and begun at Tredegar Iron Works', at the upper end of the Sirhowy valley.[8] The ironworks had been founded in 1800 by Samuel Homfray, and housing development must have started soon afterwards, for within two years the first furnaces had been completed and were in use. An Ordnance Survey drawing of 1813 shows a rudimentary gridlike pattern of streets – though none were earlier than 1809 according to Powell's *History of Tredegar* – plus a road that conveniently 'bypasses' Homfray's mansion (Bedwellty House) and park. By about 1820 a new main road (Morgan Street) had been constructed between and parallel to two of the earlier streets (North Lane and South Lane), and where it crossed Market Street/Iron Street

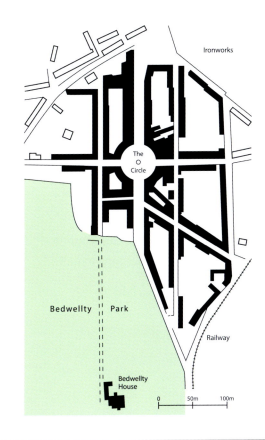

191 Tredegar, Monmouthshire. Planned layout with buildings (in black) existing *c*.1826.

at right angles, a large circular market place (later known as The Circle) had been created in the manner of a Renaissance piazza. (191) In 1858 a monumental, 22 m-high, cast-iron town clock atop a Tuscan column – designed and made by Chas. Jordan of Newport – was placed at the centre of The Circle as a decorative focal point. (192)

In 1899 the Tredegar Iron and Coal Company set out to create a new urban village to serve their colliery in the neighbouring Rhymni valley. This was to be Abertyswg, a self-contained community with similar terraced street patterns laid out on either side of a triangular park, around which were built the town's principal buildings: church, chapels, school, hospital, miners' institute, police station, hotel, bank and shops. By 1910 the town was virtually complete, and though not a model urban village in the sense of a 'garden city' as advocated by Ebenezer Howard, it was, nevertheless, a leap forward and a prototype in 1911 for Oakdale Model Village, near Blackwood ■

192 Tredegar, the Town Clock in the centre of The Circle.

13 Country Houses and Planned Towns, 1800 to 1915
References

1   R. Suggett, *John Nash: Architect-Pensaer*, p. 124.

2   R. Dixon and S. Muthesius, *Victorian Architecture*, p. 55.

3   H.-R. Hitchcock, *Architecture: Nineteenth and Twentieth Centuries*, p. 267.

4   R. Hayman, 'Architecture of Beaumaris in the Nineteenth Century', *Archaeologia Cambrensis*, 153 (2004), 112.

5   Quoted by H. *Carter in The Towns of Wales*, p 303.

6   Thomas Nicholas, *Annals and Antiquities of the Counties and Families of Wales*, vol. II (1872), p. 805.

7   N. Thompson and C. Williams, *Robert Owen and his Legacy*, p. 226.

8   A. Rees, *The Cyclopaedia*, vol. 6 (London, 1819).

14

Religion and Education, 1880 to 1915

Anglican Churches

In 1811 the inevitable schism between the Established Church in Wales and the 'methodists' took place when the latter began ordaining their own ministers, became Methodist and seceded from the Anglican Church. Yet, despite dwindling congregations as a result of the growing strength of Nonconformity and a lack of bishops able to preach in Welsh (at least until 1870, when Dr Joshua Hughes was appointed to the see of St Asaph), there was much rebuilding by the Anglican Church throughout the nineteenth century. This was due partly to the number of older churches that were in an advanced state of dereliction through neglect, and partly to the need to build new churches to serve recently formed parishes in the expanding towns of the industrial areas.

When church building resumed in earnest, it continued in a revived tradition of medieval church architecture, that is in the Romanesque or Gothic style. Nearly all the new churches were designed by professional architects, many working from London offices. Amongst local architects working for the Anglican Church in the south were John Prichard, G. E. Halliday and E. M. Bruce Vaughan. In the south-west R. K. Penson and E. H. Lingen-Barker (of Hereford) were amongst the favourites, while in the north the most popular were John Douglas (of Chester), Henry Kennedy, John Lloyd and John Welch. In mid-Wales the territories of the church architects seem to have been more restricted, with comparatively little overlapping; here some of the most popular were J. B. Fowler, R. K. Penson, S. W. Williams, and T. H. Wyatt. Many of the architects worked in more than one part of Wales.

The early buildings of the Established Church, such as St Katherine (1808), Milford Haven, and St Mary (c.1811), Tremadoc, tend to be plain and raw Gothick. Few books had, by then, been published on medieval architecture, and architects were consequently very unsure of the correct handling of stylistic details. Capel Colman at Boncath, near Cardigan, designed by Daniel Davis (1835), is, with its strange mixture of rendered walls, round-headed openings, naive slate pinnacles and clumsy parapets, typical of the unsure touch.

In the fast-growing industrial towns of the south, churches in the cheapest 'Romanesque' style were built by the iron companies for their workers. The earliest of these was an octagon-shaped church built by Richard Crawshay for his workers at the Cyfarthfa Ironworks, Merthyr Tydfil. Now only a crumbling shell, B. H. Malkin noted in 1803 that 'a spacious and elegant chapel-of-ease has just been erected.'[1] Other churches built by the ironmasters were St John, Dowlais (1827), St George, Tredegar (J. Jenkins, 1836), and Glyn-taf (T. H. Wyatt, 1838). The visually more satisfying neoclassical church of St David, Rhymney (Philip Hardwick, 1839–43) should also be mentioned here as being probably the last of its kind to be built in Wales.

Romanesque was also the style often favoured for the 'economical' churches built with the aid of parliamentary funds, under the Church Building Act of 1818, to serve the expanding population in the 1830s and 1840s. The best of these 'Commissioners' Churches', as they were known, is St Mary, Butetown, Cardiff (Thomas Foster of Bristol, 1843). At the east end it has two large and powerful towers with pyramidical stone roofs, while between the towers there is an arcade of sham windows fronting onto a small apse. The bold and cavernous interior has massive round columns with Byzantine capitals supporting stark semicircular arches; these in turn support a flat ceiling. In mid-Wales Thomas Penson was responsible for Christ Church (1839–44), Welshpool, in Romanesque style with rubble stonework outside and some elaborate terracotta decoration inside. At St Garmon (1841–2), Betws Garmon, Gwynedd, George Alexander was able to produce a 'Romanesque' church with a strong Celtic flavour in keeping with its wild surroundings.

The change to a style based on an understanding of the Gothic architecture of medieval churches was, as in England, largely due to Augustus Welby Northmore Pugin, who was convinced that Gothic architecture was not only superior to classical architecture but also morally more suitable. Pugin had helped Charles Barry with the design for the new Houses of Parliament in 1835 and had also done all the Gothic detailing, and in the following year published his influential *Contrasts*, in which he compared different types of contemporary buildings with those of the Middle Ages.

John Prichard (1817–86), a pupil of Pugin, was probably the most important Welsh-born architect of the mid-nineteenth century. By 1845 he was in charge of the restoration of Llandaf Cathedral in an early Gothic style, and as diocesan architect was responsible for many of the churches and schools in Glamorgan and occasionally further afield. One of the earliest new churches with which he was involved was St Teilo (1849–51), Merthyr Mawr, where he collaborated with Benjamin Ferrey, a former pupil of A. C. Pugin and follower and biographer of A. W. N. Pugin. Mostly Prichard's restoration work was conservative and well

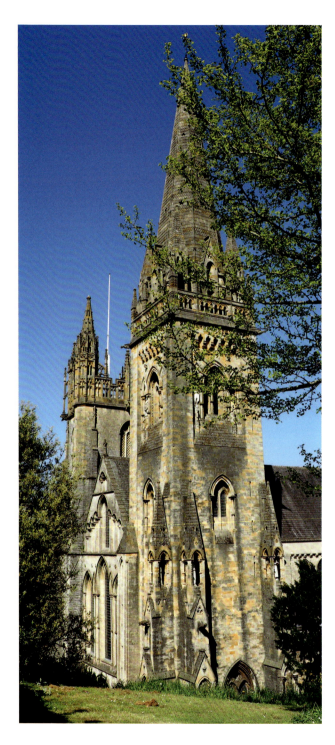

193 Llandaf Cathedral, Cardiff, the south-west tower.

194 St Mary's Church,
Abbey Cwmhir,
Radnorshire.

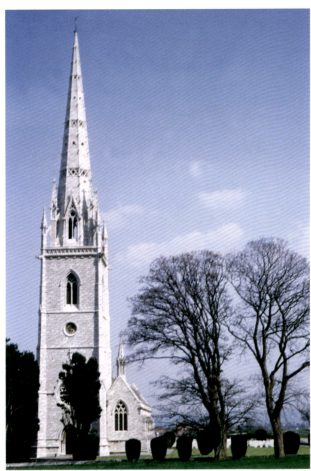

195 St Margaret's Church,
Bodelwyddan,
Flintshire.

executed, but at the south-west corner of Llandaf Cathedral he was inspired to add a splendid tower with a lofty octagonal spire, designed in 1860 but not built until 1867–9. **(193)** A similar tower and spire had been designed previously by Prichard for St John, Newport (1859). Although he was not one of the most original of architects; nearly all his churches are the fruit of true scholarship and are excellently detailed. One of his finest works is St Catherine (1875–82), Baglan, Glamorgan, a cruciform church with a tall spire and a rich interior that included mosaic floors, alabaster panelling and arches with coloured voussoirs.

Many of the better churches in the industrial valleys are by John Norton. His Christchurch (1859), Ebbw Vale, is a bold structure, built in red sandstone. The tower and spire (added 1884) is unusual in having circular turrets and spirelets at the corners. St David (1865), Neath, and St Catherine (1886), Pontypridd, are both large churches where Norton used black and red polychromatic brick decoration inside. Their spires formed prominent landmarks, that challenged the engulfing tides of Welsh Nonconformity around them. Another good church (although harshly detailed) with a fine spire is St Elvan (A. Mosley, 1852), Aberdare.

Further north, in the Severn valley, Thomas Penson was also designing Gothic Revival churches, his St David (1847), Newtown, being a yellow brick building with a strong vertical emphasis. Inside, it has elaborate but delicate decorative mouldings to the nave arcade arches. St Mary (1866), Abbey Cwmhir, Radnorshire, was designed by Poundly and Walker in French Gothic style, with slate roofs striped in two colours. **(194)** Over the porch a tower rises dramatically to a spire split half-way up by a ring of colonettes. The more conventional interior is enlivened by some beautiful stained glass windows. The same firm were responsible earlier (1863) for a similar church at Llanbedr-Dyffryn-Clwyd, Denbighshire.

The most striking church of this period in northern Wales is without doubt St Margaret, Bodelwyddan (the so-called 'Marble Church'), near Abergele. **(195)** It was designed (1856–60) by John Gibson, Barry's assistant on London's new Houses of Parliament. From the outside it is extraordinarily

196 St Augustine's Church, Penarth, Glamorgan.

197 St Philip's Church, Caerdeon, near Barmouth, Meirionnydd.

neat and tidy, 'Middle-pointed Gothic', perfectly symmetrical from the west end, and dominated by a slim tower with a beautiful spire (62m high) built in white limestone. A nearby church which also deserves mention is G. E. Street's rather harsh but visually effective St Mary, Towyn, near Rhyl. It was designed in 1873 as part of a group that also contains a school and vicarage. The church is neatly linked to the vicarage by its vestry. Both the strongly patterned roof and gable tower of the church are unusual in this part of Wales.

With the exception of Llandaf, all the Welsh cathedrals were restored by the prolific Sir George Gilbert Scott between 1860 and 1875. The most important of these was St David's, where in 1862 he rebuilt Nash's Romanesque west front with a watered-down but stylistically purer version of the medieval original. The most delightful of Scott's many church restorations in Wales was the rebuilding of Pen-pont (1865), near Brecon. The original round tower was rebuilt and capped by a circular spire, and a full-width apsidal chancel, covered by a steep roof and a high wagon ceiling, was added at the east end of the building.

Polychromatic architecture, or 'constructive colouration', as it was sometimes called, had become a popular feature of fashionable churches after mid-century. One of the finest examples in Britain of this kind of decoration can be seen at St. Augustine (1866), Penarth. (196) Here William Butterfield used yellow Bath stone and pink sandstone for the columns and arches, and raw red brickwork filled with black-and-white diaper work for the walls to produce a warm, colourful space, all in marked contrast to the church's sober light grey limestone exterior.

Even more unusual was St Philip, Caerdeon, set on a hillside overlooking the Mawddach estuary near Barmouth. (197) It was designed by the Revd John Louis Petit, apparently on the model of a rustic Alpine church, as a private chapel for his brother-in-law, the Revd William Edward Jelf. Built in 1861–2, it has an L-shaped plan formed by the nave, chancel and south transept. Externally, it is distinguished by a massive three-bay porch at the internal angle and a tall, slab-shaped bellcote rising dramatically above the chancel arch and roof.

Generally speaking, the late nineteenth-century churches seem to lack the conviction and inventiveness of churches built during the middle years of the century.

198 Caldey Abbey, Pembrokeshire.

There were, of course exceptions that stood out among the many mediocre and uninspired churches, and such a case is St German, Cardiff, by G. F. Bodley and T. Garner in 1884. In Decorated Gothic style, it has flying buttresses outside, while the graceful interior has a welcome simplicity and soaring spaciousness emphasised by clusters of tall slender columns supporting a panelled wagon ceiling to give it a moving, cathedral-like atmosphere. The side chapels are roofed with graceful ribbed stone vaulting.

Another exception is the church of St Mark, Brithdir, by Henry Wilson, an 1895–8 precursor of the Arts and Crafts movement in Wales. Sited in the foothills of Cadair Idris, near Dolgellau, the church made no attempt to ape past styles, for the architect intended that it should look 'as though it had sprung out of the soil, instead of being planted on it'. As far as possible indigenous materials like granite and local slate were used, and columns and medieval mouldings avoided. The high roof slopes steeply down almost to head level, and projects beyond the west gable to shield a massive stone cross; windows are tall, angular slots in the walls. The interior, though darkish with largely concealed light sources,

glows with colour – the nave painted a warm cream and the chancel walls red ochre with a blue ceiling vault and a copper altar in front of a single slim lancet window.

Finally, mention should be made of two interesting monastic communities (both Anglican) established in the mountains of Powys and an island off the Pembrokeshire coast. The community at Capel-y-ffin in the Black Mountains was founded by Father Ignatius in 1869. Of the church, begun in 1872 to a design by Charles Buckeridge based on the transitional Romanesque-Early Gothic of nearby Llanthony Priory, only the three-bay chancel was built, and even this was abandoned, c. 1920, when the vaulting collapsed. Fortunately, the whitewashed claustral buildings (begun by Buckeridge in 1870) have survived. Quadrangular in layout around a small cloister, three of the ranges are two-storey with many paired lancet windows, while the south range is single-storey. The monastery passed to the Caldey community in 1908, who later sold it to the artist Eric Gill in 1924 as a self-supporting community. Gill formed a chapel in the north range, with inscriptions by himself and a Crucifixion painting by David Jones.

The Caldey community of Benedictines was founded in 1906 on an island near Tenby, Pembrokeshire. The original idea by Dom Aelred Carlyle was for a vast, grandiose monastery on the cliff top and, further down, a quadrangular boys' school known as the Abbey Gatehouse. Funds ran out, and neither the Abbey nor the Gatehouse were built as intended. Instead, the present monastery was built 1910–15 to the designs of John Coates Carter on the site of the 'Gatehouse'. Later still, the community left the Anglican Church and joined the Roman Catholic Cistercians, whose mother house was Scourmont Abbey, Belgium. The monastery as designed by Carter forms a spectacular group of whitewashed buildings with red-tiled roofs around a small cloister, all in a vague kind of Rhenish-Romanesque style with great semicircular arches to the ground floor and narrow lancet windows above. (198) Projecting from the north-west corner of the complex is a large octagonal kitchen of medieval inspiration, and from the west wing a tall, cylindrical tower topped by a conical spire.

Capeli Cymru

During the nineteenth century the rising tide of Nonconformity displaced Anglicanism as the main religious force in Wales and the *capel* (plural: *capeli*) took the place of the church in the lives of most people. With 6,000 or so chapels built during little more than a century, this was as true of the agricultural uplands in the north and west as of the mining valleys in the south. In rural villages and mining towns throughout Wales the *capel* often became the most important public building, both spiritually and culturally as well as physically. The rapid urbanization of the mining valleys in the south was paralleled by an equally rapid growth of Nonconformism, so that in the two Rhondda valleys alone, more than 150 chapels were built, mostly between 1870 and 1900.

The intense activity of the chapel builders gave rise to a distinctive style of religious architecture, which was largely based on classical rather than Gothic forms, as at Capel Peniel, Tremadoc, where the neo-Greek chapel stands out in contrast to the neo-Gothic Anglican church on the opposite side of the road. Peniel, built to adorn Madocks's new town, was an early harbinger of the style that was to dominate chapel building in Wales. It was erected in 1810–11, but, due to a lack of money, without the intended portico; it was not until 1849 that the classical pedimented portico with its Tuscan columns was finally added. **(199)** The design appears to have been based on Inigo Jones's design for St Paul's Church (1638), Covent Garden.

The majority of chapels in the earlier years were not architect-designed, but were usually the products of local builders, often chapel members, who gleaned their ideas from the illustrated catalogues of their period. This created a common architectural character, despite the multitude of Nonconformist sects, with a unity of expression that could be seen as forming a kind of 'Celtic' vernacular. There were, of course, some local variations, particularly in details such as window tracery.

Nonconformist chapels were often designed by ministers, as artisan-architects. In a number of cases the minister had been originally apprenticed as a carpenter or builder, and was responsible for the design of many chapels

other than his own. The most prolific of all the chapel designers was, according to Stephen Hughes, the Revd Thomas Thomas, better known as Thomas Gladwr, 'who designed some 900 chapels in addition to Sunday schools and day schools, houses, and at least one substantial college (Brecon Memorial College, 1867–9), in locations over the whole of Wales', mostly for the Congregationalists and Welsh Independents.[2] Another prolific artisan-architect was the Revd William Jones of Capel Jerusalem, Ton Pentre, in the Rhondda. He was reputed to have 'designed over 200 chapels and created a new age in the style of these buildings' during the latter part of the nineteenth century, by designing large, open chapels.[3] Earlier in the century, the Revd Thomas Morris of Llandeilo Fawr (known as 'Ten Chapel Tom') was building or enlarging chapels in Cowbridge, Pontypool, Newport and London, while the Revd Evan Harries was responsible for a number of Calvinistic Methodist chapels

199 Peniel Chapel, Tremadoc, Caernarfonshire.

200 Capel Soar-y-Mynydd, Ceredigion.

201 Ebenezer Welsh Independent Chapel, Dinas Mawddwy, Meirionnydd.

in the Merthyr Tydfil area. Other known preacher-architects Wales were William Davies, of Rhymney, and his son Aaron Davies, William Humphreys of Swansea, and Joshua Watkins of Llanwenarth and Carmarthen.

From about the middle of the century onwards more and more chapels – especially those in the larger towns – began to be designed by professional architects. The best known of these architects were Richard Owen of Liverpool, with 250 chapels (mostly in northern Wales) attributed to him, John Humphreys who worked in the Swansea area, George Morgan in the Carmarthen area, William Gabe in

the Merthyr Tydfil area, Evan Griffiths in Aberdare and David Jenkins in Llandeilo.

The chapel designers avoided the kind of ceremonial ritual associated with traditional church worship, and as a result did not require an elaborate layouts. Instead, their buildings were designed simply as a kind of 'people's theatre' to cater for the most important element of the service – the *pregeth*, the sermon. Consequently, galleries (usually on three sides) were an important feature in all but the smaller chapels. The simple layouts reflected the theological basis of Nonconformity, which was intended to reassert the fundamental message of Christianity and, at the same time, provide a neutral background to the hell-fire *hwyl* of the preaching.

The gradual development of the chapel style can be seen most clearly in the industrial towns where, because of the phenomenal increase in population, there was an exceptional concentration of chapels for mostly Welsh-speaking congregations. During the earliest phase of chapel building the vernacular tradition of the eighteenth-century meeting houses was followed, with the pulpit located at the centre of one of the long walls, entrances (one for men and the other for women and children) on either side and a symmetrical arrangement of tall windows. Most of the earlier chapels, such as the Unitarian (1795), Bridgend, and Gellionen (1801), Pontardawe, appear to have been built in this manner before being replaced by later rebuilding. Bwlchnewydd (1833), near Carmarthen, and Capel Cymer (1834), Rhondda, are typical of many smaller chapels built in this way during the early part of the nineteenth century. Some *capeli*, such as the remote, upland chapel of Soar-y-Mynydd (1828), near Tregaron, were built with an adjoining house and stable under the same roof. **(200)**

From about 1830 onwards chapels were normally built at right angles to the street, with the preacher's pulpit at the far end and the entrance front in the gable wall next to the street. From now on the architectural emphasis was reserved for the entrance front, where the design is focused on a centralized door (or doors), around which windows – usually tall and round-headed – are positioned symmetrically below the triangular roof-end and a centrally placed name plaque as, for instance, at Ebeneser (1867), Dinas Mawddwy, Meirionnydd. **(201)** Welsh chapels have often been accused of façadism because of the emphasis on the front elevation. But the criticism misses the point, for as with many Italian Renaissance churches by Alberti and others, the front 'no longer *represents* the building behind, rather, it *expresses* the building, its nature and function rather than its size, form or structure.'[4]

As chapels became larger, particularly in the towns, neoclassical features such as pediments, columns or pilasters, cornices and balustraded parapets, were increasingly used. Crane Street Baptist chapel (J. H. Langdon, 1846), Pontypool, is probably the most unequivocal expression of neo-Greek influence in a Welsh chapel. On the outside there is a bold and correct Doric portico, while inside the only natural lighting was from above in the manner of a Greek temple. Often the earlier and mid-century 'classical' chapels – such as the Congregational (1820) in Ruthin, Naval (1834) in Pembroke Dock, Zion (1841) in Merthyr Tydfil, Tabernacle (1850) in Bridgend, Zion (1857) in Llanelli, and Seion (Revd T. Thomas, 1862) in Tal-y-Sarn – have flattish facades with pilasters and simple pediments or balustraded parapets. Cefnywaun (1869) in Deiniolen, Arfon, is a fine example of this type, its main front being an exercise in the orchestration of circles: a fine wheel window in the centre flanked by two smaller circular windows and another small circular window in the pediment. **(202)**

In many later chapels the main classical features are fuller and more emphatic, so that the whole facade becomes boldly articulated, while the interiors often have richly decorated ceilings. These chapels were nearly always designed by professional architects such as George Morgan, whose chapels in Carmarthen (English Baptist, 1872), Swansea (Mount Pleasant, 1875), and Newtown (Baptist, 1881) have majestic Corinthian porticos. **(203)** Capel Bethesda (by W. W. Gwyther, 1863), at Mold, was also designed in grand style with a similar portico. Capel y Tabernacl (J. Hartland, 1865), Cardiff, has neither columns nor pediment, but a refreshingly restrained appearance with a broad sweep of large, stained glass windows above an array of entrance doors with stair towers on either side.

202 Cefn-y-waun, Deiniolen, Caernarfonshire.

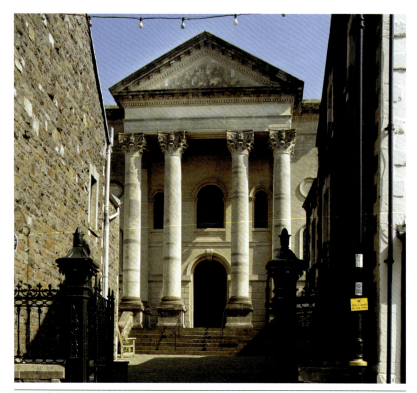

203 English Baptist Chapel, Carmarthen.

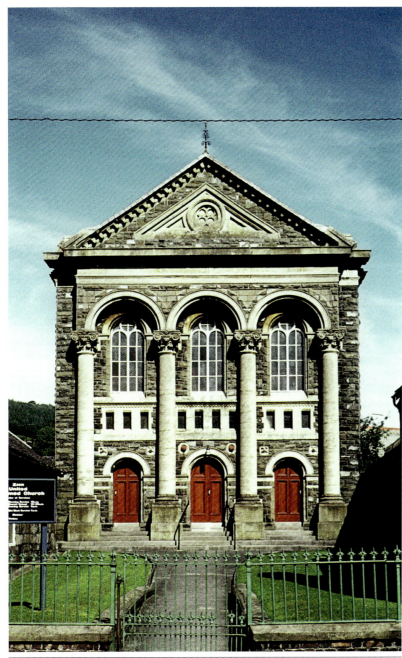

204 Zion, Llanidloes, Montgomeryshire.

A mannerism found in chapels of this period designed by John Humphreys was the use of semicircular arches, instead of horizontal architraves, to link columns (single or paired) together over the entrance portico. Humphreys was responsible for a number of bold chapels in the Swansea area, the best known of which is Morriston's famous Tabernacle (1873), the great 'Cathedral of Welsh Nonconformity', with its extraordinary spire and splendid 1,500-seat interior. Another excellent example of Humphrey's work, but on a smaller scale, is Zion (1878) at Llanidloes. **(204)**

Even before some of the above chapels were completed the signs of stylistic decadence were showing themselves. During the latter part of the nineteenth century there was a general deterioration in chapel design, with a sense of proportion and of style being lost. Elevations, tended to become gaudy and heavy with overdecoration and overstatement. In many cases the lower line of a pediment was broken by a semicircular arch and the mannerist result was usually coarse and clumsy. Where, however, the device was used with care and understanding it could form the basis of a dramatic facade, as with some of the later chapels by the Revd Thomas Thomas at Maesteg (Siloh, 1876) and at Maesycwmer (Tabor, 1876). Where elements of different styles were used in conjunction, as happened in many chapels at the end of the century, the outcome was usually aesthetically disastrous, although even amongst these there were notable exceptions, as for instance Capel Salem (1899), Senghenydd (near Caerphilly), where the result of mixing styles was boldly effective.

Something of a revival in chapel architecture took place during the early twentieth century with the work of W. Beddoe Rees, of Cardiff, who, as a leading Nonconformist and author of *Chapel Building – Hints and Suggestions* (1903), was able to specialize in chapels. Amongst Rees's most original chapels was the thousand-seat Bethania (1908), Maesteg, designed in Beaux Arts style with much Portland stone and Ionic columns above the entrance, and Ebeneser (1908–9), Llandudno, a neo-baroque design in red brick, square on plan but with a circular interior under a ribbed dome.

Apart from a few exceptions, such as Ebeneser (by John Lloyd, 1826), Caernarfon, and Croes Goch (1858), near

St David's, chapels designed in medieval styles were mostly confined to some of the larger towns along the northern coastal strip or the industrial south. On the whole, these often English-language chapels were rarely able to compete with the more wealthy Anglican churches in the quality of their architecture, although again there were some exceptions.

The most unusual chapel of this class in Wales was the Romanesque-style Beulah, at Margam Groes, near Port Talbot. It was erected in 1838 to the reputed design of C. R. M. Talbot of Margam Abbey, who provided the land and the materials. Octagonal in plan, and high for its size, it has two slim, round-headed windows under a small circular window in each bay, all surmounted by Lombardic friezes of close-set arches beneath the overhanging roof. **(205)** Equally notable is the Romanesque-style Baptist chapel at Castleton, (R. G. Thomas, 1857), between Cardiff and Newport). It has a polychromatic facade of Old Red Sandstone and multi-coloured bricks with Lombardic corbelling and a huge wheel-window in the centre of the entrance front's projecting bay.

Of the 'Gothic' chapels, St Andrew's, Swansea, and Capel Pembroke Terrace, Cardiff, stand out. St Andrew's (John Dickson, 1862–4) was originally built for the Scottish Presbyterians and has a large, five-light Geometric window in the centre and tall, eye-catching flanking towers that become octagonal above roof level and are crowned with pinnacles. The robust French-Gothic front of Capel Pembroke Terrace (Henry C. Harris, 1877) towers above the street flanked by octagonal turrets. The interior, with its red-brick walls and cream and black diaper work echoes the polychromatic interiors of Butterfield's churches. When Harris exhibited his design at the Royal Academy in London in 1878, it earned an ironic snigger from *The Builder* that 'at this rate of progress in ecclesiastical architecture, the Welsh Calvinists will hardly know themselves soon!'[5]

Roman Catholic Churches

In 1851 there were, according to the Religious Census of that year, only twenty Catholic churches in Wales, and of those almost half were in Monmouthshire. By then there were

205 Beulah Chapel, Margam Groes, near Port Talbot, Glamorgan.

something like 20,000 Irish-born inhabitants, of whom most were Catholic by religion. As the numbers of Irish continued to grow, so did the strength of the Roman Catholic Church, with a diocese based on Newport.

The earliest churches were mostly the work of the Catholic specialist Joseph John Scoles, of London. These included churches such as St Winefride (1833), Holywell, a neoclassical edifice (extended in 1909 and 1912), St Mary, Newport (1840, early Gothic), St David, Cardiff (1842, neo-Norman), St Mary, Bangor (1844, neo-Gothic), St Illtyd, Dowlais (1846, neo-Gothic; enlarged 1894 with red-brick chancel and stub transepts) and St Alban, Pontypool (1846, neo-Norman).

More interesting visually were some of the churches built during the middle years of the century by Charles F. Hansom, of Bristol, who favoured the Geometric-Gothic style. The earliest were St Xavier and St David Lewis, Usk, built in 1847 with Old Red Sandstone, to which Hansom added a campanile-like tower in 1865, and also St David's Priory, Swansea. The shapely church of St Peter, Roath, in Cardiff, was built in 1861 in Pennant sandstone with bands of Bath stone. The side aisles have multiple gabled roofs giving a concertina-like elevations, to which a fine tower was added at the south-west corner in 1884 by J. J. Hurley.

The church of Our Lady of Dolours, Wrexham, was built in 1857 for the ironmaster Richard Thompson, to the design of Edward Welby Pugin (son of Augustus Welby Pugin) in Decorated Gothic style, with a broach spire and straight pointed heads to windows. It became the pro-cathedral of the Menevia diocese in 1907. Another Roman Catholic church to become a cathedral (in 1916) was St David, Charles Street, Cardiff, built 1884–7 to replace Scoles's earlier church of the same dedication. Designed by Pugin and Pugin, it has a bulky presence distinguished by a five-light window with Geometric tracery and a four-stage tower with a stumpy spire. The interior, entered under a gallery supported on segmental arches, was largely gutted by bomb damage in 1941 and was later restored by F. R. Bates, who installed hammer-beam roof trusses over the nave and a circular window with hexagonal tracery.

Of the early twentieth-century churches, two designed by F. A. Walters are of interest. St Mary of the Angels, Canton, was built 1907 (tower added in 1916), and St Joseph's, Penarth, was built in 1915 (completed 1928). Both were boldly designed in simplified neo-Norman style, with large recessed bays between plain pilasters externally and more ornate interiors with transitional Gothic details (French-influenced in St Mary's and Italianate at St Joseph's).

Educational Buildings

The provision of buildings for both lower and higher education in Wales was limited and wholly inadequate for much of the nineteenth century. Serious education for the working classes during the first half of the century was largely carried out in schools built by the Established Church through the National School Society, which by 1847 still accounted for roughly half of the schools in Wales. The other half was made up of Nonconformist Sunday Schools (usually held in the chapels themselves), schools erected by the British School Society from about 1840, works schools, and private-venture schools that were often little more than child-minding establishments. Amongst the earliest schools were some of the works schools like the neo-Gothic school erected at Llandygai, near Bangor, in 1813 by Anne Pennant in memory of her husband Richard, the Penrhyn quarry owner, and St Peter's School (again neo-Gothic) at Blaenafon, erected in 1816 by Sarah Hopkins in memory of her brother Samuel, the co-owner of the ironworks. Fortunately both buildings survive, the latter as a visitor centre. Another interesting school from the early days was at Penley, Flintshire, where the Madras School – as it was known after the monitorial system of teaching first used in India by Andrew Bell – was built in 1811 with two classrooms under a thatched and hipped roof.

Most of the early schools that survive 'have the traditional single-storey schoolroom, with stone walls and slate roofs'.[6] The National school (1821) in Amlwch, Anglesy, on the other hand has two separate hip-roofed classrooms linked to a two-storey block combining an entrance (through a wide segmental arch) and teacher's accommodation. There were also occasional two-storey schools with a classroom on each floor, one for boys and the other for girls. Other two-storey schools, such as the diminutive building at Nolton (1810), Pembrokeshire, used the upper floor as a classroom and the ground floor for the teacher's accommodation.

Many of the earlier schools, such as the little two-classroom National school (Ellis Davies, 1840), Llangollen, with its simple, Tudoresque windows, were designed and erected by local builders. By the middle of the century, however, professionals were being used more and more; amongst these were county surveyors like John Lloyd in Caernarfonshire, and Thomas Penson in Flintshire, and architects like John Prichard, who (with his partner John Seddon) was responsible for many fine National schools in Glamorgan and Monmouthshire. On the whole the Church-supported National School Society was able to find the money for more interesting designs – such as the picturesque school at Llandeilo, Carmarthneshire, by W. M. Teulon, 1860 – **(206)** more easily than the chapel-supported British School Society. In both cases, the designs adopted were usually Gothic-inspired, or occasionally Tudor or Jacobean. When money was available, however, the British schools could sometimes rise to the occasion, as at the Central School, Dowlais, where Lady Charlotte Guest (translator of *The Mabinogion* into English in 1846), engaged Sir Charles Barry to design a new school with seven classrooms 'in the late Gothic style reminiscent of Tintern Abbey' at a cost of £7,000.[7] It had a great window with Perpendicular-style tracery to light the central hall and thin, curved iron brackets to support the roof. Larger in size, but far less interesting, was Ysgol y Comin, Aberdare, designed by chapel architect Evan Griffiths. Built in 1866 to accommodate 230 boys on the ground floor and 230 girls on the first floor, it was an almost totally plain, two-storey, fourteen-bay cement-rendered building with tall, regularly spaced windows and, at either end, a teacher's house.

The provision of endowed grammar schools and private boarding schools intended for children of the (mostly

207 Christ College, Brecon.

Anglican) middle classes progressed slowly during the first half of the century. Although extensions were carried out at Hawarden and Ruabon schools in the north, it was not until the middle of the century that further existing grammar and public schools began to be rebuilt or extended. They included Bala (Wigg and Pownall, 1851), Christ College, Brecon (J.P. Seddon, 1862–73), Cowbridge (John Prichard, 1849–52), Monmouth (W. Snoke, 1865–95), Swansea (Thomas Taylor, 1853–69), and Welshpool (George Gilbert Scott, 1853). Of these, Christ College, Brecon – re-established in 1853 as a public school at the Dominican Friary – was the most significant. **(207)** A competition to reconstruct the school in Gothic style was won by Prichard and Seddon in 1859, with designs for classrooms, dormitories, octagonal kitchen and master's residence. Building work began two years later, but after the dissolution of the partnership in 1862 John Seddon appears to have been in sole charge, including the restoration of part of the friary church as the school's chapel. In 1880–2 a new library, by J. B. Fowler in early Gothic style, was erected in the space between the school house and the chapel.

206 National School, Llandeilo, Montgomeryshire.

A few new public schools were also established during this period. The earliest was Llandovery College for boys (Fuller and Gingell, 1849–51), built in purple and grey stone (since rendered) in Tudor style, with the main hall on one side of a central entrance tower and three-storey dormitories on the other. Two sister schools, each intended for thirty orphan girls, followed at Denbigh and Llandaf in 1858–9. Both were designed by Herbert Williams of London in Late Gothic style as romantic structures in stone with tall entrance towers surmounted by steep, pyramidal roofs.

In 1870 the passing of the Elementary Education Act led to locally elected education boards building large numbers of non-denominational elementary schools between 1870 and 1914 to fill the gaps left by voluntary schools. As the schools became larger, their plans changed from simple layouts based on a large schoolroom to more complex layouts with a number of classrooms laid out on either side of a corridor or around a central hall. Many architects who had previously specialized in designing churches or chapels now began designing 'board schools', as they came to be known. This also provided them with the opportunity to design buildings in something other than the Gothic style; red-brick buildings with Dutch gables, for example, became popular for many board schools. Cardiff was even noted for 'the size and variety of the Board Schools', by *The Builder* in 1897, which went on to state that 'they are not built by an official architect on one model, but vary very much in style and appearance.'[8]

The Welsh Intermediate Education Act of 1889 made authorities responsible for building secondary schools as well as providing higher-grade education. The new schools provided accommodation for teaching a wider range of subjects, some of which required specialized rooms or laboratories. Consequently, secondary schools tended to be larger than elementary schools, often two- or three-storey buildings with complex layouts. Most were designed with separate entrances for boys and girls, while some were planned, at least in the early days, with boys' classrooms and girls' classrooms on different floors.

Purpose-built colleges for advanced education in Wales were virtually non-existent at the beginning of the nineteenth century. The first to be built was St David's College, Lampeter, in 1822–7 to prepare students for the Anglican ministry. Designed by C. R. Cockerell in late Gothic and Tudor style (though he was a 'classicist'), the college (now Lampeter University) was built in the form of a rather stark, two-storey quadrangle, after the model of Oxford's colleges. The four ranges intersect at the outer corners and have slim, octagonal towers to the internal corners. A battlemented entrance tower marks the centre of the south range, while the north range has a projecting centre section (incorporating a library on the first floor) with a chapel on one side and the hall on the other.

The South Wales and Monmouthshire Training College (now Trinity College), Carmarthen, was designed by Henry Clutton (1847–8) for training teachers for the National (Anglican) schools. Its main two-storey, rubble-stone front is set between the gables of flanking side wings, and has a curious division of ground-floor windows – 'Decorated' windows to the hall on the left-hand side and flat-headed Perpendicular windows and doorway to the library and entrance on the right. Above these is a row of narrow lancets, with steep-roofed dormers incorporating double lancets to the roof.

Architecturally superior to the two colleges mentioned was St Deiniol's Library by Douglas and Minshull, at Hawarden, Flintshire. This was a centre for Christian learning and study, based on W. E. Gladstone's collection of 30,000 books, which was built in two stages: the library section in 1899–1902, and the residential section in 1904–6. Late Gothic in design, the two-storey building is ashlared sandstone to an H plan with a storeyed entrance porch at the centre of the main front. (208) The library half is fully detailed with crenellated and pinnacled parapets and varying window treatment, while the residential part to the right of the porch is much plainer, though this hardly detracts from the overall impression when seen from a distance. The chief interest inside is the library itself, with its open timber roof and all round gallery.

When the University of Wales was formally founded in 1893, three existing colleges became part of the new university, thus realizing, almost four hundred years later, one of Owain Glyndŵr's great unfulfilled dreams. The college at Aberystwyth had begun life in 1864 as a fantastic

209 Old College, Aberystwyth.

neo-Gothic seaside hotel that incorporated Nash's triangular house for Uvedale Price, with John Seddon as its architect. When funds ran out before completion, the building was taken over in 1872 to become a college, and Seddon was recalled to make the necessary alterations, resulting in an even more extravagant mixture of Gothic styles with pinnacled roofs and castellated towers. In June 1885 a fire gutted much of the unfinished building, after which Seddon, with John Coates Carter as his partner, was reappointed architect. The north range was rebuilt in a simpler manner,

while the upper storey of the triangular south wing was reclad in stone and an octagonal tower with spire and high-level mosaics by C. F. A. Voysey was added at the sharp end. (209) The rear elevation is dominated by a pair of circular towers, one incorporating the ceremonial stairs and the other enclosing a full-height staircase.

A limited competition for the University College of South Wales and Monmouthshire (now Cardiff University), situated in the 'neoclassical' surroundings of Cathays Park, Cardiff, was won in 1903 by the gothicist architect W. D.

Caroe. The result was a rather stilted 'English Renaissance' scheme for a very long, mainly two-storey, Portland stone building around a large rectangular courtyard, with frequent variations in design. It was built in stages over a long period (1905 to 1962) that further reduced its integrity. At the rear, a three-storey block, containing a fine library with a stone-panelled barrel ceiling, projects into the Great Court, splitting it into two parts.

Of all the university buildings, the University College of North Wales (now Bangor University) is the finest architecturally. Dramatically sited on the crest of a hill, it suggests some great medieval cathedral with a handsome castellated tower rising majestically above the roofs of the town. **(210)** Designed by Henry T. Hare in a limited competition, the Renaissance-style, sandstone building with its light-coloured Preseli slate roofs was erected in 1907–11. The plan is based on two offset courtyards, with three-storey wings on the lower side, two-storey wings further back, and a central tower tying the design together where they all meet. There are many gables and gablets and a variety of windows, some with detached pediments and others based on late Gothic archetypes. The library with its panelled, timber barrel-vault ceiling occupies the west side of the great court. The smaller, stepped court has an Arts and Crafts feel about it and is closed on the north side by the Prichard Jones Hall ∎

14 Religion and Education, 1880 to 1915
References

1   B. H. Malkin, *The Scenery, Antiquities and Biography of South Wales*, p. 179.

2   Stephen Hughes, 'Thomas Thomas, 1817–88: the first national architect of Wales', *Arch. Camb*, 152 (2003), 69.

3   *Crynhodeb o Hanes Jerusalem, Ton* [Summary of the History of Jerusalem, Ton] (Ystrad [Rhondda], 1920), p. 13.

4   K. Downes, 'The Façade Problem in Roman Churches, c.1540–1640', in Jill A. Franklin et al., *Architecture and Interpretation* (Boydell Press, Woodbridge, 2012), pp. 262–3.

5   *The Builder*, 18 May 1878.

6   M. Seaborne, *Schools in Wales 1500–1900*, p. 88.

7   *The Builder* (1855), p. 462.

8   Quoted by M. Seaborne, *Schools in Wales*, p. 181.

15

Civic and Communal, 1800 to 1915

Some of the most successful works of architecture of the nineteenth century were the public and communal buildings erected in the more prosperous county towns and in the growing centres of importance. As with most churches, chapels, schools and country houses, the outward appearance of these buildings reflected the historic styles of the past. In the earlier part of the century most buildings could be clearly identified with one or other of the historic styles: educational buildings tended to be 'Gothic' or 'Tudor', while public buildings were proudly 'classical' to symbolize the civic

virtues. In the latter part of the century, the range of buildings was far wider and the question of which was the most 'appropriate' style became more difficult to decide. Many were, at least in Wales, virtually new types of buildings, e.g. art galleries, museums, workmen's institutes. They required new and more flexible solutions. By then archaeological knowledge had deepened and become more precise, so that there was a bewildering range of styles and periods from which to choose. Each had its own adherents, who often tended to use it irrespective of the building's function.

Nineteenth-century Civic Buildings

The architectural Greek Revival was a late starter in Britain, for already in the late eighteenth century the 'Greek' movement had been popularized in Germany by Johann Winckelmann and Friedrich Gilly, and in France by Claude-Nicholas Ledoux. Academically purer than Renaissance architecture and less eclectic than baroque, the 'noble simplicity and quiet grandeur' of the neo-Greek manner made it an ideal vehicle of design for civic and cultural buildings.

One of the earliest attempts at something along these lines in Wales (apart from Capel Peniel, Porthmadog), and rather more home-spun Tuscan than Greek, was the attractive Shire Hall, Dolgellau, by Edward Haycock. It was built in the tough local granite in 1825 as the Assizes, with a large courtroom in the centre flanked by modest side wings. (211) The main facade of the courtroom has an overhanging pediment, with flat pilasters and segmental-headed windows below, while the projecting wings mimic this on a smaller scale. The Shire Hall (now Brecknock Museum), Brecon, is an altogether purer design by T. H. Wyatt and David Brandon, 1839–43. (212) Built in Bath stone, it has a fine entrance portico with four fluted Doric columns (plus two similar columns to the inner porch), architrave with triglyphs, and pediment. The bold entablature is continued on the outer bays, although the shallow pilasters are curiously to one side only. The polygonal rear wall of the courtroom was once faced with Ionic columns.

Without question one of the most powerful neo-Greek public buildings, and one of the most Ledoux-like structures, was Bridgend's superb Town Hall, by David Vaughan of Bonvilston, near Cardiff. It was on an island site near the town centre, and completed in 1843. The full-width, pedimented portico was fronted by colossal unfluted Doric columns, apparently influenced by images of the great temples in the western Greek colonies, such as Paestum and Segesta, rather than by the precepts of Athens. Sadly, the Town Hall was ungraciously demolished in 1971, after having been officially scheduled as a 'building of exceptional architectural interest'. Equally grand was Swansea's Old Guildhall and Assizes (1848–52), by Thomas Taylor of London. It had a strange plan, with each side different from the others. What held the Bath stone building together visually, however, was the use of round-headed windows to both floors, and arrays of Corinthian columns on three sides of the upper floor, the columns and entablature breaking forward at the end bays. It was reconstructed in 1993–4, keeping only the external walls, as the Dylan Thomas Centre.

After the mid-century, the Greek style gave way to Roman-inspired or even Gothic-inspired styles. The County Hall and Assize Court, Caernarfon, by the county surveyor John Thomas, 1863, was, for instance, neo-Reniassance. Here, against a background of squared, rock-faced rubble walls, the richly detailed portico stands out, complete with fluted Doric columns on pedestals, engraved entablature and heavily dentilled pediment surmounted by a blindfold figure of justice.

Many new town halls in the rural market towns tended to continue along the path set by the eighteenth-century courts with combined market halls and assizes. The bold, Italianate town hall at Llandovery, by R. K. Penson, 1857–8, for example, is on an island site and has its first-floor courtroom above an arcaded market hall open on three sides. At the rear are police cells and the court entrance under a square tower with pyramidal roof and bell-turret. Cardigan Guildhall, by R. J. Withers, 1858–60, follows roughly the same plan but has decorative, brick and Bath stone pointed arches to the ground floor market. (213) Above is a large assembly hall with hipped roof and lit by tall two-light windows with blank, pointed arches. Further along is the

211 Shire Hall, Dolgellau, Meirionnydd.

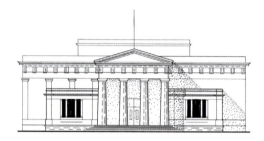

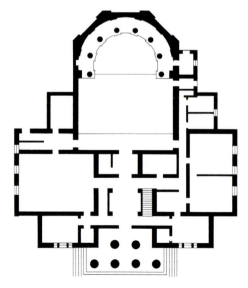
212 Shire Hall, Brecon, elevation and plan.

213 Town Hall, Cardigan.

At Llanelli, the Italianate Town Hall by William Griffiths (1885) – a fine, carefully composed building with a central clock-tower – was built without the need for an accompanying market; instead the council chamber occupies the first floor of the central block, with lower ranges on either side. Merthyr Tydfil's red-brick, neo-Renaissance Town Hall (E. A. Johnson, 1896–7) was built with a block for council offices facing the street and another block at the rear of the courtyard for county courts. The council block has a flamboyant entrance hall with a sweeping Imperial staircase and a large stained glass window behind. In 2007 the building was converted to a community centre, the courtyard roofed over and the building renamed the Redhouse.

Early Twentieth-century Civic Grandeur

As the new century dawned neoclassicism remained the favourite mode for civic buildings. This was the case with Pontypridd's new Council Offices (Henry T. Hare, 1903–4), although here the neoclassicism appears more relaxed and less contrived than in some other buildings of its type. Hare's design, which won in competition, accepted the functional relationship between the councillors' areas and the offices by proposing two interconnecting ranges at right angles to each other. The former, a three-bay pavilion with an arcade of round-headed arches below and three, triple-light windows above, recalls earlier market-and-courtroom models, though in this case the arcade fronts a deep entrance hall and the windows light the council chamber. The block is faced in sandstone, variously smooth (with relief carving), channelled or hammered, and has flat pilasters and a balustraded parapet framing the elevation and only partially screening the pitched roof behind. The end wall is gabled and has a Venetian window to the upper storey. The office block at the rear of the council pavilion, but also in sandstone, forms an eight-bay, two-storey range with second-floor dormer windows in a mansard roof.

A few miles south of Pontypridd is Cathays Park in Cardiff, famous as a civic centre but containing far more than just a few municipal buildings. Indeed, the park's

entrance under a stumpy clock tower, and at the lower end a cross-range which once housed a small grammar school. The composite type of market-and-courtroom continued late into the century with buildings like Abergavenny's Town Hall (Wilson and Wilcox, 1869–71), a handsome French-Gothic structure with a massive, copper-topped clock tower at the corner. Here, the pointed arches of the market were glazed in for comfort. Maesteg's Town Hall (Henry C. Harris, 1881), is vaguely Dutch Renaissance with a steep, hipped roof and double-decker lantern; its projecting centre bay has a wide, round-headed entrance leading to the market, and above, a continuous, timber-framed window.

development over nearly a century to include some of the nation's principal buildings – however architecturally un-Welsh they might appear – is a singular reflection of Cardiff's growth in importance, validating as much as anything its claim to city status and national capital. The 'finest civic centre in the British Isles', as it has been called,[1] was the result of a far-seeing vision by a few councillors, sensible conditions laid down by the landowner (Lord Bute), and proposals by the borough engineer (William Harpur) in 1899. It was largely built through the wealth created by the iron and coal industries of the Valleys during the nineteenth and early twentieth centuries.

Altogether, the civic centre is an extraordinary assemblage of white, Portland stone buildings, in effect a permanent exhibition of architectural styles and tastes of the late nineteenth century and the twentieth century. (214) Of the eight public buildings begun before the First World War, all except for one were the result of open or limited architectural competitions. Four buildings served local authority or government functions, viz. the City Hall, Law Courts, Glamorgan County Hall, and Welsh Insurance Commission – the last never getting beyond a few foundations due to the outbreak of war. The other four were for educational and leisure purposes, viz. University College, Technical College, University of Wales Registry and the National Museum.

The City Hall project was won by Lanchester, Stewart and Rickards in a competition held in 1897 for both a Town Hall (as it then was) and Law Courts. With these two early buildings the architectural trend for classicism and Portland stone was set for the rest of the Park. The vigorously modelled City Hall, begun in 1900 and completed in 1905, occupies with great self-assurance the dominant position at the centre of the southern group of buildings, a position admirably suited to show off its imaginative design, a concept heavily influenced by Austrian arboque with overtones of French baroque. (215) In principle, the City Hall forms a hollow rectangle on plan with, at first floor, a circular Council Chamber linked via a shining Marble Hall to a vaulted Assembly Hall. Externally, it appears as a large, two-storey building with an elaborate centre section with

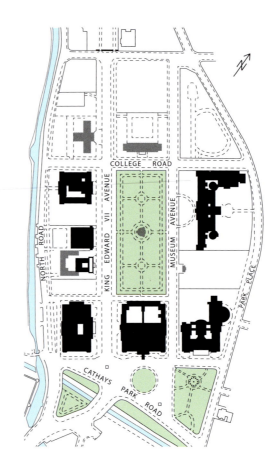

214 Cathays Park, Cardiff. Buildings built between 1900 and 1914 shown black; buildings built between 1918 and 1939 shown grey.

lead-covered dome (above the Council Chamber) to the south front, corner pavilions and a splendid, 60 m-high clock tower with a flamboyant upper part, rising above the west front. Flanking the City Hall on the left are the Law Courts (1900–5), by the same architects, but in a more restrained yet closely related manner. While clearly from the same stable, the Courts building is sufficiently different to stand on its own, but in a balanced composition. Rectangular in plan, it faces the City Hall's west front and secondary entrance. A broad flight of steps leads up to a slightly projecting centre

215 City Hall, Cathays Park, Cardiff.

216 Glamorgan County Hall, Cathays Park, Cardiff.

section with twin entrance loggias with Ionic columns and twin cupola-topped turrets above. Inside, there is a beautiful, three-bay Courts Hall, lit by high-level semicircular windows beneath a segmental ceiling with saucer domes.

One of the finest buildings in Cathays Park is the Greco-Roman-style Glamorgan County Hall (now part of Cardiff University) that lies behind the Law Courts. Winner of the 1908 competition, it was designed by Vincent Harris, along with his colleague Thomas Moodie, and built 1909–11. The main facade is monumental in scale with five central bays set back behind a portico of coupled Corinthian columns between outer pavilions, all surmounted by a continuous entablature with a heavily dentilled cornice and an attic storey fronted by a balustrade. **(216)** The side elevations are comparatively simple, with arched ground-floor windows, while the rear elevation has an elaborate overhanging first-floor balcony carried on stone brackets. The D-shaped Council Chamber inside is an impressive space with ashlared walls and a near-hemispherical ceiling.

Assembly Rooms, Theatres and Workmen's Institutes

For most of the nineteenth century facilities for leisure were limited to the upper or middle classes, there being virtually no provision for the working classes apart from public houses. The earliest building erected simply for leisure may have been the Public Bathhouse (now Laston House) at Tenby, a pleasing five-bay building with a curved porch (incorporating a Greek inscription) and windows set below blank arches. It was designed by S. P. Cockerell and built in 1810 for Sir William Paxton, who wanted to take advantage of the new vogue for sea bathing.

By now Assembly Rooms for social occasions and entertainment had become popular in fashionable resorts. Cockerell had already (in 1804) prepared a design for Assembly Rooms at Swansea's seafront, but this had been rejected. The later history of the building, which was built by subscription, is confused, for though the local architect William Jernegan 'provided a new design [in 1810] ... the rooms were built over many years, and [only] opened in

1821.'² In fact there were two parallel buildings, each of the same size and height. The earlier building (demolished since 1975, when inspected by the author) had a plain but well-proportioned elevation facing – but set well back from – Pier Street; it was lit by tall windows and had a graceful oriel to the upper floor. The later, five-bay building faces on to Cambrian Place. Externally the lower storey has channelled masonry, half-round Doric columns and a central entrance, while the upper storey has tall windows to light the ballroom, each with incised panels below and above (217) – the circular windows being added later. At some time the space between the two buildings was roofed over and a grand, top-lit, open-well staircase inserted to serve both parts.

At much the same time Aberystwyth got its own elegant Assembly Rooms in Laura Place, near the castle. Designed by George Repton, and built 1818–20, it comprises a hipped central block with tall, round-headed windows, and slightly projecting pedimented wings with lower roofs on either side. Later, Assembly Rooms designed by James Wilson of Bath were built in 1854 at King Street, Carmarthen.

217 Assembly Rooms, Cambrian Place, Swansea.

The Italianate-style building was subsequently remodelled as the Lyric Theatre in 1936.

Outside the largest towns there was little in the way of purpose-built theatres during the earlier part of the nineteenth century. In some market towns, such as Brecon, Carmarthen and Monmouth, town halls were used for productions by travelling performers. A few of the larger estates like Wynnstay also had their own private theatres, but mostly there were few facilities available apart from the popular portable theatre.

Swansea, however, had had a theatre since 1785, and another one, the New Theatre, opened in 1807. In 1864 the first of the town's Music Halls opened, followed by the Star Amphitheatre in 1869 and the Pavilion Music Hall in 1888. The Palace Theatre, a mansard-roofed, neo-baroque building designed by Alfred Bucknall and E. W. Jennings, also opened in 1888. The neoclassical Grand Theatre, by William Hope, was built in 1897, and remodelled a century later, by McColl Associates without obliterating the main front's projecting ends, with their steep roofs, or altering the original interior.

Cardiff's first real theatre, the Theatre Royal on the site of the future Park Hotel, did not open until 1826. This was followed by the neoclassical Philharmonic Theatre in 1876, the Venetian-Gothic Prince of Wales Theatre in 1878, and the neo-Renaissance Grand Theatre in 1880. Of the three the Prince of Wales (W. D. Blessley and T. Waring), in Wood Street, survived longest, finally closing as a live theatre in 1961 and later reopening in 1999 as a pub to reveal much of its former auditorium. The New Theatre (Ernest Runtz and Ford, 1906), Park Place, has a lively, curved entrance bay in red brick with coupled Ionic columns and entablature to the upper storey, between octagonal turrets with domes.

Despite its rural setting, mid-Wales was also able to acquire a few theatres. Brecon – birthplace of the actress Sarah Siddons (1755–1851) – gained a playhouse when the old Guildlhall was altered in 1888 to incorporate a theatre. Two years later the opera singer Adelina Patti (1843–1919) had a small, 150-seat theatre built alongside her home at Craig-y-nos (a castellated mansion of 1841–3), near Ystradgynlais. The theatre (by Bucknall and Jennings, of Swansea) was

218 Craig-y-nos Castle, Glyntawe, Breconshire, the Theatre.

219 Garth Pier, Bangor, Caernarfonshire.

intended to be a miniature La Scala that incorporated ideas from Wagner's Bayreuth. Internally it is lined with Corinthian columns and has a movable floor; **(218)** externally the entrance front has Doric pilasters. Aberystwyth's Coliseum Theatre (J. Arthur Jones, 1904) – now the Ceredigion Museum – had a stone and yellow terracotta facade with domed cupolas either side of a pilastered gable; it was built above a shopping arcade and had two balconies inside. The arrival of the railway in 1865 encouraged Llandrindod's development as a spa town, but it still had to wait almost half a century before getting a theatre and concert hall in the shape of the Grand Pavilion (R. Wellings Thomas, 1912) – a large rendered, rectangular building with a glazed cupola and semicircular windows, but now without its corner domes.

Theatres in the north were largely restricted to the coastal resorts. Rhyl appears to have been the earliest to get a theatre when the Winter Gardens (Owen Edwards) opened in 1876; the theatre, however, seems not to have survived beyond 1897. Llandudno's (former) Grand Theatre (G. A. Humphreys, with Edwin Sachs, 1901) is a rather plain red-brick structure, enlivened with yellow terracotta to the gable. Some theatres

were associated with piers, such as Llandudno's octagonal-shaped Pier Pavilion (B. Nelson, 1883-6), a 2,000-seat iron and glass structure at the landward end of the 1876-8 pier; the pier itself was demolished in 1994 after a fire. The Victoria Pier (Mangnall and Littlewoods, 1899-1900) at Colwyn Bay supported an even larger, 2,500-seat pavilion; both pier and pavilion were burnt down in 1922, and another pier and pavilion were built in 1934.

Seaside piers were also erected at Aberystwyth (Eugenius Birch, 1865), to which an iron shed-like pavilion with a semi-circular roof with dormers (George Croydon Marks) was added in 1896, and at Penarth (H. F. Edwards, 1895), where a small wooden theatre (1907) was sited at the end of the pier, and later a shell-concrete, Art Deco-style pavilion with octagonal corner towers (L. G. Mouchel and Partners, 1927-8) was built at the landward end. The most ambitious pier in Wales was Bangor's Garth pier (John James Webster, 1896), which at 475 m long reaches two-thirds of the way across the Menai Straits. **(219)** It has highly decorative ironwork and Hindu-looking kiosks at intervals and a small, multifaceted pavilion with onion-shaped roof at the end. Closed in 1971, it was later restored and reopened.

During the latter part of the nineteenth century institutes for promoting professions and crafts, usually for men, began appearing. One of the earliest was the Mechanics' Institute (K. W. Ladd, 1862–3), Pembroke Dock, a simple, arcaded building of little architectural interest. There was also a Mechanics' Institute (Lawrence and Goodman, 1875) at Griffithstown, near Pontypool, and a Working Men's Free Institute (Benjamin Lawrence, 1868) in Monmouth, both neo-Gothic, one French and the other Italian. In Swansea, the Working Men's Club and Institute (Benjamin Williams, 1885) was a red-brick and Bath stone, three-storey (plus dormered attic) building in an eclectic style borrowed from France. At the other end of the scale is the South Wales Institute of Engineers (E. W. M. Corbett, 1893), in Cardiff, a decorative building of red brick and terracotta in free classicism.

More evocative, perhaps, are the miners' halls and institutes that became important parts of the social fabric and visual environment of the coalfields in the south and north during the late nineteenth and early twentieth centuries. Surprisingly, nothing similar arose in the slate-quarrying areas of Gwynedd in the north-west. In the southern Valleys virtually every town had a miners' institute, often providing a hall, library, reading room and games rooms. Amongst the earliest are neo-Renaissance institutes at Blaina (F. R. Bate, 1892), Blaengarw (Jacob Rees, 1894) and Blaenafon (E. A. Landsdowne, 1894), the latter with dramatic front in rock-faced pennant sandstone and dressed-stone pilasters, curved pediments and triple doorway. **(220)** Inside, there is a 1,500-seat hall. The Nixon Workmen's Institute (Dan Lloyd, 1899), Mountain Ash, has a 1,500-seat theatre and a swimming pool, as well as a Wren-style yellow-brick elevation with red-brick pilasters and a pedimented doorway enriched with glazed terracotta in various colours. Another large and architecturally interesting workmen's institute is that at Aberaman (Thomas Roderick, 1909), with a red-brick main front with stone dressings, three pedimented doorways and a large central mullioned window.

Miners' institutes continued to be built well into the twentieth century, and even after the First World War despite a downturn in mining. That at Newbridge, Monmouthshire, had been built in 1907 in red and yellow brick with stone dressings; a large Memorial Hall (Memo) with a dance hall on the ground floor and a theatre above – elegantly decorated in Art Deco fashion with simplified patterns and bold colours – was added in 1924 next to the earlier building. At Rhosllanerchrugog, near Wrexham, an ambitious neo-baroque institute was built as late as 1926 (John Owen and F. A. Roberts) in red brick and Portland stone, with a Doric portico. Probably the last Miners' Hall (now a theatre) to be built was at Ammanford (J. O. Parry, c.1935), Carmarthenshire, again in neoclassical style with giant Ionic columns under an entablature.

220 Workmen's Hall & Institute, Blaenafon, Monmouthshire.

Other Communal Buildings:
Museums, Galleries and Libraries

The oldest museum in Wales is the rather stately Royal Institution of South Wales (now the Swansea Museum) – around the corner from the Assembly Rooms – founded in 1835 as the Swansea Philosophical and Literary Society. It was designed by Frederick Long of Liverpool in 1838, completed in 1841 and opened in 1845. A scholarly, nine-bay building with a portico supported on giant Greek Ionic columns; the two-storey side bays are marked by pilasters and tall windows on the ground floor and square, recessed panels to the upper floor.

Five years later, the Roman Legionary Museum was opened in Caerleon. Now, only its splendid Greek Doric portico of Bath stone remains above ground, the remainder having been demolished for the erection of a new museum in 1987. Designed by H. F. Lockwood, it was originally built as a temple-like structure, lit from above through a glazed roof.

A museum which never got built was the Museum of Welsh Culture proposed by the charismatic Dr William Price in a document published in March 1838. It was to be built by public subscription at Glyn-taf, near Pontypridd, as 'a Tower of one hundred feet high ... near Y Maen Chwyf; the space within the Tower to be divided into eight apartments for a Museum, and surmounted by a Camera Obscura'.[3] Unfortunately the money raised was never enough, and there were also legal issues, so that twenty years later all that had been built were two, white-washed, three-storey round towers with octagonal roofs intended to be the gateway to the main museum tower. (221)

Apart from temporary exhibitions at various National Eisteddfodau – starting in 1862 at Caernarfon, where Owen Jones of Crystal Palace fame had designed the pavilion – there had been little provision for displaying the visual arts in Wales, except in private galleries, until the founding of the Royal Cambrian Academy of Art in 1882. Spurred on by people like Edwin Seward, who had just won the 1880 competition for a Cardiff Free Library and Art Gallery, the

221 Druid Towers (Round Houses), Glyn-taf, near Pontypridd.

The Architecture of Wales

Academy first planned to make Cardiff its headquarters and build a permanent gallery there. Instead it settled for Plas Mawr, Conwy, in 1885, where it remained until 1993.

Shortly after the Academy's change of mind, James Pyke Thompson had the Turner House Gallery (Edwin Seward, 1887–8) built in Penarth to house his collection of Turner paintings. A vaguely neo-Renaissance pavilion of red brick and red stone with a hipped roof, its central bay forms a wide, recessed arch under a pediment. The two-storey interior is top-lit and has a large opening between the floors, and is now used as a photography gallery.

The Mostyn Art Gallery, Llandudno, was built for Lady Mostyn in 1901–2 to showcase the work of women artists and encourage the arts and crafts. Designed by the estate architect G. A. Humphreys, it is a curious three-storey (plus roof dormers) by five-bay building in red brick and terracotta, with angular oriels on the first floor, semicircular windows to the second floor and an angular, slate-covered spire in the centre. It closed in 1914, but reopened in 1984 with the name Oriel Mostyn, later shortened to Mostyn.

Swansea's major gallery, the Glynn Vivian Art Gallery (Glendinning Moxham, 1909–11), was founded by way of a bequest from Richard Glynn Vivian, heir to the family of industrialists that had turned Swansea into the metallurgical centre of the world. It has a dramatic baroque-style facade in red brick and Bath stone. The central five bays have a florid central doorway with blocked Doric columns; tall angular windows to the lower storey and plain red brickwork above with a heavily dentilled cornice at either end; and bold, slightly projecting, pedimented two-storey bays with channelled Bath stone, deeply recessed windows and giant Ionic columns. The gallery was extended in 1974 with a glass-and-concrete addition, and was remoddled in 2016 by Powell Dobson.

One of the most significant buildings to be erected in the Valleys during the middle years of the nineteenth century was the Guest Memorial Library at Dowlais, Merthyr Tydfil, a surprisingly brave attempt at neoclassical architecture in a working-class area. It was built in 1863 as a memorial to Sir Josiah Guest at the expense of his widow, Lady Charlotte, who had Sir Charles Barry to design it. Laid out in the form of a Latin cross, it has pediments on all four faces. The portico on the main front has Tuscan columns carried on a podium supported on piers of rock-faced limestone. During the steel-making era it became the GKN Recreation Centre, and was later converted to domestic use.

During the first decade of the twentieth century many towns in Wales, along with those in England and Scotland, benefited from the provision of local libraries funded by the Carnegie Trust, a bequest that had been set up by the US steel magnate Andrew Carnegie. Altogether seventeen Carnegie Libraries were built in Wales. Amongst the more interesting are a couple of neo-baroque designs: the 'Old Library' (now council offices), Wrexham, a competition winner by Vernon Hope (1906–7) in brick and stone with near-continuous first-floor windows; and the small library in Corporation Road, Newport, by C. F. Ward (1906–7), a single storey building with T-shaped plan and wide, segmental arches over the entrance doorway and side windows. In addition, there is the delightful Cathays Library, Cardiff, an Arts and Crafts design described in the next chapter.

Towards the end of the nineteenth century a movement to acquire a national library and national museum along the lines of those in Scotland and Ireland began to gain ground. It was not until 1904, however, that the government in London approved the idea in principle and appointed a Privy Council committee to determine their location. A number of towns petitioned for either one or both institutions, and in the following year it was decided to establish a National Library in Aberystwyth and a National Museum in Cardiff. Following this, Royal Charters were granted to both institutions in 1907.

In 1909 the National Library was temporarily housed in the Assembly Rooms while a competition was set up to choose a design for the new library to be built on a site overlooking the town. The competition was won by Sydney Kyffin Greenslade, with a pompous neoclassical design in Portland stone on a granite base, more appropriate to a dense urban site than the green hills above Aberystwyth. (222) The Library was planned as a cross within a square, the entrance and administration being in the west wing and the book

222 National Library of Wales, Aberystwyth.

stacks at the rear. The north and south wings were built in 1911–16. They contain an impressive Readers' Room (north) and Gregynog Gallery (south), both with curved and coffered ceilings and central cross vault. The west wing overlooking the town was built 1935–7 to a modified design by Adams, Holden and Pearson. The main facade has channelled stonework to the two lower floors, plain stonework and flat pilasters elsewhere, tall round-headed windows to highlight the projecting ends of the north and south wings, and giant, recessed Ionic columns to flank the first-floor entrance porch reached from two flights of external steps. The north and south fronts are also of Portland stone, but the stackroom block (1928–65) at the rear, a hollow rectangle is in purple brick. (The development of the University campus by Sir Percy Thomas and others on the Penglais site behind the National Library, from 1935 onwards, has moderated the incongruity of the competition design to a certain extent, but of course the campus was not envisaged at the time when the competition was held.)

A competition for the design of the National Museum on a site in Cardiff's Cathays Park, was won by Dunbar Smith and Cecil Brewer in 1910, out of 130 entries. The neoclassical design of the winning entry – apparently influenced by the work of McKim, Mead and White in the United States – was in the form of a long, hollow rectangle with galleries on all four sides, a spacious, domed entrance hall and an interior courtyard with more galleries in two separate pavilions. Construction began in 1911, but was interrupted by the First World War, so that the first part containing the extraordinarily fine entrance hall was not opened until 1927; the east wing followed in 1932 and the west wing in 1965. The north wing, by the Alex Gordon Partnership, had to wait until 1992, by which time some of the design requirements had changed. Smoother-looking and more relaxed externally than the nearby City Hall, the Museum offers an impressive, sphinx-like front to the Park, that incorporates a wide, five-bay entrance loggia with giant paired Doric columns. **(223)** Flanking the loggia are the three-bay channelled Portland stone ends to the long side wings, each with a protruding centre bay with recessed columns and a high attic storey against which are set various sculptural groups ■

223   National Museum of Wales, Cathays Park, Cardiff.

15   Civic and Communal, 1800 to 1915
References

1   John Newman, *The Buildings of Wales: Glamorgan*, p. 220.

2   Prys Morgan, 'Art and Architecture', in Glanmor Williams (ed.), *Swansea – An Illustrated History* (Swansea, 1990), p. 193.

3   Quoted by Dean Powell, in *Dr William Price* (Stroud, 2012), p. 83.

16

'Arts and Crafts' to Early Modernism, 1900 to 1939

In 1851 Owen Jones (1809–74) – son of Owen Jones of Llanfihangel Glyn Myfyr (founder of the Gwyneddigion Society in London) – was appointed superintendent of works of the Great Exhibition of Industry (and later joint director of decoration), held at Paxton's Crystal Palace in London. He is mentioned here because – as a forerunner of William Morris – the full significance of Jones's own pioneering in the improvement of wallpaper and textile design and furniture has not always been recognized. He is best remembered for his original use of colour and for his monumental encyclopedia *The Grammar of Ornament* (1856), an important work that probably influenced Morris. According to Pevsner, 'William Morris's early designs [were] crisper, lighter, and more daintily stylized, under some influence no doubt from the teachings ... of Owen Jones whose *Grammar of Ornament* he possessed.'[1]

Arts and Crafts

However, if Morris owed some debt to Owen Jones, as well as to others, the debt that we owe to Morris himself as inspirer of the Arts and Crafts movement in Britain is in no way lessened. Reacting critically to the mass-produced products on show at the Great Exhibiton, Morris's initial impact was in the 'decorative arts', including fabrics and furniture design, and not specifically in the field of domestic architecture. Imbued with fervour for good rural craftsmanship – which he associated with the pre-machine days of the Middle Ages – there were thus medieval undertones, and even Gothic Revival links, in his prints and artefacts. It was Morris's disciples – men such as C. F. A. Voysey (1857–1941), J. C. Carter (1859–1927) and H. L. North (1871–1941) – who were to carry the cleansing flame of the Arts and Crafts movement into English and Welsh domestic architecture at the end of the nineteenth century and the early years of the twentieth.

While the Arts and Crafts movement campaigned for a revival of good craftsmanship to combat the outpouring of tasteless factory-made goods produced almost everywhere, a genuine craft tradition still existed in many parts of Wales and survived at least until the First World War. The age-old masonry tradition — particularly in Gwynedd — was so powerful (even into the 1920s) as to mean the continued use of indigenous materials as a matter of course, and not just as the result of an introduced Arts and Crafts style. In this context the work of Herbert Luck North is of especial interest because his aim was to exploit the character of genuine Welsh arts and crafts traditions by the sensitive use of indigenous materials such as the local small thick slates for roofing and also slate for fencing. Though born in Leicester, he had lived with his grandparents in Llanfairfechan from an early age, and after studying in Cambridge did his articles in London with the Arts and Crafts architect Henry Wilson. It was while he was at Wilson's office that he was sent back to Wales to supervise the building of St Mark's, Brithdir. Later, in 1898, North produced a singular design for a new church at Caerhun – possibly influenced by Petit's church at Caerdeon – where he tried to achieve something of the intimate spirit of the older churches in Snowdonia, but in a new way. **(224)** The tall, narrow windows, the porch doorway and the double-nave roof were all local features, but combined in a way to produce a new vernacular inspired by both tradition and Arts and Crafts attitudes. Unfortunately the church was never built; had it been, it would surely have been a jewel amongst the hills.

It is for his domestic work, however, that North is best known. By the First World War he had designed more than a dozen houses, during a period when 'he did his most interesting domestic work, weaving together fashionable Arts and Crafts ideas and features with those he was discovering in the local vernacular buildings.'[2] They were picturesque houses, with prominent gables, steep, slate roofs and white roughcast walls, such as Beamsmore, **(225)** mostly grouped around The Close, in Llanfairfechan. At the same time he wrote, together with Harold Hughes, *The Old Cottages of Snowdonia* (1908). In this, they drew the reader's attention to the simplicity of

the old cottages ... they were planned to be absolutely suitable to the requirements of the time. We must do the same, using to the full the additional real advantages we now possess, but observing always the same simplicity. Our building, besides being thoroughly practical, should have in it (the) element of beauty and poetry which gives it an individuality ... a beauty for which many of the old cottages are so conspicuous.

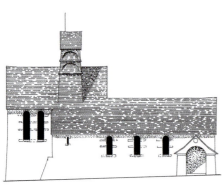

224 Proposed Church, Caerhun, near Bangor.

225 Beamsmoor, Llanfairfechan, Caernarfonshire.

226 Cottage Hospital, Dolgellau, Meirionnydd.

After the war North designed nearly twenty more houses for The Close, mostly different, but with a certain quirkiness that held them visually together, as well as a public housing scheme in Bangor. It was during this time that he wrote, again with Hughes, *The Old Churches of Snowdonia* (1924). North also designed a few churches and chapels, including some in England and a small hospital in Dolgellau, **(226)** where he showed the same kind of sensitivity and ingenuity, as well as a love of strong geometrical shapes – steep roofs outside, sharply pointed arches inside – as he had done in his earlier domestic work. In one of his last (unbuilt) designs of 1939, an Expressionist-looking chapel for St Michael's College, Llandaf, he seemed to be exploring new territory. With its octagonal tower topped by a curving roof, it had a sculptural feel, inside and out, and no hint of historicism.

At about the same time as North was producing his

Arts and Crafts buildings, Roland Lloyd Jones, the Caernarfon County Architect, was designing (from 1898 to 1928) schools in Snowdonia, usually with half-timbered gables above stepped windows, as well as some experimental 'open-air' schools where a whole elevation might be glazed and openable to let in fresh air. He was also responsible for a few Nonconformist chapels in the area, and the Prichard Jones Institute (1902–5) in the small village of Newborough, Anglesey. The Institute was designed as a neo-Tudor mansion with grey stone walls, stone mullioned windows and half-timber gables. It has an off-centre porch and three-storey clock-tower, and two unequal-length wings, one with a library (with Art Nouveau fittings) on the ground floor and hall above. The group includes six single-storey cottages, two on each side of a courtyard, with stone walls, bay windows and half-timber gables.

Frank Shayler of Shrewsbury had some interesting attempts in the Arts and Crafts medium in northern Powys, with Ysgol Maesydre (1898), Welshpool, the Free Library (1902), Newtown – striped stone and red-brick lower storey and a corner turret, and vertical studding above (now Robert Owen Museum) – a Gothicky chapel (Seion, 1904) in Llanrhaeadr-ym-Mochnant. Shayler was also responsible for the Glyndŵr Institute (1911), Machynlleth – with timber-framed and boarded upper storey and low tower with quirky broached spire – next door to the Parliament House, which he is also said to have restored.

In mid-Powys the village (1906–9) designed by the Birmingham architects Buckland and Haywood-Farmer for maintenance staff at the Elan Valley reservoirs is worth noting. Here, the dominant building is the school (Elan Valley Lodge), a rugged five-bay structure with a sweeping, half-hipped roof broken by three tall gable-topped windows, and, at the side, a tall bell-tower with saddleback roof. **(227)** The neat, stone-walled cottages, mostly in pairs, with steep roofs and ashlar-mullioned windows, look, in comparison, self-consciously out of place.

In the south it was Charles Frances Annesley Voysey – once a pupil of J. P. Seddon, and a prolific Arts and Crafts designer of small country houses, furniture and fabrics – who led the way with Tŷ Bronna, a three-storey villa on a sloping

227 Elan Valley Lodge (school), near Rhayadr.

228 Tŷ Bronna, Fairwater, Cardiff.

site on the western outskirts of Cardiff. **(228)** Although Voysey sprang from a Gothic Revival background, his mature work was based on vernacular English domestic building and on the use of traditional materials. He introduced a fresh simplicity and functional naturalness that had more in common with the twentieth century than the nineteenth. Tŷ Bronna (1903–6) is his only important work in Wales, but the feeling of unaffected charm given to it by the use of splayed buttresses, horizontal bands of windows, steep, hipped roofs and tall chimneys is typical of Voysey's work at its best. The stable block, alongside the road, follows much the same pattern.

The Arts and Crafts architect whose presence was most widely felt must have been John Coates Carter, a native of Norwich, who first assisted Seddon and then joined him in partnership in 1884. From 1889 Carter was in charge of the Cardiff office until 1904, when the partnership broke up, and then on his own In Cardiff until 1916. It was while with Seddon that he became interested in the Arts and Crafts movement and designed the Red House (1902), Victoria Road, Penarth, in that style for himself and his Swiss wife. The garden front is like a Swiss chalet with its wide, steeply sloping roof, and

semi-circular window under a bowed balcony; the entrance front is asymmetric with steep gables, arched entrance and a small turret. Inside, it has a large living room, with a beamed ceiling, a dividing arch and inglenooks. Carter was responsible for a number of other houses in the same road and, most importantly, the lovely All Saints' Parish Hall (1906). The hall, built in rock-faced stone, with boulders and Bath stone dressings, has an expressionist feel conveyed by the circular tower with conical roof, splayed and round-headed doorway, semicircular windows and wide overhanging, pantiled roof partly supported on timber braces.

Coates Carter was an enigmatic designer, and his work reflects a highly personal and idiosyncratic tendency to search for solutions beyond the mainstream architectural tides of the day, nowhere more than in the splendid monastery on Caldey Island that he designed in 1910 for the Benedictine monks (see Chapter 14). In later life Carter was still able to create distinctive buildings, as at the dramatically sited St Luke's Church (1923–6), Abercarn, with its soaring south tower. Now only a shell, due to subsidence in 1950s, the nave and aisled church of hammer-dressed sandstone remains an impressive

229 Cathays Library, Cardiff.

sight with grouped sets of tall, lancet windows and a wide four-centred entrance. Carter's last work was rebuilding the ruined and roofless church of St Teilo (or Eloi), Llandeloy, Pembrokeshire, in 1925–6, with Arts and Crafts sensitivity that created a warm and mystic atmosphere: inside, exposed stone walls, low roof with multi-angled ribs, a splendid rood screen and a painted reredos (possibly by Carter himself).

Another Cardiff firm versed in the Arts and Crafts was Speir and Beavan, who won a competition for the delightful Cathays Public Library in 1906. Built in Pennant sandstone with large areas of Bath stone to a symmetrical 'butterfly' plan, it comprises two lofty, hall-like wings joined by a low entrance block with a central turret and spire. **(229)** Functionality is achieved by providing spacious halls for 'reading' and 'lending', each lit by very tall Perpendicular-style windows, and a central linked area for reception. The same architects were responsible for the public library (1907–8) at Hanbury Road, Newport – a neo-baroque building in glazed brick and Portland stone with the three main spaces divided internally by Tuscan columns supporting segmental arches.

Other buildings that fall into the Arts and Crafts role are Mounton House near Chepstow, by H. Avray Tipping and Eric Francis (1912–14) – a splendid example that despite its size and formal symmetry still seems to reflect the vernacular tradition, partly as a result of its construction in hammer-dressed stone to the projecting wings and vertical half-timbering to the whole of the centre section, and partly as a result of its carefully restrained detailing; and the cruciform, Mediterranean-style Chapel – and the Basil Webb Building at Bronllys Hospital, Breconshire, by E. T. and E. S. Hall (1920), where painted brick, roughcast render, slate-hung gables, herringbone masonry, splayed buttreses and low-eaved roofs are all in evidence.

Planned Villages

Hundreds of suburban houses built throughout Wales in the early part of the twentieth century owe their inspiration to country houses by Voysey and other Arts and Crafts architects. Indeed, in a vestigial sense the 'Arts and Crafts' design language spoken by them had a profound influence on followers such as Alwyn Lloyd, Herbert North, Beddoe Rees, and later S. Colwyn Foulkes, particularly in the development of the Garden City movement in Wales. Yet, despite a number of attempts after the co-partnership legislation of 1909 to set up public utility companies to develop Garden Cities and Garden Villages along the lines advocated by Ebenezer Howard in his book *Tomorrow: A Peaceful Path to Real Reform* (1898), progress was slow and stumbling.

The earliest attempt was Wyndham Park (originally known as Glyn Cory Garden Village) at Peterston-super-Ely in the Vale of Glamorgan, with Thomas Adams as planner in conjuction with T. H. Mawson, the garden designer. It began optimistically in 1907 on a 300- acre site with plans for hundreds of houses, together with a church and other public buildings, but by 1914 only twenty-two modernist houses had been erected. Many other planned villages had a similar fate, such as the Machynlleth Garden Village (T. Alwyn Lloyd, 1913), where 150 houses were planned, but only 13 built. Swansea had probably the most forward-looking councillors; they organized a South Wales Cottage Exhibition in 1910, followed by the erection of 'sample' houses and a 1914 plan to erect 300 sample houses at Mayhill, only to be scrapped by the First World War. Other forward-looking estates were planned in the area, such as the Townhill Estate (Raymond Unwin, 1909), and Fforest-fach Garden Village (Pepler and Allen, 1910), but neither had achieved much before war brought work to a halt. Wrexham also had its own Garden Village (G. Sutcliffe, 1913; T. Alwyn Lloyd, 1914), planned for 1,800 houses but without any public buildings until much later.

The most ambitious and successful garden village was that built between 1911 and 1916 by the Tredegar Iron and Coal Company at Oakdale Model Village, near Blackwood. The village of 660 houses was designed by Arthur F. Webb, to accommodate workers from the company's new coal mine in the valley below. It was laid out to a formal, near-radial plan, split by a broad avenue, with public buildings (including church and chapel, hospital, hotel and workmen's institute) located at the centre. (230) The houses, though mostly in short terraces, were built to a variety of designs and different materials, and included rear and front gardens as well as bathrooms.

Other pre-war attempts at garden village planning could only be, without some public buildings, partially successful. These included Barry Garden Suburb (by Raymond Unwin, with T. Alwyn Lloyd), with 210 houses completed by 1914; Rhiwbina Garden Village (by Raymond Unwin, 1912, with A. H. Mottram, T. Alwyn Lloyd and H. Avray Tipping) for 300 houses. Most of the remaining garden villages, though well intentioned, ended up being little more than suburban housing estates.

One that could not be seen as dull, or even as a 'garden village' in the Howard sense, is Portmeirion, the seaside village in Gwynedd by Clough Williams-Ellis, who, as both client and Arts and Crafts-trained architect, was able to design and build it from 1925 onwards to please himself. Hugging a small valley overlooking a sandy beach and the sea, it is a picturesque folly writ large, with bright colour-washed cottages, domes, towers and rescued bits of historic architecture. (231) 'The many-layered creation was', according to Richard Haslam, 'in part a visual and architectural idea; in part a demonstration … that a beautiful coastal site could be enhanced by a thoughtful architect.'[3] Though in one sense a folly that seems, in its vibrant mixture of forms and styles, to recall an Italian seaside village (perhaps Portofino which Williams-Ellis loved), it is also a successful holiday resort and tourist venue. Amongst Williams-Ellis's most memorable early works are the Bell Tower (1928) near the entrance, the Observatory Tower (1936–7) by the seashore, and the Town Hall (1937–8) that was designed to house a remarkable Jacobean ceiling, panelling and windows salvaged from Emral Hall, Flintshire. The construction of Portmeirion was interrupted by the Second World War, but resumed in the 1950s until more than fifty buildings (each different) had been erected.

230 Oakdale model town, near Blackwood, Monmouthshire.

Williams-Ellis's other work in Wales during this period was very limited, but included a purpose-designed Youth Hostel at Maeshafn, Denbighshire. This was a strictly symmetrical, two-storey building of 1931 with weather-boarding and a pseudo-pediment. Though normally an eclectic designer, Williams-Ellis could produce modernist work when required, as at the lively Laughing Water Restauarnt (1933), in Kent (sadly demolished after the Second World War).

Revivalism

While the Arts and Crafts movement was only a transient episode in the story of Welsh architecture (as elsewhere in Britain), revivalism of various sorts continued to be a potent source for design over a longer period, with many architects (or their clients) preferring to dwell on the past and fall back on historic styles. Churches, schools and local libraries, for example, mostly continued to be built in some form of 'Gothic' well into the twentieth century, while other types of buildings were often classical in inspiration.

Of all the buildings, perhaps only J. Ninian Comper's splendid National War Memorial had any justification for using an archaic style to connect with the past – in this case adopting a classical idiom to remember the fallen of a lost era Constructed in 1926–8 and sited at the heart of Cardiff's Civic Centre, it comprises a circular colonnade of Corinthian columns with a continuous entablature and, inside, a column clad with bronze figures of a soldier, sailor and airman, that supports a winged 'messenger of victory'.

Commercial architecture, despite its contemporary role, was no less willing to resort to the past. In the town centre of Ruthin, for instance, there are three half-timbered banks, of which only one (National Westminster) is a historic building; Barclays (F. A. Roberts, 1928) features reproductions of Exemewe Hall, while the Midland (now HSBC; T. M. Alexander, 1925) appears to be wholly twentieth century. Elsewhere, banks as far apart as Cricieth and Tregaron (both by Palmer and Holden) made their own whimsical attempts at historical character, the former (1923) with crow-stepped gables, and the latter (1924) with box-frame timbering. In Cardiff, the same architects went for a monumental, five-storey neo-Greek structure for the Butetown branch of the National Westminster Bank (1924); it has identical elevations front and back, each with giant Ionic columns and deep, overhanging cornices, and inside, in the banking hall, giant fluted Doric columns support a curved ceiling. To all intents and purposes the elevations of larger commercial buildings were little more than architects' period claddings disguising engineers' structural steel frames.

The few public buildings that were erected between the wars are generally marked by a watering-down of classical motifs, sometimes resulting in austere, but nevertheless memorable neoclassical monuments. Such is Swansea's Guildhall, the design for which was won by Percy Thomas in an open competition held in 1930. Though eschewing columns and cornices, it remains, in its axiality, massing and planning, 'classical' in all but name. The superficial Modernism of this and Thomas's Temple of Peace and Health in Cardiff may seem reminiscent of the architecture of Fascist Italy and Nazi Germany before the Second World War. In fact, both of Thomas's buildings were designed years before iconic Fascist and Nazi buildings, such as the Universal Exhibition, Rome (1938–42), and the Reich Chancellery (1938), Berlin, had been erected, and owe more to Scandinavian neoclassicism than to Italian or German authoritarianism.

The Guildhall, Swansea, was built in 1932–6 as four

232 Guildhall, Swansea.

233 Temple of Peace and Health, Cathays Park, Cardiff.

connected blocks, each with different functions, around a rectangular courtyard. From the outside it appears as a mostly two-storey Portland stone building, the lower storey forming a deeply channelled podium to the *piano nobile* above. **(232)** The main entrance is through a tall arched opening with bronze screen in a windowless pavilion on the east facade, above which sits a slightly tapered clock tower, nearly 50 m high. The south block is differentiated by a three-bay arcade forming the public entrance to the Brangwyn Hall. From the vaulted entrance hall a grand flight of steps leads up to an ante-hall, which in turn leads into the temple-like, top-lit Council Chamber, complete with Ionic columns and coffered ceiling. The Brangwyn Hall in the south block has a coffered ceiling with Art Deco pendant light fittings and walls lined with seventeen large paintings (British Empire Panels) by Frank Brangwyn. The panels, painted between 1925 and 1932, were intended as a war memorial for the House of Lords, but when the offer was rejected they went to Swansea instead.

The origins of the Temple of Peace and Health in Cardiff's Cathays Park began as a proposal funded by Lord Davies of Llandinam for a Welsh National Memorial Building to support the causes of peace and health. Davies commissioned Percy Thomas to design it, which he did in 1930 (and later revised). Foundations were laid in 1937 and the building was opened on 23 November 1938, as 'workmen were digging air raid shelters on the adjoining land ready for the Second World War'.[4] The layout is that of a T-shaped cross – the Temple forming the stem with the six-bay side wings housing administrative offices. Externally, the contrast between the domestic-looking wings with their hipped, red-tiled roofs and the formal entrance portico is striking. The tall, three-bay portico as built has plain, square columns, a change from the 1930 design, which had round, Ionic columns. **(233)** After the austerity of the exterior, the interior comes as something of a surprise: a low entrance hall with gold rosettes on the ceiling leads, via a short flight of steps flanked by large, black marble vases, to the Marble Hall, an astonishing space with black and gold square fluted columns (again, round in the 1930 design), between which hang Art Deco pendant lights, and a richly decorated ceiling with geometrically patterned borders and green and gold coffering.

The design of Newport's Civic Centre was won in competition (1936) by T. Cecil Howitt of Nottingham. Though construction work began the following year, only one wing of the Centre had been opened by 1939, the remainder not being completed until 1964. The Centre is in the form of three loosely connected Portland-stone blocks with the three-storey middle block at the top of a rise, and the two-storey, side wings stepping down the hill on either side. **(234)** The centre section of the middle block projects forward on both sides, with a tall, round-arched entrance on the west side and five tall windows (to the Council Chamber) separated by curious, sham columns at first-floor level on the east side. Above the centre section rises, as in Thomas's Swansea Guildhall, a tall, tapered clock-tower with a pyramidal cap. The main interest internally is the central stair hall with its eleven large mural panels painted by Hans Feibusch in 1961–4 to illustrate the history of Monmouthshire. In 1989–91, a modernist, two-storey Crown Court pavilion was built between the arms of the Civic Centre, partially closing off the view from the south-east.

Early Modernism

The inter-war period in Wales is often seen as largely lacking in architecturally progressive buildings, especially when compared to what was going on elsewhere. Yet, if Modernism is taken to mean that good design is related to functional efficiency, a rational use of materials and a lack of ornament, then the style was alive and kicking, particularly in the field of industry where there had been a long history of functionalist architecture, such as the bottle-shaped furnaces at ironworks and geometrically conceived headframes at collieries, or the brick-vaulted floors of the Bute Warehouse (1861), Cardiff, and the concrete frame of the Weaver Flour Mills (1898), Swansea. Another building that comes to mind is the boiler factory built at Queensferry, near Flint, c.1901–5, to designs by H. B. Creswell. Its Egyptaic appearance was largely fortuitous, the result of massive, sloping buttresses to carry the weight of travelling cranes, and an equally massive, central tower to house specialist machinery.

Surprisingly, it was in the mining industry that architectural functionalism was most clearly demonstrated, though few examples now remain. Especially notable in this respect were some of the unadorned, reinforced concrete structures such as a cylindrical coal-storage bunker (1918) at a Powell Duffryn colliery, a tall 'cubist' coal bunker (with circular openings) on stilts (1913) at Bargoed Colliery, and a surrealist collection of concrete buildings (offices, cylindrical towers, octagonal silos and a washery block on stilts) that once stood, Chirico-like, at the Wern Tarw patent fuel works (1937), Pencoed. The earliest pithead baths in Wales were erected at the Deep Navigation Colliery, Treharris, in 1916, designed by the colliery engineer G. D. Jones, and built in brick. Later baths were designed by J. H. Forshaw of the Miners' Welfare Committee, based in London, in distinctive modernist style with a strong horizontality emphasized by flat roofs and continuous strip windows. They were mostly built in concrete, as at Pig Pit (c.1930), Blaenafon, **(235)** or sometimes in brown brick, as at Penallta (1938), Gelligaer.

The 'finest modernist sanatorium to be built in Britain' before the onset of the Second World War was Sully Hospital, near Barry, built in 1932–6 for tubercular

235 Big Pit pithead baths, Blaenafon, Monmouthshire.

236 Sully Hospital, near Barry, Glamorgan.

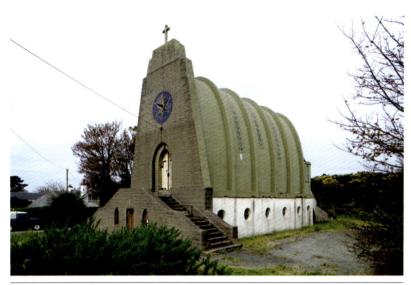

237 Our Lady of the Sea Church, Amlwch, Anglesey.

238 Odeon Cinema, Newport.

patients.[5] It was designed (in competition) by W. A. Pite, Son and Fairweather in 1932, with the purpose of allowing the maximum air and light for the treatment of tuberculosis patients. The most dramatic part is the long zigzag block that faces south across the sea, with long balconies on the straight sections and wards stepped on plan on the canted sections. (236) Behind this, on an axis, there is a tall access tower and a square administrative block, and behind that again the nurses' wing, originally shorter than the ward block, but since extended. Construction was mostly brick with white render, while the ward block is partly concrete-framed to make possible the large areas of openable glazing.

In complete contrast is the extraordinary Church of Our Lady Star of the Sea and St Winefride (RC), in Amlwch, Anglesey, designed by Giuseppe Rinvolucri and built 1932–5. The church itself is a five-bay shell-concrete vault sitting on a stone podium (the church hall) that is lit by circular windows on either side. (237) Steps lead up to a slablike west wall of stone and a first-floor entrance to the church. Inside, the walls sweep upwards in a continuous parabolic curve divided by concrete ribs with, before a conical apse, a wide arch pierced with five glass stars. Natural lighting is from three transverse bands of blue and white glazing in the curved walls.

Examples of modernist domestic architecture are hard to find, few patrons seeming to have had either the wealth or inclination to proceed in that direction. R. H. Franks designed (1935) a couple of flat-roofed, modernist houses at Borth, north of Aberystwyth, and Gordon Griffiths was responsible (1939) for an interesting flat-roofed, white-walled house with a curving stairs at Cliff Parade, Penarth. The largest modernist house by far is the Villa Marina (1936) at Craigside, Llandudno, a white, L-shaped three-storey house with horizontal strip windows, by Harry Weedon of Birmingham. At the junction of the two wings are a circular entrance hall and spiral stairs leading to the flat roof, and on the front, overlooking the sea, a large curved bow window.

Mention of Harry Weedon is a reminder that he was responsible for overseeing, between 1932 and 1939, designs for 250 cinemas across Britain in the Odeon chain for Oscar Deutsch. A number of Weedon's Odeon cinemas were built in Wales, though few have survived unaltered. The Odeon Cinema (1937–8) in Newport is one of the best, a showy, eye-catching Art Deco design with extensive areas of faience tiles (black below, buff above), vertical fins of red-brown brickwork and a bow-ended projection with circular windows. **(238)** Similar Art Deco Odeon cinemas by Weedon, with much faience work, survive in Llanelli (1938, now the Theatr Elli) and Rhyl (1937, now the Astra). Also in Rhyl were two earlier and more restrained, brick-faced cinemas by S. Colwyn Foulkes: the Plaza (1931), with recessed ground floor and tall window-like recessed panels above, and the Regal (1937, demolished). The Palace Cinema, Conwy, also by Foulkes (1935), was built in rubble stone with stepped gables in an attempt to harmonize with the historic town ■

16 'Arts and Crafts' to Early Modernism, 1900 to 1939
References

1   N. Pevsner, *Pioneers of Modern Design* (third edn), p. 43.

2   A. Voelcker, *Herbert Luck North*, p. 10.

3   R. Haslam, *Clough Williams-Ellis*, p. 18.

4   Sir P. Thomas, *Pupil to President*, p. 32.

5   M. Cherry, *Building Wales: Adeiladu Cymru*, p. 12.

17

Late Modernism, 1940–1985

The outbreak of the Second World War in September 1939 led to the cessation of all non-essential building construction throughout Britain, except for work on military sites. During the six years of war there was more destruction than construction, with sporadic air raids on Cardiff, Newport, Swansea and Pembroke Dock. Swansea, in particular, was badly hit during 1940–1, resulting in the devastation of its town centre and the loss of six churches and chapels. It was to be nearly a decade before the building industry was able to get going again on anything like a normal scale. Thus, for

instance, the construction of Carmarthenshire County Hall (designed by Percy Thomas in 1935), though begun in 1939, was not completed until 1955.

A general election in July 1945, two months after the end of the war in Europe, brought in the first majority Labour government in British history; it was to have a far-reaching effect on the building industry and architecture. In addition to nationalizing many basic service industries, the government passed the New Towns Act in 1946 and the Town and Country Planning Act in 1947 (effective from July 1948) – the one intended to reduce overcrowding and provide a better life for many, the other intended to improve the quality and design of buildings everywhere. There were also government restrictions on materials in short supply and how they were to be used, all of which tended to slow down the building process.

Industrial Buildings

Apart from the need to provide new housing to make up for losses caused by enemy action and the lack of construction during the war years, the most urgent need was to put industry back on its feet. This meant building new factories, and where possible making them more efficient than before. Most were cheap, lightweight factories of little architectural interest on industrial trading estates. One of the first purpose-designed factories of architectural quality was the British Nylon Spinners' factory (now unoccupied) near Pontypool, designed by Sir Percy Thomas & Son and built 1947–8 for the production of nylon yarn. It comprises a series of steel-framed low blocks clad in brown brick with strip glazing, and at one end a massive rectangular brick tower (where gravity is used in the spinning process) with a colossal central window panel divided vertically by concrete fins.

The Rubber Factory at Brynmawr, Blaenau Gwent, was completed three years later on a windswept site 300m above sea level. Visionary in both social and architectural terms, it was an extraordinary example of factory design at its most innovative. Designed in 1946 by the young Architects' Co-operative Partnership, with Ove Arup as the

engineer, it was beset by problems caused by shortage of materials, so that it was not completed until 1951 at almost twice the original cost estimate. It was a two-storey building with mostly storage space on the lower floor. The main production space on the upper floor was covered by nine (3 by 3) 80 mm thick, gently curved shell concrete domes based on a German system evolved in the 1930s. **(239)** The domes were supported at the corners by V-shaped pillars, and pierced at intervals with circular lights, and had glazed panels along each side, giving the space inside a sculptural quality that resulted, as Reyner Banham wrote, in 'one of the most impressive interiors built in Britain since St Paul's'.[1] Rectangular areas on two sides were covered by parallel lines of concrete vaults, while the administration block on a third side had an entrance hall with a curved shell concrete roof that appeared to float above it. Unfortunately the factory was forced to close in 1982 owing to difficulties in obtaining sufficient orders, and was eventually demolished in 2001 despite being the first post-war building to be listed (Grade II*) and a lengthy conservation battle.

The Steel Company of Wales (SCOW) was created in 1947 by combining the four main steel and tinplate combines in the south. The new company, along with Richard Thomas and Baldwin (RTB), completely dominated sheet steel production after the war. The first of a new group of steel-making plants was established by SCOW at Port Talbot, where the Abbey Works were erected in 1948–52, with parallel rolling mills – each over 1 km long – externally designed by Sir Percy Thomas & Son as trains of squarish bays clad in yellow corrugated steel and divided by lower glazed sections. There was also a four-storey office block. The Abbey Works were followed by the Trostre Steelworks (1952–6) for SCOW at Llanelli, and the 4 km-long Spencer Steelworks (1958–62) for RTB at Llanwern near Newport, each with Sir Percy Thomas & Son as external designers. Both of these were later demolished, leaving only an attenuated Abbey Works in production.

Wales's first nuclear power station was built in 1959–63 in a remote area on the shore of Llyn Trawsfynydd reservoir in Snowdonia. The external designer was Sir Basil Spence with Dame Sylvia Crowe as landscape consultant. It comprises two blocky reactor towers, each 55 m high, clad with precast concrete using local aggregate, and each articulated with vertical panels and horizontal bands of seemingly tiny windows. Though decommissioned as far

240 Inmos Microprocessor
Factory, Duffryn,
Newport.

indicate the industrial manufacture of radio-isotopes. A long external corridor links the manufacturing laboratories to two fully glazed, circular office and amenity blocks.

The innovative Inmos Microprocessor Factory, near Newport, was an early example of high-tech architecture, designed by Richard Rogers & Partners and built in 1982. With a brief that demanded speed of design and construction, the building was conceived as a logical 'kit of parts' that could be prefabricated off-site. The factory is visually dominated by exposed tubular steel roof trusses supported by tie rods from tall steel towers along a central circulation spine, together with service ducts and pipes. **(240)** The overall plan is a rectangle eight bays deep on either side of the central spine, with production areas to the north, and offices and amenity rooms to the south, all with external walls of steel frames filled with glazed or opaque panels.

back as the 1990s, it remains an uncomfortable blot on the landscape which no amount of greenery can alleviate. A second nuclear power station was built at Wylfa Head near Cemaes, Anglesy, in 1962–71 with the same landscape designer but with Farmer & Dark as external designers. The two 55 m-high cylindrical reactor towers have faceted faces and are joined by a turbine house, all encased in concrete.

One of the most intriguing buildings of the early 1970s was the Parke-Davis Pharmaceutical Centre at Llanfihangel Pontymoile, near Pontypool. It was built in 1971–3 for research and manufacturing, and was designed by the Percy Thomas Partnership as a series of single- and two-storey pavilions unified by the use of grey facing bricks and continuous strip windows with wide, overhanging roofs faced with vertical corrugated cladding. Another research and manufacturing centre by the same firm of architects is the Amersham International Research Centre set alongside the river Taff at Whitchurch, Cardiff, built in 1974–81. At first sight, the extensive use of buff-coloured glass-reinforced plastic panels, strip glazing and rounded corners on the three low-lying rectangular blocks suggests a sophisticated laboratory environment, with only the 50 m-high ventilation shafts to

Residential Buildings

Despite the impoverishment of the early post-war years, a large number of houses and flats were constructed in Wales, '87 per cent of which were built by local authorities' between April 1945 and the end of 1951.[2] Amongst the earliest houses to be erected were prefabricated types (or 'prefabs' as they were commonly known), provided by the government under the Housing (Temporary Accommodation) Act of 1944 to replace destroyed houses or to rehouse ex-servicemen and their families. They were mostly single-storey bungalows of factory-made parts that came to site in sections with pre-assembled wiring and plumbing for erection by unskilled labour. There were four basic types with similar layouts but made from different materials, including aluminium like the B2 Type re-erected at the St Fagans National Museum of History. With their fitted kitchens, bathrooms and built-in wardrobes, prefabs were in many ways superior to the older, brick-built terrace houses that had previously dominated the Valleys and larger towns.

A notable housing estate with traditionally built houses from this period is a development at Brynmawr, Blaenau Gwent, designed by Yorke, Rosenberg & Mardell, and built in 1949–50 for workers at the Rubber Factory. It comprises a mix of five short terraces facing down the slope and a three-storey block of flats, all with central heating and rubber floors. The two-storey terraces have low, mono-pitch roofs, and the block of flats a double-pitch roof; each has random-laid sandstone gable walls and colour-washed long walls. Though very large by comparison, the planning of the Gaer Estate (c.1946–51), Newport (by Johnson Blackett, county borough architect), was tackled in much the same way, with a mixture of two-storey and three-storey terraces off single-sided cul-de-sacs stepping down the hillside. The terraces vary in length, some short, others long and serpentine, as they follow the site's curving profile, and are faced in brick or colour-washed render, and have slightly tilted mono-pitch roofs with wide overhangs.

With the growth of car ownership and traffic generally in the 1950s, consideration was given to the possibility of segregating pedestrians from vehicular traffic in residential areas, as had been tried in Radburn, USA, in 1930. The principle of segregation known as 'Radburn planning' was first introduced to Britain at Queen's Park Estate, Wrexham, in 1950–6. Designed by the Wrexham Borough engineer and surveyor, J. M. Davies, in consultation with Gordon Stephenson, the housing estate is divided into eight 'superblocks' in each of which the terraces of houses front onto green areas accessed by footpaths, while vehicular access is from short cul-de-sacs at the rear. Radburn planning was later used in the design of a number of neighbourhood units at Cwmbran New Town, particularly the Fairwater neighbourhood (Gordon Redfern, 1963–6). The system was also used on other sites in Wales, such as Maen-du, Brecon, (by Robertson, Francis & Partners, 1975), where mono-pitch, timber-framed and timber-clad terraces, accessed by winding footpaths, step down the hillside in parallel rows.

Also designed as a segregated development was the Duffryn Housing Estate, Newport, where an almost continuous chain of nearly 1,000 two-storey houses with mono-pitch roofs weave back and forth around the perimeter of a 39 ha site to form a series of twenty-two courts facing onto a vast, partly wooded green space. The winner of a 1974 competition, the design by a consortium of six firms led by L. G. Mouchel & Partners was based on the theoretical ideas of Richard MacCormac, and built in 1976–9. The lower storeys are brick-faced, with cream-coloured panels and tile cladding above. A group of old persons' housing at the south-west corner of the site was built around a grid of small courtyards. The development includes a primary school, but economic cuts prevented a proposed district centre from being built.

Few individual private houses were built in the immediate aftermath of the Second World War. One of the earliest one-off houses of interest is Talar Wen, Llangadog, designed by Dewi-Prys Thomas and completed in 1953 for his brother-in-law Gwynfor Evans, the long-term president of Plaid Cymru. L-shaped in plan with juxtaposed pitched roofs, it is bedded into the slope, its outer elevations looking across Dyffryn Tywi while the inner ones look onto a sloping garden court. With white-rendered walls, dark stained timber panels and slate roofs, it manages to suggest both modernist and vernacular inspiration.

Further north to Rhyl, the local architect Patrick Garnett designed his own house in The Boulevard in 1961–2 in a way that owed something to the International Style of Mies van der Rohe and Philip Johnson in its free plan and use of steel and glass. The living area, on the fully glazed – except for a single panel of vertical timber boarding – and flat-roofed upper floor, oversails a car port and ground floor entrance hall faced in grey brick.

By contrast, Cardiff architects Hird and Brooks used white-painted brick and black-stained timber for the Capel House, Llandaf, in 1966 in a building clearly inspired by Danish architecture. Planned as two staggered wings linked by a through entrance hall, most rooms face the garden with large windows, presenting blank walls – separated from the overhanging roofs by narrow clerestory windows – to the world outside.

At Penglais, Arberystwyth, local architect Ifan Prys Edwards produced Bryn Aberoedd in 1968, a house in the International Style, but hard-edged and angular. Built over a dark-brown brick podium containing garages, the lower floor is also dark-brown brick, but set back. Above this,

241 Part of Little Ochard estate, Dinas Powys, Glamorgan.

242 Hafan Elan estate for the elderly, Llanrug, Caernarfonshire.

the main living areas – all in white-painted aluminium and storey-height glass – are cantilevered forward in two boxy projections (one further forward than the other) with a glass-fronted balcony in between.

Private housing estates were few and far between and generally small during the post-war period, while those of architectural interest are rare. In this respect, Dinas Powys, in the Vale of Glamorgan, must be unique with a trio of innovative private housing estates. The first of these, Little Orchard, designed by Cardiff architects T. Glyn Jones and John R. Evans, and completed in 1968 and 1973, has six flat-roofed houses using (inside and out) exposed, ribbed concrete panels. The boldly designed landscaping here allows the upper floors, with storey-height windows and cantilevered balconies, to sit on raised mounds, while garages and workspaces are sunk into the ground at road level. (241) The Mount (1975), by Hird & Brooks, has sixteen single-storey houses in three types, each based on their earlier Capel House in Llandaf and using a common language of white-painted brick, flat roofs and exposed timber structures. Nearby Merivale (1976), by the same architects, has eleven single-storey dwellings, some of a T-shaped patio layout, and all of fair-faced brickwork with very shallow pitched roofs.

Housing the elderly and handicapped necessitated different forms of building. The Albert Prince of Wales Court, Porthcawl, built in 1970–3 for the elderly to designs by the Percy Thomas Partnership for the Royal Masonic Benevolent Institution, is laid out around a pair of courts with a series of staggered residential units around one court and communal rooms and a chapel around the other. The single-storey and two-storey buildings are constructed in light grey brick with slate monopitch roofs.

The Cefndy Home for the Mentally Handicapped in Rhyl was a hostel for twenty-four people that managed to retain a domestic, non-institutional character by the use of buff-coloured bricks, timber, tiled monopitch roofs and an informal layout and massing. Designed by the Bowen Dann Davies Partnership of Colwyn Bay and completed in 1975, the complex has three house units grouped around small garden courts, and linked to a communal block and warden's quarters. Each house has two bedroom wings – both accommodating four residents – and a living/dining area.

The Hafan Elan estate (1980) for the elderly in Llanrug, near Caernarfon, is even more relaxed and domestic in character. **(242)** Also designed by the Bowen Dann Davies Partnership, it consists of a series of short single-storey terraces around two irregularly shaped and well-landscaped courts that have a feeling of warmth and intimacy. Steep, slate roofs (on one side only of each block) and rough stone walls reinforce the rural character, 'tying' the development to its surroundings in a seemingly natural way.

Churches, Chapels and Buildings of Remembrance

Amongst the buildings damaged by enemy action in the Second World War were a number of churches, including the Anglican and Roman Catholic cathedrals in Llandaf and Cardiff, and St Mary's parish church in Swansea, each of which was gutted and made roofless during air raids in 1941. Llandaf Cathedral was handsomely restored between 1949 and 1960 by George Pace. He replaced Prichard's open timber roof over the nave with an almost flat, timber-panelled ceiling that paradoxically seems to give the interior a greater impression of height and dignity and a more 'cathedral-like' atmosphere than formerly, while probably more akin to the original thirteenth-century ceiling. The most striking new feature inside, however, is the great parabolic concrete arch (Ove Arup, engineer) on the site of the medieval pulpitum. It carries a cylindrical organ case and a superb aluminium sculpture of *Christ in Majesty* by Jacob Epstein. A new Welsh Regiment Memorial Chapel (known as the David Chapel), with apsidal end, curved ceiling and deeply recessed windows, was added (1953–6) on the north side of the cathedral, accessed from the north aisle. Pace was also the architect for the new free-standing chapel at St Michael's College, Llandaf. Completed in 1959, its blank, slightly curved stone end walls and asymmetric roof gives it a simple yet sturdy character. **(243)** The side walls are pierced by batteries of random-placed, deep-set windows of varying sizes, all presumably inspired by Le Corbusier's

chapel at Ronchamp, France.

As Llandaf Cathedral was being restored, St David's Roman Catholic Cathedral, Charles Street, Cardiff, was being carefully repaired and reconstructed by F. R. Bates, Son & Price, of Newport. They added hammer-beam roof trusses over the nave and a circular west window with hexagonal tracery. St Mary's Church, Swansea, was rebuilt in 1957–9 largely as before, under the supervision of Leslie T. Moore and Sir Percy Thomas. The main alteration was the replacement of the medieval Herbert Chapel with a Lady Chapel, accessed through three arches in the chancel wall.

The Anglican Church in Wales had little need to build new churches in the post-war years as the great majority of parish churches remained unscathed. The situation was different as far as the Roman Catholics were concerned; they were still endeavouring to catch up, and consequently built more new churches. One of the earliest was St David's

243 St Michael's College Chapel, Llandaf, Cardiff.

Church, Newport, designed by F. R. Bates, Son & Price, again apparently inspired by Le Corbusier's Ronchamp Chapel. Built in 1963, it has an apsidal end, groups of tiny windows and a tilted roof.

In the north a group of Roman Catholic churches by the practice of S. Powell Bowen (later, Bowen Dann Davies) deserves mention for its sustained quality of design. The Church of Our Lady of Lourdes, Benllech, Anglesey (S. Powell Bowen, 1966) is notable for its careful composition of rectangular volumes and steep, monopitch slate roofs, that progresses from entrance to sanctuary, with the tallest monopitch and clerestory window above the altar. The low-pitched roofs of the Church of Christ the King, Towyn, Denbighshire (Bowen Dann Davies, 1974) meet at different levels, providing space for a clerestory window above the main body of the church. The internal walls are faced in brick and the ceilings are timber-boarded. St Illtud's Church, Rhuddlan (Bowen Dann Davies, 1976), is long and low, and more domestic in character, with roughcast walls, narrow

bands of windows, and again a clerestory window where the roofs meet above the sanctuary.

Like the Anglican Church, the Nonconformists had little need to erect new chapels, apart from a few in the suburbs of larger towns. A couple of chapels in Cardiff and one in Wrexham are of interest. St David's Church, Fairwater, Cardiff (Alex Gordon & Partners, 1961) was built following the inauguration of a small Lutheran mission in the city. The box-like building is topped by a concrete butterfly roof that appears to 'float' above dark brown brick walls. Inside, the altar is lit indirectly from hidden side windows. Bethany Baptist Chapel, Rhiwbina, Cardiff (J. Morgan Harries, 1964) has a zigzag concrete roof that sweeps proudly up over the altar at one end. Inside, the concertina-like roof is supported by slender concrete piers. There are full-height strip windows on either side of the altar and a thin band of clerestory lighting between wall tops and roof. The Calvinistic Methodist Capel-y-groes at Wrexham (Bowen Dann Davies, 1982) is less assertive, its dominant feature being a wide,

244 Capel-y-groes (Calvinistic Methodist), Wrexham.

245 Llwydcoed Crematorium, near Aberdare, Glamorgan.

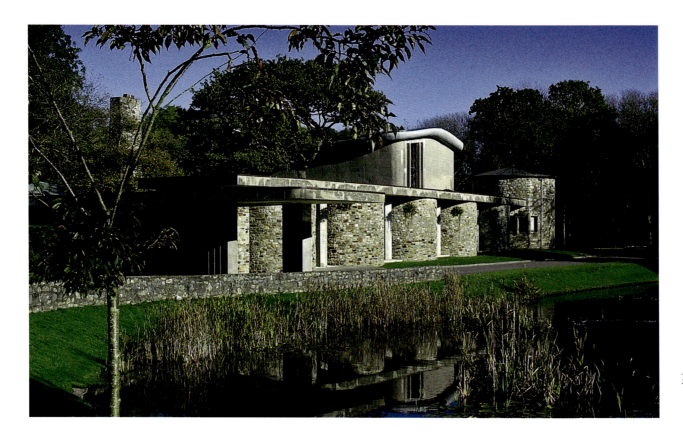

246 Coychurch (formerly Mid-Glamorgan) Crematorium, near Bridgend.

spreading tiled roof that echoes an irregular floor plan. **(244)** Walls are brick-faced, and there are some hardwood corner windows. Nearby is a free-standing brick tower out of which rises a slim metal cross.

In a county that was once the centre of the movement by Dr William Price to legalize cremation it is not perhaps surprising that Glamorgan (as it was) has a number of crematoria. Of the four built in Glamorgan in the post-war years, three built within a year or so of each other are of particular interest. The first was the Margam Crematorium (by F. D. Williamson & Associates, 1969), overlooking the Eglwys Nunydd Reservoir. All in white concrete, it has a wide forecourt with a deep fascia behind which the furrowed columns and vertical windows of the main building rise with, on the right-hand side the tall angular incinerator chimney.

The Llwydcoed Crematorium (by H. M. R. Burgess & Partners, 1970) is more ecclesiastical in appearance in its mountain setting with a structure that appears to have grown outwardly from an inner core. **(245)** It is in fact a tightly disciplined arrangement of three top-lit chapels with slate roofs forming a kind of splintered pyramid and a series of open-wreath courts. The Coychurch Crematorium (by Fry Drew Knight and Creamer, 1970), comprises a pair of linked memorial chapels beside a small lake. The larger chapel is approached by way of a covered passage, marked by a row of curved stone walls on one side and multiple vertical panels of stained glass on the other; the chapel itself has a concrete end wall with off-centre vertical window and a curved concrete roof. **(246)** Originally there was a tall concrete cowl rising above the roof and enclosing a cross, all reminiscent of Le Corbusier's Ronchamp

Chapel, but this was unfortunately demolished in 1993.

In a somewhat different category is the Memorial Chapel built to commemorate the farmsteads and Capel Celyn Calvinistic Methodist chapel (1821) of Cwm Treweryn, Meirionydd, that were drowned by the controversial reservoir built for Liverpool Corporation in 1964–5. Sited at the northern edge of Llyn Celyn, the chapel (by R. L. Gapper, City of Liverpool) is simply built with a steep mono-pitch roof and rubble-stone walls, and, between the curving end wall and side wall, a full-height window to illuminate the otherwise dark but moving interior. Inside, are three slate slabs inscribed with the names of occupants of the former burial ground.

Educational Buildings

There was a considerable advance in school architecture during the period, with much thought given to environmental improvement for children. Two primary schools give an idea of some of the better ones. One of the first schools to be built after the war was Ysgol Gynradd Beaumaris, in Anglesey. Designed in the County Architect's department under N. Squire Johnson, it was erected as early as 1947, and has a central brick entrance tower with a long, white-rendered two-storey splayed wing on either side. Abermule School and Community Centre, Montgomeryshire, by County Architect Herbert Carr (1951), follows a broadly similar layout; it has a red-brick hall with hipped roof and vertical strip windows at the centre and, on either side, low, flat-roofed and splayed entrance wings connected to single-storey flat-roofed classroom blocks.

At the secondary level of education, the 1944 Education Act advocated a divisive split between grammar schools and secondary modern schools, and this is what mostly happened until the 1970s, though a number of local authorities in Wales would have preferred multilateral secondary schools. Initially, only Anglesey went down the multilateral route as the pioneer of comprehensive education in Britain. Ysgol Syr Thomas Jones, Amlwch, (named after a local doctor who had proposed that education on the island should be open to all) was erected in 1952 as Britain's first purpose-built comprehensive school. Designed in the County Architect's department, it has a widespread, asymmetrical layout in staggered blocks pivoted around a four-storey, stone-clad entrance tower with pitched roof. To the right of the tower is a slightly curved, white-rendered two-storey communal block with individual windows; to the left there are two three-storey classroom wings expressed externally by a stone-clad ground-floor plinth, and above that horizontal bands of white render and continuous windows.

Another innovative educational institution was Atlantic College, the international sixth-form college founded by Kurt Hahn in 1962 in the grounds of St Donat's Castle, Vale of Glamorgan. New teaching blocks, student and staff accommodation, and a quadrangular administration block, mostly in black brick with flat roofs designed by Alex Gordon & Partners, were built in the following years mainly to the south of the access road on the east side of the castle. Though resolutely modern, they do not detract from the historic architecture of the twelfth- to sixteenth-century castle. Other buildings, such as the long two-storey range of the seventeenth-century Cavalry Barracks below the gardens, were restored and converted to new uses by the same architects in 1978–81.

At the higher education level, the University of Wales and some colleges were involved in considerable expansion from the 1950s onwards due to increasing numbers of students. At Cardiff University (formerly University College of South Wales) development was initially confined to the Ranch Site adjoining the original building in Cathays Park. There, a timid neoclassical V-plan Arts building (Sir Percy Thomas, 1962) and two multi-storey buildings (Sir Percy Thomas & Son, 1967 and 1968) with alternating bands of Portland stone and continuous windows were erected.

Swansea University (formerly University College of Swansea) was the first in Wales to develop an out-of-town campus, at Singleton Abbey Park. Following a masterplan by Sir Percy Thomas & Son, the buildings were initially grouped around an axial main drive, the earliest being a faintly classical Natural Science building (1957) and College House (1962), both two-storey structures in brown brick. Later buildings included multi-storey structures with externally visible frames and much glazing, such as the thirteen-storey residential towers (1960–8) and the eight-storey Engineering building (1973) based on an H-plan layout. The Taliesin Theatre and Arts Centre (by Peter Moro, opened 1984) stands out as a carefully modelled building with a non-rectangular, polygonal footprint, repeated by the upper part of the auditorium as it rises above the main roof level. The oblique angles continue into the foyer with balconies at different levels, and the auditorium with a pair of canted balconies.

At Aberystwyth University (formerly University College of Wales, Aberystwyth) a new campus was begun on Penglais Hill behind the National Library. A scheme by the Percy Thomas Partnership in 1964 proposed long, terraced blocks parallel to the contours and stepping down the site, with communal buildings grouped around a central concourse. Though gradually diluted, the plan's general feeling of spaciousness survives. The concourse – marked by a slim bell-tower that acts as a reference point as well as a heating flue – is raised above road level and approached via wide stairs from below. The Great Hall (1970) forms the nucleus of the building complex on the east side of the platform. **(247)** The main facade is monumental in character, but geometrically simple: a glazed rectangle – through which part of the auditorium protrudes – within a grey outer rectangle, all overhanging a continuous strip of ground-floor glazing. Inside, the foyer continues beneath the sloping undersides of the auditorium. The Hugh Owen Library (1976) on the north side is essentially a three-storey rectangular building, each floor stepped forward of the lower floor, with the grey uppermost floor marked by groups of vertical slot windows. The Students' Union (1973), to the south, is long and low, with a single deep band of continuous windows between bands of grey panelling.

Architecturally, the most adventurous colleges were at Carmarthen, and Harlech. At Trinity College, Carmarthen, the Architects Co-Partnership was brought in to develop the site with students' hostels to the west side of the original building and a communal block to the south, all completed in 1964. The women's hostels are mostly in a two-storey,

split-level block around a court, while the men's hostel is an eleven-storey tower. The communal block has an auditorium with a roof that sweeps sharply upwards at one end, and is partly surrounded by single-storey, fully-glazed dining rooms. The twelve-storey Hall of Residence at Coleg Harlech (Colwyn Foulkes & Partners, 1968) is faced with precast concrete panels and window frames, and has its entrance on the fifth floor, accessed via a bridge from a cliff at the rear.

Buildings for Leisure
A feature of the period was the number of new theatres built in different parts of the country. Some, such as those mentioned above at Carmarthen and Swansea, were built as integral parts of higher education campuses. Cardiff University had no out-of-town campus, and consequently both its concert hall and its theatre were located on the fringes of Cathays Park, within easy reach of the general public. The Music Department's Concert Hall (Alex Gordon Partnership, 1970) is faced in red brick to complement its

247 Great Hall and Bell Tower, Aberystwyth University, Penglais, Aberystwyth.

248 Music Department Concert Hall, Cardiff University, Cardiff.

249 Theatr Clwyd, Mold, Flintshire.

Jacobean-style neighbour, Aberdare Hall, while at the same time acting as a foil to the white buildings of the civic centre. Relying on carefully chosen materials and excellent detailing, the facade expresses the building's different functions with a cantilevered panel above the central entrance, an unbroken face of brick fronting the 400-seat concert hall, and narrow slot windows denoting the practice rooms. **(248)** The Sherman Theatre (Alex Gordon & Partners, 1974), Senghennydd Road, is a virtually windowless block in dark brown brick and lacks the subtlety of the concert hall. (Note: the exterior has since been radically altered.) It was built as a joint contract with the Students' Union in Park Place.

A remarkable theatre that also began life as part of a higher education institution, but was later operated by a separate body, is Theatr Harlech, at Coleg Harlech. Challengingly at odds with its setting, it was designed by Colwyn Foulkes & Partners as a 'brutalist' concrete and copper-clad, polygonal structure raised on legs, with meeting rooms below. It is currently closed.

Theatr Clwyd, on the outskirts of Mold, is a complex and irregularly massed structure of squares and rectangles that reflects an interior mix of foyer, main theatre, studio theatre, television studio and film theatre. **(249)** Designed by the County Architect R. W. Harvey, and completed in 1976, it is faced in warm red, hand-made bricks with lead fascias and flat roofs.

St David's Concert Hall (by the Seymour Harris Partnership, 1978–82), Cardiff, was built on a confined city-centre site, and hence has a limited street frontage, with some of the raw concrete upper floors jetted outwards and others hidden behind the steeply inclined and lead-lined roof. Inside, a small entrance foyer leads to a complex system of stairs, escalators and upper foyers to reach the auditorium built above shops. The 2,000 seat auditorium is roughly octagonal in plan and has seven balconies cantilevered outwards at different angles.

A number of public libraries date from this period. Aberdare's neat two-storey Central Library (Stephen Thomas & Partners) was built in the austere International Style. Completed in 1963, it is essentially a long, flat-roofed block with the upper storey projecting forwards on slim columns on both the entrance front and an adjacent side. Both floors have fully-glazed sections.

Brecon's County Library (J. A. McRobbie, County Architect, 1969) is prominently sited at the side of a rising street. The lowest floor of the three-storey building is set back on two adjacent sides beneath the serrated outline of the two upper storeys; these have a sawtooth configuration of narrow, vertical glazing between angled slabs of pale brick. Interesting and eye-catching, but restless.

The Public Library in Tredegar (by Powell, Alport & Partners, 1975) is located on a sloping site at the junction of a side street with The Circle. It has a chunky feel with blank walls of light grey brick rising from a battered, red-brick plinth. The deep-set entrance and ground-floor windows appear as if carved out of the solid, as does a windowless brick oriel projecting above the corner bay.

Only two new museum buildings of note – both branches of the National Museum of Wales – were built during the Late Modernist period. The Welsh Industrial and Maritime Museum in Cardiff Bay was designed by H. M. R. Burgess & Partners, completed in 1976 and unfortunately demolished in 1999 to make way for an insipid shopping centre. The red-brick exterior rising from a sloping plinth with a deep, overhanging glazed roof supported on steel stanchions, was simple but well detailed. The interior was a veritable hall of power, its exposed space-frame roof, reused engine-house windows, iron staircase and open wells forming an appropriate background to massive exhibits.

The Gallery and Administration block of the Welsh Folk Museum (now St Fagans National Museum of History), St Fagans, was designed by Sir Percy Thomas & Son in a style that reflected the influence of Scandinavia, coincidently the birthplace of the open-air folk museum movement in the late nineteenth century (250). It was built in two phases (1967–8 and 1971–2) using pale grey facing bricks and a grid of exposed concrete columns and beams. The potential impact of a large building on a rural environment was mitigated by utilising the sloping ground to create two rectangular courts, with two-storey units facing the public entrance but only single-storey units facing the folk park. (251) The three galleries (two of which are top-lit) were arranged so that visitors followed a rising sequence around the public court. Major alterations to the interior, by Purcell, were carried out in 2017.

Among the leisure buildings erected for more energetic purposes, was the Empire Pool (by John Dryburgh, the city architect), Cardiff. Completed early in 1958 in time for that year's Empire Games, it was a rather staid-

250 Main Building, National Museum of History, St Fagans.

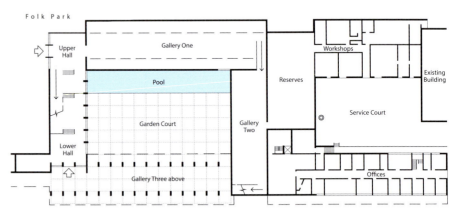

251 Plan of Main Building, National Museum of History, St Fagans.

looking building in brown brick with a fully glazed entrance portico set slightly forward in a concrete frame. Daylighting elsewhere was by rows of small, square windows in concrete frames. The gables of the segmental-vaulted roof over the swimming pool, were clad in a chequerboard effect of blue and white tiles. The building was demolished in 1997 to make way for a new national rugby stadium.

The Brecon Beacons Mountain Centre, completed in 1966 at Llanilltud, is an innovative mix of steep, vernacular-like roofs and exposed concrete columns that fit well in the mountainous landscape. **(252)** Designed by Colwyn Foulkes & Partners, it is partly surrounded by an open gallery, which, like the exhibition and information centre, is accessed at upper-floor level, while the restaurant and stone-clad lower floor are accessed at a lower level.

The dominant feature of the Plas Menai National Outdoor Pursuits Centre (Bowen Dann Davies, 1982), on the shore of the Menai strait, is the massed array of wide, overhanging roofs descending towards the water which, together with a limited palette of materials – slate, granite, white roughcast and dark-stained timber – have created a building in harmony with the mountainous background of Snowdonia. **(253)** According to Richard Weston, it was received by many 'as the most persuasive built manifesto of the search for a Welsh architecture', a claim difficult to refute.[3] Strung out around partly enclosed and sheltered courtyards, the building contains teaching rooms, canoeing pool, boat stores, climbing wall and residential accommodation ∎

17 Late Modernism, 1940–1985
References

1   Rayner Banham, *Age of the Masters* (London, 1976),
        p. 62.

2   Quoted by Martin Johnes, *Wales Since 1939*
        (Manchester University Press, 2012), p. 39.

3   Richard Weston, 'Revisiting our roots', RSAW,
        Touchstone, 10 (Spring 2002), 18.

18

Recent Developments, 1985–2017

by Simon Unwin
(with thanks to Patrick Hannay)

Wider issues influence the architecture that time produces. The 1980s government of Margaret Thatcher asserted a neoliberal ideology that has prevailed into the twenty-first century. Climate change has raised concerns about the responsible use of resources to preserve the environment. There have been global financial crises, the latest in 2008, which provoked a period of prolonged austerity in the UK. And, almost at the centre point of these three decades, the second millennium turned into the third. In Wales, major industries (mining and docks) have been lost or much reduced, whilst others (services, education, arts and media) have grown. As in other parts of the UK, cities have expanded, while the countryside has become increasingly a place of recreation and refuge. In the midst of this, Wales acquired its own National Assembly following a referendum in 1997. All these issues have influenced the recent architecture of Wales.

Cardiff Bay

The redevelopment of Cardiff's largely redundant docklands began in the early 1980s. The Cardiff Bay Development Corporation (CBDC) was set up in 1987 after initial proposals by the Welsh Office and South Glamorgan County Council. From the start, the plan was to build a barrage across the bay at the mouth of the Taff and Ely rivers to turn tidal mudflats into a lake and make the area generally more attractive. This was completed in 1999. But the earliest commitment of faith in the docklands redevelopment was the county council's decision in 1983 to build a new County Headquarters, designed by its own architects and completed in 1987, just as CBDC was being formed.

Under CBDC, projects in the Bay were to be financed other than by local or national government funding. The master plan for the Inner Harbour area was developed by a US firm – Benjamin Thompson and Associates, responsible for the successful Harbourplace in Baltimore, Maryland (1980). CBDC also commissioned: Martorell Bohigas Mackay (Barcelona) to make proposals for the links between the Bay and city centre; Nicholas Hare Architects (London) to consider the Oval Basin (now Roald Dahl Plas) adjacent to Frame's Pierhead Building; and Alsop, Lyall and Störmer (London) to provide an architectural treatment for the barrage.

In 1990, to market the development to prospective investors as well as to garner public support, CBDC commissioned Will Alsop (Alsop, Lyall and Störmer) to design the Cardiff Bay Visitor Centre (254) – a plywood oval tube, covered in PVC sheeting, that housed a large model of the dockland area as it would be in the future. It was entered like an aeroplane, via steps that could be winched back into its body. Its oval end window framed a fine view across the

254 Cardiff Bay Visitor Centre ('The Tube'), Cardiff.

bay to Penarth Head surmounted by Butterfield's distinctive St Augustine's Church. At the time 'The Tube', as it was nicknamed, projected a dynamic vision of the Bay's future. Intended to last only a few years, it was a rare example of non-traditional architecture liked by the public. Relocated in 1993 (without the framed view and 'aeroplane' steps), it was finally dismantled in 2010.

Another early contribution to the development of Cardiff Bay was the Techniquest building (Ahrends, Burton, Koralek, 1995). Housing permanent exhibitions aimed at stimulating scientific imagination, the galleries were built into the steel skeleton of an old docklands engineering workshop. Standing nearby, prominent in a privileged position on the edge of the bay, is the St David's Hotel (Patrick Davies for Rocco Forte Group, 2000), with its huge non-functional roof feature representing sails, a ship's bow-wave, or perhaps a pair of dragon's wings.

The most notorious project of the Bay's early history was the plan for a Cardiff Bay Opera House. It was to be a 'Millennium' project financed by the National Lottery, newly set up by John Major's government in 1993. An architectural competition held that year was won by Zaha Hadid; it would have been her first UK building. Controversy ensued (discussed at length elsewhere;[1] arguments occasionally resurface even twenty years later). The outcome was that the Millennium Commission refused Lottery funding in 1995. The project was reinvented as the Millennium Centre, awarded to the Cardiff-based Percy Thomas Partnership, designed by Jonathan Adams (previously of Will Alsop's practice) and completed in two phases, 2004 and 2009, with the help of Lottery funding and money from the National Assembly for Wales. Its massive 'dome', clad in bronze-tinted stainless steel and surmounting Welsh slate walls, is the hub of the Bay. On the front, in huge letters illuminated at night, is poet Gwyneth Lewis's bilingual inscription, 'CREU GWIR FEL GWYDR O FFWRNAIS AWEN – IN THESE STONES HORIZONS SING' (the Welsh words translate as 'Forging truth like glass from the furnace of inspiration').

Following the 1997 referendum result, another architectural competition awarded the design of a new building for the National Assembly to Richard Rogers Partnership. Known as the Senedd, it was opened by Queen Elizabeth II in 2006. **(255)** Like a modern interpretation of an ancient temple protecting the hivelike debating chamber at its heart, it projects its authority across the bay from a plinth of Welsh slate. With its prominent wind cowl helping to ventilate the building naturally, and warmed by earth heat exchangers, the building was lauded for its environmental efficiency and nominated for the 2006 RIBA Stirling Prize.

In the early years of the twenty-first century, the BBC, encouraged by government to diversify its operations geographically, decided to create in Cardiff a Centre of Excellence for Drama. It opened the Roath Lock building, with its 300 m-long facade designed by Fashion Architecture Taste (FAT, in collaboration with Cardiff's Holder and Mathias), in 2011. Consequently, through television series such as *Casualty*, *Dr Who*, *Torchwood* and *Sherlock*, locations in and around Cardiff often masquerade as different parts of this or other worlds.

The Cardiff Bay Development Corporation was dissolved in 2000. Interviewed thirty years after it was set up, Lord Crickhowell (who as Nicholas Edwards had been Secretary of State for Wales at the time) remarked: 'I think [Cardiff Bay] has been an immense success. There's a whole

255 The Senedd, Cardiff Bay, with the Millennium Centre behind.

generation who has no idea what it was like before. We cannot contemplate Cardiff without the bay. It's the centre of the city – it's highly successful.'[2] Whatever its undoubted successes in reinhabiting derelict brownfield land, a balanced view would be that it could have been better. Even with the advantage of its new lake (around the perimeter of which public access has thankfully been preserved) and that fine view of Penarth Head, it has not, because of its clash of disparate buildings, found the strength of identity that great places possess – except perhaps as a place for a stroll and an ice cream or drink on a summer evening. Considered generally, some have argued that the development lacks consistent design quality and visual integrity. It certainly has not, as Lord Crickhowell asserted, become 'the centre of the city'. It stands as a testament to the limited ability of neoliberal policies to deliver an integrated, humane and beautiful urban environment.

Cardiff City Centre

Wales is known as 'the land of song', but it is a land of rugby too. One of the reasons suggested for the Cardiff Bay Opera House's failure to attract Lottery funding was that the millennium would be better marked by a less elitist building – a rugby ground to replace the city centre's ageing Cardiff Arms Park. The Principality Stadium (Lobb Partnership) opened in 1999. Suggestions by some that the nation's new home of rugby should be built on the outskirts of the city had been resisted. Its masts and the massive structure supporting its retractable roof stand like a medieval cathedral at the centre of its community, a landmark visible for miles around.

Though Cardiff Bay has not found a strong identity, the city centre, in the face of the competition the Bay was once expected to present, has retained vitality even in the face of national UK economic challenges and the emergence of the Internet as a major retail forum. This has been helped by some particular initiatives. The St David's Shopping Centre (1981) was significantly extended southwards in 2009 (St David's 2, Benoy and Chapman Taylor) incorporating Hayes Apartments (Glenn Howells Architects) and a large hidden

256 Royal Welsh College of Music and Drama, Cardiff.

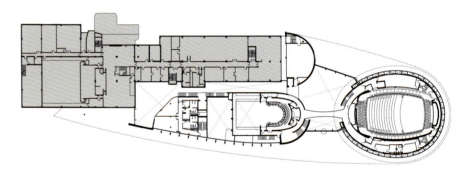

257 Royal Welsh College of Music and Drama. First floor plan, with the original building shown in grey.

multi-storey car park. A new Central Library (Building Design Partnership) opened the same year. The achievement of these coordinated projects is not so much in their individual architecture as in their integration with older components of the city's heart – especially The Hayes and the historic arcades – helping maintain Cardiff's quality as a habitable place.

Reversing its 1970s policy of moving people out of the city, Cardiff has been keen to revive city-centre living.

A number of apartment blocks as well as hotels have been constructed, notably the Altolusso residential block (Holder and Mathias Architects, 2005) just north of the main railway line. To accommodate growing service industries, new offices have been built, especially around Callaghan Square (laid out in 2000 at the northern end of the historic Bute Street link to the Bay, and once considered as the site for the Assembly building), and in the so-called Capital Quarter, opposite the Altolusso block, just to the south of the railway.

Cardiff has benefited from the substantial growth of higher education. Many new student residences accommodate increased student numbers. In 2013 Cardiff University completed its Hadyn Ellis Building (Nightingale

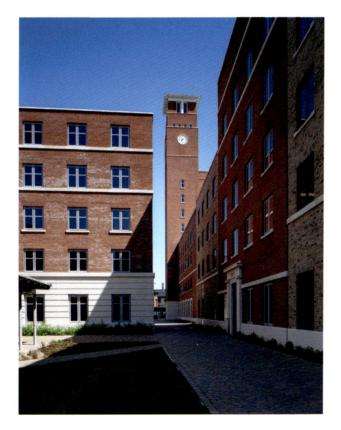

258 Swansea University's
      Bay Campus, Swansea.

Associates) housing facilities for health-related research. Its Brain Research Imaging Centre (IBI Group) opened in 2016. The first building of the University of South Wales's city-centre campus – The Atrium (Holder and Mathias, 2007) – houses the Cardiff Faculty of Creative and Cultural Industries. But the most congenial recent building in the city (also part of the University of South Wales) is the substantial extension to the Royal Welsh College of Music and Drama (BFLS Architects, now Flanagan Lawrence, 2011), situated on North Road between the Civic Centre and Bute Park. (256 and 257) The new addition (which partly conceals the 1970s Raymond Edwards Building) houses the Richard Burton Theatre and the Dora Stoutzker Hall. The intimate character and exemplary acoustics of the latter (Arup Acoustics) have quickly established it as a music venue of international quality. At the new building's heart is a generous and lofty foyer – used for socializing and informal performances – with a grand view through its large glazed wall into the seasonally changing well-treed landscape of Bute Park.

Culture-related Projects outside Cardiff

Just as London attracts more investment than the rest of Britain, so Cardiff is favoured over other parts of Wales. Even so, notable projects have succeeded elsewhere, mainly through public initiatives often involving National Lottery and European Union funding.

Swansea became a city in 1969, and Newport in 2002. Both have made their own attempts at developing redundant dockland and other ex-industrial sites, though not on the same scale as Cardiff's. Both have wanted signature buildings. The Riverfront Theatre and Arts Centre (Austin-Smith Lord) was opened in Newport in 2004. In Swansea's Maritime Quarter, the Dylan Thomas Centre (Rock Townsend), occupying the city's Old Guildhall, opened in 1995; and the National Waterfront Museum (Wilkinson Eyre), incorporating a 1901 warehouse that had formerly been converted into the Swansea Industrial and Maritime Museum, opened in 2006. Again, to accommodate burgeoning higher education, Swansea University's new Bay Campus (Porphyrios Associates and

Hopkins Architects) was opened in 2015 on land previously occupied by British Petroleum. **(258)** Influenced by the neo-traditionalist philosophy advocated by Prince Charles, some of the large buildings on this extensive seaside campus try to appear as if built incrementally in earlier times; and the Great Hall at its heart takes its influence from ancient Rome.

Further west, the National Botanic Garden of Wales, another Millennium project, opened near Llanarthne in 2000. At its heart is the Great Glasshouse (Foster + Partners, 2000) which finds its place in the long history of great British conservatories, stretching back to Decimus Burton and Joseph Paxton in the mid-nineteenth century, by boasting the largest unsupported span of any glasshouse in the world. **(259)**

Architect Percy Thomas Partnership's 1960s work at University College of Wales, Aberystwyth, was mentioned in the previous chapter. It incorporated an arts centre, the facilities of which have been subsequently expanded. In 2000, a cinema, studio theatre and dance studio were added (Smith Roberts Associates). And in 2006, Thomas Heatherwick won a competition to design sixteen studios for arts-related businesses. Paired in eight 'sheds' distinctively clad in crumpled stainless steel foil, they were completed in 2009. **(260)**

Funding has been forthcoming to support arts-related projects in northern Wales too. Alongside Caernarfon's Victoria Dock, the Galeri Creative Enterprise Centre (Richard Murphy Architects, 2005) also houses start-up studios, together with a theatre and rehearsal spaces. The Ruthin Craft Centre reopened in 2008 after a major transformation (Sergison Bates). And the most recent major arts-related project in Wales, the Pontio Arts and Innovation Centre at Bangor University (Grimshaw Architects) was completed in 2016, accommodating Theatr Bryn Terfel plus a studio theatre, a cinema and various teaching and innovation facilities.

259 The Great Glasshouse, National Botanic Garden of Wales, Llanarthne, Carmarthenshire.

260 The Creative Units at Aberystwyth University.

Environmentally Responsible Architecture

By legislation, all new building has to be environmentally responsible, but some architects adopt sustainability as a governing ideology. Wales has been home to the Centre for Alternative Technology (CAT) since the 1970s. Situated in a disused quarry near Machynlleth, it is devoted to promoting sustainable development through demonstration and education. Various additions have been made during the following decades. Three of these were designed by Pat Borer and David Lea. The site is entered by a water-balanced cliff railway; their first collaboration was to design its stations (1992). The adjacent AtEIC (Autonomous Environmental Information Centre), incorporating a shop and using walls of rammed earth, was completed in 2000. And the WISE (Wales Institute for Sustainable Education) building opened in 2010. **(261)** This is the largest of the Centre's buildings and accommodates its postgraduate courses, a café, and accommodation for residential courses. Using renewable natural materials and passive energy strategies, it is an object lesson in sustainable architecture. It also draws on historical precedent: the courtyard was influenced by the Zen rock gardens of Japan; and the interior of the circular lecture hall, with its 7.2 metre-high rammed earth walls, refers back to the 3,000-year-old Tomb of Agamemnon at Mycenae.

261 Centre for Alternative Technology, near Machynlleth. Early drawing of the WISE Building by David Lea.

In 1999 the National Museum of Wales, together with the BBC and Redrow Homes, held a competition to design a House for the Future. It was won by the London firm of Jestico and Whiles, designed by Welsh School of Architecture graduate Jude Harris, and built at the St Fagans National Museum of History in 2000. The design of Tŷ Gwyrdd was informed by the idea that the future would be challenged by environmental issues; it benefits from passive solar gain, is highly insulated with sheep's wool, and was originally fitted with a ground- source heat pump (subsequently replaced) as well as solar panels and photovoltaic cells.

Smaller Projects around Wales

In the early 1980s architect Christopher Day helped the Nant-y-Cwm Steiner School in Pembrokeshire to alter a century-old Board School according to Rudolf Steiner's principles of place-making. Based in nature and aimed at nurturing self-expression free of restrictive rules, these advise against the right-angle and in favour of intimate spaces related to inhabitation ('cwtches', as we would say in Wales). At the end of the 1980s, Day added a Kindergarten, a new building in which Steiner's principles could be followed more thoroughly. (262) It accommodates two circular classrooms with irregular windows, shallow-domed ceilings and inhabited walls containing 'child caves', all under the blanket of a grass roof.

Maggie's, the cancer charity, was set up by Maggie Keswick Jencks and her husband, landscape designer and architectural historian Charles Jencks, shortly before she died in 1995. The first Maggie's Centre for cancer care opened in Edinburgh in 1996 (designed by Richard Murphy, who designed Galeri in Caernarfon). The charity's tenth centre, and the first in Wales, was opened at Singleton Hospital, Swansea, in 2011. The eminent Japanese architect Kisho Kurokawa, a friend of the Jenckses, died shortly after designing it in 2007; the building was completed by Garbers and James Architects of London. The building's plan resembles the cutter from a food processor but is based on the idea of a galactic whirlpool around a still centre. (A second centre in Wales is planned for Velindre Hospital in

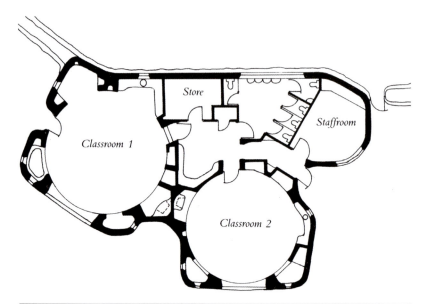

262 Steiner Kindergarten, Nant-y-Cwm, Pembrokeshire.

263 Visitor Centre and Watersports Centre, Llandegfedd Reservoir, near Pontypool.

Cardiff, to be designed by Dow Jones Architects.)

The Visitor Centre and Watersports Centre, on the banks of Llandegfedd Reservoir near Pontypool, were designed by Chepstow-based architects Hall & Bednarczyk for Dŵr Cymru Welsh Water. (263) It opened in 2015. Entered via the upper of two floors, it is a modern version of a temple in a picturesque landscape. It plays the classical trick of taking the visitor through a doorway in a screen wall before revealing an expansive panorama, which here includes the reservoir's mysterious valve tower standing in the water like a sinister mausoleum.

The Llandegfedd Visitor Centre and Watersports Centre is one of a number of visitor centres built in Wales, which include one for Castell Henllys (an Iron Age hillfort in north Pembrokeshire, 1993), the Welsh Wildlife Centre near Cilgerran Castle (1994) and the St David's Information Centre (2000), all designed by Peter Roberts (the first two when with Niall Phillips Architects, the last through his own practice, Smith Roberts Architects). There are others at Caerphilly Castle (Davies Sutton Architects, 2003);

the World Heritage Centre Big Pit, Blaenavon (Purcell Architects, 2008); the Hafod Eryri–Snowdon Summit (Ray Hole Architects, 2009); and Copper Kingdom in Amlwch (Donald Insall Associates, 2013).

Conservation Projects

In 1975, the Royal Commission on Ancient and Historic Monuments in Wales published *Houses of the Welsh Countryside* by its secretary, Peter Smith. It was, and remains, an exemplary overview of the traditional regional architecture of Wales, and includes references to Tŷ Mawr, Castell Caereinion, a rare survival of a fine timber-frame house in Montgomeryshire dating back to the fifteenth century. Smith himself had discovered it in ruins in 1971. There were lengthy discussions about moving the house to the National History Museum, St Fagans; but in 1997–8 the house was restored where it had always stood (Michael Garner for Cadw) in recognition of the vital relationship traditional rural houses have with the land in which they sit. (264)

Two other important houses that could easily have been lost are Sker House – a large sixteenth-century house set amongst Kenfig Burrows near Porthcawl – and Llwyn Celyn – an early fifteenth-century house in the Monmouthshire Black Mountains. Both endured years of difficulty. Sker was eventually restored in 2003 (Davies Sutton Architects) for the Buildings at Risk Trust, and Llwyn Celyn in 2017 (John C. Goom Architects) for the Landmark Trust.

It is usual for conservation projects to become sagas. Another is that of Cardigan Castle, which, although partly inhabited until the 1990s, had become progressively more dilapidated and overgrown. It was finally opened to the public in 2015 after a widely praised restoration by Purcell Architects for Cadwgan Building Preservation Trust.

Modern Houses of the Welsh Countryside

Peter Smith's book would be very different for the first two decades of the twenty-first century. Whilst local authority social housing everywhere has languished, some clients

264 Tŷ Mawr, Castell Caereinion, near Welshpool, Montgomeryshire.

265 Malator, Nolton, Pembrokeshire.

266 Stormy Castle, Gower, interior.

have found themselves able to build sophisticated houses in the Welsh countryside, especially on the coast.

Malator (also known as the 'Telletubby House') is a small earth-sheltered holiday home in the Pembrokeshire Coast National Park (Future Systems, 1998). It was one of the first houses to adopt a more adventurous, non-vernacular approach to houses in the Welsh countryside. Under its grassy mound it is almost invisible from the landward road; its main eye-shaped glass wall looks out across St Bride's Bay to the setting sun. **(265)**

Also in the Pembrokeshire National Park, the Hampshire-based architect John Pardey designed Trewarren House (2011), which enjoys magnificent views across the Newport Estuary. In the same year the London practice of Featherstone Young completed a daring house, part of which is cantilevered dramatically over the Ysgir river in the Brecon Beacons National Park; it is appropriately called Tŷ Hedfan ('Flying House'). Other distinguished contemporary houses in the Welsh countryside include the prize-winning Stormy Castle on the north Gower coast, **(266)** designed in 2013 by the Penarth-based practice of Chris Loyn (Loyn & Co.) which was also responsible for the remarkable Outhouse in the Forest of Dean (shortlisted for the 2016 RIBA Stirling Prize).

All these recent houses owe a debt to twentieth-century Modernism but add wit, twenty-first century sophistication and the use of much improved materials and construction systems. Perhaps this is best exemplified in Cefn Castell (2015), a crisp composition of white planes

267   Cefn Castell, near Cricieth, Caernarfonshire.

and glass walls that would not be out of place on the hills overlooking Las Vegas. **(267)** It was designed by Manchester's Stephenson Studio for the coastal site of an old cottage near Cricieth on the Llŷn peninsula.

That sophistication is also apparent in the work of younger practices based in Wales. For example, Hall & Bednarczyk (architects of the Llangedfedd Visitor Centre and Watersports Centre) completed Carreg a Gwydr ('Stone and Glass') in rural Monmouthshire in 2011, while Hyde + Hyde (Swansea) completed their Cliff House in 2014 and Silver House in 2017, both on the Gower peninsula. To add to the internationally distinguished architects represented in Wales, in 2016 the celebrated minimalist John Pawson completed The Life House (Tŷ Bywyd) on a remote site near

Llanbister in mid-Wales for the author Alain de Botton's 'Living Architecture' series of holiday houses, which aims to improve 'public perceptions of modern architecture'.

Meanwhile other influential individuals have preferred to look backwards in time. Poundbury near Dorchester (conceived in the 1980s) is well known as representing the Prince of Wales's view of how residential settlements in twenty-first century Britain should be. The same influence has been exercised in Wales at Coed Darcy, on land previously occupied by the Llandarcy oil refinery near Neath. An initial scheme designed by classical and traditional architect Robert Adam in 2006 was found uneconomical, and so, in 2007, a much larger neo-traditionalist scheme was instigated by developers St Modwen (also responsible for Swansea University's Bay

Campus). Set on hills and reminiscent of a nineteenth- and early twentieth- century 'Valleys' town, Coed Darcy has found itself somewhat isolated from the infrastructure necessary for the hoped-for community life. A more integrated neo-traditionalist housing project can be found at Loftus Garden Village in Newport (Alan Baxter Architects and others, for Pobl Housing Association). Here, on a large brownfield site previously occupied by the Pirelli Cables factory, new streets continue the existing pattern, opening up into landscaped spaces and bringing green belt into the city.

Looking Forward ...

In the early decades of the twenty-first century the issues outlined at the start of this chapter largely persist. Docklands have been redeveloped, while some communities associated with past industries continue to struggle. There has been some progress in attracting new industry, though in 2014 (the beginning of the most recent funding period) large areas of Wales remained eligible for the highest level of European Union structural funding. Following the 2016 referendum, the consequences of the UK's negotiations to leave the EU are at the time of writing unknown. Areas of success include the growth of education and the creative industries – most notably the major expansion of the BBC's activities in Cardiff. Central Square, **(268)** immediately north of Cardiff Central Station, is under construction and will include the new Welsh headquarters for the BBC, designed by Foster + Partners (to be completed in 2019). The Welsh Government's Twenty-first Century Schools programme is underway, promising better learning environments for children of all ages. Maybe social housing will come back into favour. Cardiff University's expansion continues with plans for a new Centre for Student Life on Park Place (Fielden Clegg Bradley Studios), and an ambitious Innovation Campus on Maindy Road. The rich variety of contemporary architecture is being embraced in all these initiatives. The architecture of Wales will be worth watching in the next three decades ∎

268 Artist's impression of Central Square, Cardiff, showing the new headquarters of BBC Wales in the centre.

18 Recent Developments, 1985–2017
References

1   Nicholas Crickhowell, *Opera House Lottery: Zaha Hadid and the Cardiff Bay Project* (Cardiff: University of Wales Press, 1997).

2   Natalie Crockett, 'Cardiff Bay: What has 30 years of development achieved', BBC News website, 13 August 2017, available at *bbc.co.uk/news/uk-wales-40681940* (accessed October 2017).

Appendix 1: *Glossary of Welsh Architectural and Building Terms*

Abaty	abbey
Bangor	wattle
Beudy	cow shed
Bwa	arch
Bwthyn	one or two-roomed cottage
Capan	lintel
Capel	chapel
Carreg	stone
Castell	castle (L: castellum)
Cegin	kitchen (L: culina)
Cerrig diddos	crow-steps (on gable or side of chimney)
Clas	cloister
Commote	medieval land division
Croglen	rood screen
Croglofft	small loft in roof of house
Cromen	dome, vault
Cwpwl	truss
Cwpwl bongam	cruck-truss
Drws	door
Eglwys	church
Eglwys gadeiriol	cathedral
Ffenestr	window (L: fenestra)
Grisiau	stairs (L: gressus = step)
Hafod	summer (farm) house; often of a temporary nature only
Hendref	winter (or main) farmhouse
Lintal	sill or cill (L: limen)
Llan	churchyard
Llech	slate
Llys	court (mansion)
Maen	stone
Maen clo	keystone
Maen hir	standing stone (menhir)
Maerdref	royal village
Melin	mill
Melin wynt	windmill
Mur	wall (L: murus)
Mynachdy	monastery
Nenbren	roof beam, ridge-piece
Neuadd	hall
Oriel	balcony, gallery
Pandy	fulling-mill
Penllawr	passage between upper and lower ends of a long-house
Pen-isaf	lower end of a long-house
Pen-uchaf	upper end of a long-house
Pont	bridge (L: pons)
Porth	doorway or gateway (L: porta)
Taflod	loft
Talcen grisiog	crow-stepped gable
Talcen tŷ	gable-end or pine-end
To	roof (L: tego)
To gwellt	thatch
Tomen	motte (L: tumulus)
Twmpath	motte
Tŵr	tower (L: turris)
Tŷ-clom	clay (or clod) house
Tŷ cyfrifol	gentry house (house of account)
Tyddyn	smallholding or croft
Tŷ-hir	long-house
Tŷ-unnos	one-night house, i.e. house erected between sunset and sunrise
Ysgubor	barn
Ystafell	room (L: stabellum)

Appendix 2:
RIBA Awards in Wales 1923 to 2018

Compiled by Jonathan Vining and Mary Wrenn

The Royal Institute of British Architects has operated two award schemes over the last hundred years: the Architecture Bronze Medal, which was instituted in 1923 and continued until 1965, and subsequently the RIBA Architecture Awards.

In the early decades, the allocation of awards was rather haphazard across the UK, until the system was rationalized in 1966 so that awards could be made consistently on an annual basis at the same time across the whole of the UK. Since then, the RIBA award scheme has undergone several adjustments with the aim of promoting excellence of design achievement. Commendations were introduced in 1973 and later dropped; and at one stage the eligibility criteria stated that a building could not be considered for an award until two years after completion.

The most recent review came in 2012 when the RIBA took steps to consolidate the additional regional schemes that had gradually proliferated across the UK since the 1970s. The result was the creation of a two-tier system of awards, at regional and national (UK) level. In Wales this first phase of the RIBA Awards was established as the RSAW Welsh Architecture Awards (RSAW is the RIBA in Wales). Category prizes were also introduced, such as 'Client of the Year' or 'Small Project of the Year'.

The RIBA Awards now present a progressive linked route from regional awards through to the Stirling Prize, first awarded in 1996 (previously known as Building of the Year) to recognise 'the greatest contribution to British architecture in the past year'.

All the buildings and practices listed here have achieved an award at either regional, national or category level. For more information on the level of RIBA award won by specific schemes and Welsh practices shortlisted for the RIBA Stirling Prize and other UK awards and prizes, contact **rsaw@riba.org**.

Winners of RIBA Bronze Medals

1930

– South addition to James Howell
  and Company's store, Cardiff
  Ivor Jones and Percy Thomas

1935

– The Guildhall, Swansea
  Ivor Jones and Percy Thomas

1946

– The Temple of Peace and Health, Cardiff
  (built 1937–8)
  Percy Thomas

1953

– Denbighshire Technical College, Wrexham
  Saxon, Smith and Partners

1955

– Sports pavilion, University College of South
  Wales and Monmouthshire, Llanrumney,
  Cardiff
  T. Alwyn Lloyd and Gordon

1958

– Kardov depot and office, Ystrad Road,
  Fforestfach, Swansea
  Smith, Wilson and Cox

1961

– St David's Lutheran Church, Fairwater, Cardiff
  T. Alwyn Lloyd and Gordon

1964

– School of Social Studies, University
  College of Swansea
  Sir Percy Thomas and Son

Winners of RIBA Commendations (1974–86)

1974

– University Hospital of Wales, Heath Park,
  Cardiff (built 1963–71)
  *S W Milburn & Partners, in association
  with M. Harding and J. Surtees*

1974

– Sherman Theatre, Senghennydd Road,
  Cardiff
  Alex Gordon and Partners

1975

– Albert Edward Prince of Wales Court,
  Penylan Avenue, Porthcawl
  Percy Thomas Partnership

1976

– Arts and Social Sciences Library,
  University College Cardiff
  Faulkner-Brown, Hendy, Watkinson, Stonor

1977

– Hugh Owen Library, University College
  of Wales, Aberystwyth
  Percy Thomas Partnership

1978

– Roman Catholic Church of St Illtyd, Maes
  Onnan, Rhuddlan
  Bowen Dann Davies

– Office Cleaning Services offices, Cardiff
  Road, Llandaf, Cardiff
  Holder & Mathias Partnership

1979

– Marine Terminal, Amlwch and Rhosgoch
  Architects Design Group

– Melrose Centre, Shotton
  *Bowen Dann Davies Partnership in association
  with Clwyd County Architect*

1982

– Trinity Court housing, Paradise Street, Rhyl
  (built 1977–8)
  Bowen Dann Davies Partnership

– Hafan Elan housing for older people, Llanrug
  Bowen Dann Davies Partnership

1983

– Whitbread brewery, Magor
  Frederick Gibberd, Coombes and Partners

1984

– Holiday cottages, North Rogeston,
  near Haverfordwest
  Ralphs and Mansell

– Capel-y-groes, Powell Road, Wrexham
  Bowen Dann Davies Partnership

1986

– Plas Menai (National Outdoor Pursuits
  Centre), Llanfairisgaer, Caernarfon
  Bowen Dann Davies Partnership

– Hanover Court housing for older people,
  Bryn Euryn Farm, Llandrillo-yn-Rhos
  Brian Lingard & Partners

Winners of RIBA Awards for Architecture (1966–2011)

1966

– E. M. Edwards works, Llandarcy
Alex Gordon and Partners

1967

– Temporary laboratories, University College of South Wales and Monmouthshire, Cathays Park, Cardiff
Alex Gordon and Partners

1970

– Great hall, bell tower and Sudents' Union, University College of Wales, Aberystwyth
Percy Thomas Partnership

1971

– Llwydcoed Crematorium, near Aberdare
HMR Burgess + Partners

1973

– Parke-Davis & Company research and manufacturing centre, Llanfihangel Pont-y-moel, Pontypool
Percy Thomas Partnership

1976

– Cefndy Hostel for people with learning difficulties, Cefndy Road, Rhyl
Bowen Dann Davies Partnership in association with R. W. Harvey, Clwyd County Council

1982

– Amersham International radiochemical centre, Forest Farm, Cardiff
Percy Thomas Partnership

1988

– Llyn Madoc, Llangollen
Graham Bromilow Associates

– Ystradgynlais Community Hospital, Swansea
William H. Simpson, Welsh Health Common Services Authority

– Coleshill Home and Social Centre, Llanelli
Alex Gordon Partnership

1989

– South Glamorgan County Hall, Atlantic Wharf, Cardiff
J. R. C. Bethell, County Architect

– Ferrara Quay, Maritime Quarter, Swansea
Halliday Meecham Partnership, in collaboration with Robin Campbell

– Llys Picton housing for older people, Carmarthen
Alex Gordon Partnership

– Studio 13, architectural studio, Abergavenny
Brown and Parnaby Architects

1990

– Amersham International research products laboratory, Forest Farm, Cardiff
Percy Thomas Partnership

– Eveswell Junior and Infants School, Newport
K. P. Jones, Gwent county architect

– Plantasia, North Dock, Swansea
Percy Thomas Partnership

1991

– Cardiff Bay Visitor Centre, Cardiff
Alsop Lyall & Störmer

1992

– Lower Treginnis Farm, St David's
Niall Phillips Architects

– Arts centre, Tŷ Isaf Farm Barn, Treuddyn, near Mold
Pankaj Patel, Andrew Taylor Architects

1994

– Castell Henllys education centre, Eglwyswrw
Niall Phillips Architects

1995

– British Airways avionics facility, Llantrisant
Percy Thomas Partnership

– Welsh Wildlife Centre, Teifi Marshes, Cilgerran
Niall Phillips Architects

1996

– Techniquest science discovery centre, Stuart Street, Cardiff
Ahrends Burton & Koralek

– NCM Credit Insurance offices, Harbour Drive, Cardiff
Holder Mathias Alcock

– Tŵr Brynkir folly, Gwynedd
Adam and Frances Voelcker

1997

– Swansea Foyer, Alexandra Road, Swansea
PCKO Architects

1998

– Conservatory, Broadleys Cottage, Denbigh
Sanders & Stonebridge Architects

- Control Techniques research and
  development facility, Newtown
  Arup Associates

2000

- Perthcelyn Community Primary School,
  Mountain Ash
  Rhondda Cynon Taf County Borough Council

- The Great Glasshouse, National Botanic
  Garden of Wales, Llanarthne
  Foster + Partners

2001

- Aberystwyth Arts Centre,
  Aberystwyth University
  Smith Roberts Associates

- Private house, Raisdale Road, Penarth
  Loyn & Co. Architects

2002

- Low-energy factory, Baglan Energy Park,
  Port Talbot
  *Neath Port Talbot County Borough Council,
  in association with the Welsh School of
  Architecture, Cardiff University*

2004

- Sker House, Kenfig, Porthcawl
  Davies Sutton Architects

2005

- Galeri creative enterprise centre, Caernarfon
  Richard Murphy Architects

- Wales Millennium Centre, Bute Place, Cardiff
  Capita Percy Thomas

2006

- The Senedd, Cardiff
  Richard Rogers Partnership

- National Waterfront Museum, Swansea
  Wilkinson Eyre Architects

2008

- Blaenavon Heritage Centre
  Purcell Miller Tritton

2009

- Penderyn Distillery visitor centre, Penderyn
  David Archer Architects

- Ruthin Craft Centre
  Sergison Bates architects

2010

- Margam Discovery Centre, Margam Park,
  Port Talbot
  *Design Research Unit Wales, Welsh School
  of Architecture, Cardiff University, with
  Loyn & Co. Architects*

- Creative business units, Aberystwyth Arts
  Centre, Aberystwyth University
  Heatherwick Studio

- Cardiff Central Library
  BDP, executive architect Stride Treglown

- Chapter Arts Centre refurbishment,
  Canton, Cardiff
  Ash Sakula Architects

- Sleeperz Hotel, Saunders Road, Cardiff
  Clash Associates and Holder Mathias Architects

- Hafod Eryri, Snowdon summit building
  Ray Hole Architects

- Skypad Teenage Cancer Trust Unit,
  University Hospital of Wales, Cardiff
  *Orms Designers + Architects, executive architect
  Stride Treglown*

2011

- University of South Wales, Newport City
  Campus, Usk Way, Newport
  BDP

- Tŷ Hedfan, Brecon
  Featherstone Young

- Mostyn gallery, Llandudno
  Ellis Williams Architects

- UWIC School of Management, Llandaff
  Campus, Cardiff
  Austin-Smith:Lord

- Students' Union, University of Glamorgan,
  Trefforest
  Rio Architects

- WISE Building, Centre for Alternative
  Technology, Machynlleth
  Pat Borer and David Lea

- Blue Door private house, Chepstow
  Hall & Bednarczyk Architects

Winners of RIBA Awards 2012–17

(The list includes RIBA Regional Awards (Welsh Architecture Awards) and RIBA National Awards)

2012

– Royal Welsh College of Music and Drama, North Road, Cardiff
BFLS

– Beacon Heating showroom, Newcastle Emlyn
Rural Office for Architecture

– Carreg a Gwydr private house, Monmouthshire
Hall & Bednarczyk Architects

2013

– Trewarren private house, Newport, Pembrokeshire
John Pardey Architects

– Petravore private house, Cyncoed, Cardiff
Hyde + Hyde Architects

2014

– New Barn private home and studio, Newcastle Emlyn
Rural Office for Architecture

– Stormy Castle private house, Llanmadog, Gower
Loyn & Co. Architects

– Old Farm Mews, Dinas Powys
Hoole & Walmsley Architects

– Copper Kingdom visitor centre, Amlwch
Donald Insall Architects

– Galilee Chapel, St Illtyd's Church, Llantwit Major
Davies Sutton Architects

2015

– Cardiff School of Art & Design, Cardiff Metropolitan University, Llandaff Campus, Western Avenue, Cardiff
Austin-Smith:Lord

– Cefn Castell private house, Cricieth
Stephenson Studio

– Cliff House, Southgate, Gower
Hyde + Hyde Architects

– Denbigh Hwb, Smithfield Road, Denbigh
John McCall Architects

– Private house, Llanishen, Cardiff
Loyn & Co. Architects

2016

– Llandegfedd Visitor Centre and Watersports Centre
Hall & Bednarczyk Architects

– Welsh National Sailing Academy and Events Centre, Pwllheli
Ellis Williams Architects

– Cardigan Castle conservation works and new restaurant
Purcell

– Burry Port Community Primary School
Architype and Carmarthenshire County Council

– Cardiff and Vale College, City Centre Campus, Dumballs Road, Cardiff
BDP

2017

– Silver House, Gower
Hyde + Hyde Architects

– The Chickenshed, private house, Monmouthshire
Hall & Bednarczyk Architects

2018

– Yr Ysgwrn, Trawsfynydd
Purcell

– New In-Patient Unit, St David's Hospice, Newport
KKE Architects

– Pontio Bangor University Arts and Innovation Centre
Grimshaw

Royal Gold Medal for Architecture

1939

– Percy Thomas, in recognition of his lifetime's work and significant influence on the advancement of architecture.

Select Bibliography

Abbreviations:

Arch. Camb.	Archaeologia Cambrensis: Journal of the Cambrian Archaeological Association
Cadw	Cadw: Welsh Historic Monuments
NMW	National Museum of Wales
RCAHMW	Royal Commission on the Ancient and Historic Monuments of Wales
UWP	University of Wales Press

Architects Working in Wales

Darby, Michael, *John Pollard Seddon: Catalogue of Architectural Drawings* (London: Victoria and Albert Museum, 1983).

Davey, Elaine, *A National Architect? The Percy Thomas Practice and Welsh National Identity* (Ph.D. thesis, 2013).

David, Farmer, *John Humphrey, God's Own Architect* (Swansea: Royal Institution of South Wales, 1997).

Haslam, Richard, *Clough Williams-Ellis: RIBA Drawings Monographs No. 1* (London: Academy Editions, 1996).

Hughes, Stephen, *Thomas Thomas, 1817–88: The First National Architect of Wales, Arch. Camb.*, 152 (2003), 69–166.

Jones, Jonah, *Clough Williams-Ellis: The Architect of Portmeirion* (Bridgend: Seren, 1996).

Richards, H. P., *William Edwards, Architect, Builder, Minister: A Short Biography* (Cowbridge: D. Brown & Sons Ltd, 1983).

Suggett, Richard, *John Nash, Architect in Wales* (Aberystwyth: NLW and RCAHMW, 1995).

Thomas, Sir Percy, *Pupil to President: Memoirs of an Architect* (Leigh-on-Sea: F. Lewis, Publishers, Limited, 1963).

Voelcker, Adam, *Herbert Luck North: Arts and Crafts Architecture for Wales* (Aberystwyth: RCAHMW, 2011).

Book Series

Buildings of Wales:

Haslam, Richard, Julian Orbach and Adam Voelcker, Adam, *Gwynedd* (New Haven and London: Yale University Press, 2009).

Hubbard, Edward, *Clwyd* (Cardiff: UWP, 1994).

Lloyd, Thomas, Julian Orbach, and Robert Scourfield, *Carmarthenshire and Ceredigion* (New Haven and London: Yale University Press, 2006).

Lloyd, Thomas, Julian Orbach, and Robert Scourfield, *Pembrokeshire* (New Haven and London: Yale University Press, 2004).

Newman, John, *Glamorgan* (Cardiff: Penguin / UWP, 1995).

Newman, John, *Gwent / Monmouthshire* (Cardiff: Penguin / UWP, 2000).

Scourfield, Robert, and Richard Haslam, *Powys* (New Haven and London: Yale University Press, 2013).

Cadw Guides to Ancient and Historic Wales (all London: HMSO):

Burnham, Helen, *Clwyd and Powys* (1995).

Lynch, Frances, *Gwynedd* (1995).

Rees, Sian, *Dyfed* (1992).

Whittle, Elisabeth, *Glamorgan and Gwent* (1992).

General Bibliography

Aldhouse-Green, Miranda, and Ray Howell, *Celtic Wales*, second edn (Cardiff: UWP, 2017).

Arnold, C. J., and J. L. Davies, *Roman and Early Medieval Wales* (Stroud: Sutton Publishing, 2000).

Avent, Richard, *Cestyll Tywysogion Gwynedd / Castles of the Princes of Gwynedd* (London: HMSO, 1983).

Baker, Mark, and Greg Stevenson, *50 Buildings that Built Wales* (Cardiff: Graffeg, 2016).

Barley, Maurice, *Houses and History* (London: Faber and Faber, 1986).

Beresford, Maurice, *New Towns of the Middle Ages: Town Plantations in England, Wales and Gascony* (London: Lutterworth Press, 1967).

Bowen, E. G., *Saints, Seaways and Settlements in the Celtic Lands*, second edn (Cardiff: UWP, 1977).

Bowen, H. V. (ed.), *Buildings and Places in Welsh History* (Llandysul: Gomer, 2013).

Brewer, Richard J., *Caerwent Roman Town* (Cardiff: Cadw, 2006).

Britnell, W. J., R. J. Silvester, R. Suggett and E. William, 'Tŷ-draw, Llanarmon Mynydd Mawr, Powys – a late-medieval cruck-framed hallhouse-longhouse', *Arch. Camb.*, 157 (2008).

Brunskill, R. W., *Houses and Cottages of Britain: Origins and Development of Traditional Buildings* (London: Victor Gollancz, 1997).

Brunskill, R. W., *Illustrated Handbook of Vernacular Architecture* (London: Faber and Faber, 1970).

Brut y Tywysogyon ('The Chronicle of the Princes'), Red Book of Hergest Version (Cardiff: UWP, 1955).

Burton, Janet, and Karen Stöber, *Abbeys and Priories of Medieval Wales* (Cardiff: UWP, 2015).

Caple, Chris, *Excavations at Dryslwyn Castle, 1980–95* (London: The Society for Medieval Archaeology, 2007).

Carter, Harold, *The Towns of Wales: A Study in Urban Geography* (Cardiff: UWP, 1965).

Chadwick, Nora, *The Celts* (Harmondsworth: Penguin Books, 1971; reprinted with revisons, 1997).

Cherry, Monica, *Building Wales / Adeiladu Cymru* (Cardiff: Welsh Development Association, 2005).

Creighton, O., and R. Higham, *Medieval Town Walls: An Archaeology and Social History of Urban Defences* (Stroud: Tempus Books, 2005).

Crickhowell, Nicholas, *Opera House Lottery: Zaha Hadid and the Cardiff Bay Project* (Cardiff: UWP, 1997).

Crosssley, Fred H., and Maurice H. Ridgeway, 'Screens, Lofts and Stalls in Monmouthshire', reprinted from *Arch. Camb.*, 108 (1959).

Cumming, Elizabeth, and Wendy Kaplan, *The Arts and Crafts Movement* (London: Thames & Hudson, 1991).

Cunliffe, B. *Britain Begins* (Oxford: Oxford University Prress, 2013).

Darley, Gillian, *Villages of Vision: A Study of Strange Utopias* (Nottingham: Five Leaves Publications, 2007).

Davies, John, *A History of Wales* (London: Penguin Books, 1994).

Davies, John, *The Making of Wales* (Stroud: Sutton Publishing, 1996; new edn, Stroud: The History Press, 2009).

Davies, R. R., *Conquest, Coexistence and Change: Wales 1063 –1415* (Oxford: Oxford University Press, 1987; reissued as *The Age of Conquest*, 1991).

Davies, V. Eirwen, *Gruffudd ap Cynan, 1055 –1137* (Cardiff: UWP, 1959).

Davies, Wendy, *An Early Welsh Microcosm: Studies in the Llandaff Charters* (London: Royal Historical Society, 1978).

Davis, Paul R., & Lloyd-Fern, Susan, *Lost Churches of Wales and the Marches* (Stroud, 1990).

Davis, Paul R., *Castles of the Welsh Princes* (Talybont, 2007).

Davis, Paul R., *The Forgotten Castles of Wales* (Logaston, 2011).

Day, Christopher, *Places of the Soul* (The Aquarian Press, Wellingborough, 1990).

Dixon, Roger, and Muthesius, *Victorian Architecture* (Thames & Hudson, London, 1878).

Dodd, A. H., *The Industrial Revolution in North Wales* (UWP, Cardiff, 3rd edn, 1971).

Edwards, Ifor, *Gwaith Haearn-bwrw Addurnol Yng Nghymru: Decorative Cast-ironwork in Wales* (Gomer, Llandysul, 1989).

Edwards, Nancy (ed.), *Landscape and Settlement in Medieval Wales* (Oxford, 1997).

Edwards, Nancy (ed.), *The Archaeology of the Early Medieval Celtic Churches* (Leeds, 2009).

Evans, Wyn, *St David's Cathedral* (Yr Oriel Fach Press, St David's, 1981).

Fox, Celina, *The Arts of Industry in the Age of Enlightenment* (Yale University Press, New Haven & London, 2009).

Fox, Sir Cyril, and Raglan, Lord, *Monmouthshire Houses: Part 1, Medieval; Part II, Sub-Medieval; Part III, Renaissance* (NMW, Cardiff, 1951, 1953, 1954).

Fox, Sir Cyril, *The Personality of Britain* (Cardiff: NMW, 1959).

Fox, Sir Cyril, and Lord Raglan, *Monmouthshire Houses: Part 1, Medieval; Part II, Sub-Medieval; Part III, Renaissance* (Cardiff: NMW, 1951, 1953, 1954).

Gam, Richard, 'Gruffudd ap Cynan and the Romanesque Church of Penmon, Anglesey', in N. Edwards (ed.), *The Archaeology of the Early Medieval Celtic Churches* (Leeds: Maney Publishing, 2009).

Gerald of Wales, *The Journey through Wales; The Description of Wales* (London: Penguin Books, London, 1978).

Gilpin, William, *Observations on the River Wye, and several parts of South Wales etc., relative chiefly to Picturesque Beauty: made in the summer of the year 1770* (London: Pallas Athene edn, 2005).

Guest, Lady Charlotte, *The Mabinogion* (facsimile of 1877 edition) (Cardiff: John Jones Ltd, 1977).

Gwyn, David, *Gwynedd, Inheriting a Revolution* (Chichester: Phillimore, 2006).

Hilling, John, B., *Cardiff and the Valleys* (London: Lund Humphries, 1973).

Hilling, John B., *The History and Architecture of Cardiff Civic Centre* (Cardiff: UWP, 2016).

Hilling, John B., *Llandaf, Past and Present* (Barry: Stewart Williams, 1978).

Hilling, John B., 'Wales', in *Modern British Architecture since 1945* (London: Frederick Muller Ltd, 1984).

Hislop, Malcolm, *Castle Builders* (Barnsley: Pen & Sword, 2016).

Hitchcock, Henry-Russell, *Architecture: Nineteenth and Twentieth Centuries*, third edn (Harmondsworth: Penguin, 1969).

Hogg, A.H.A., and D. J. C. King, 'Castles in Wales and the Marches – Additions and Corrections', *Arch. Camb.*, 119 (1970), 119–24.

Hogg, A.H.A., and D. J. C. King, 'Early Castles in Wales and the Marches', *Arch. Camb.*, 111 (1963), 77–124.

Hogg, A.H.A., and D. J. C. King, 'Masonry Castles in Wales and the Marches', *Arch. Camb.*, 116 (1967), 71–132.

Hughes, Harold and Herbert L. North, *The Old Churches of Snowdonia* (Bangor: Jarvis & Foster, 1924; Capel Curig: The Snowdonia National Park Society, reprinted with new Introduction and Notes, 1984).

Hughes, Stephen, *Copperopolis: Landscapes of the Early Industrial Period in Swansea* (Aberystwyth: RCAHMW, 2000).

Hughes, Stephen, Brian Malaws, Medwyn Parry and Peter Wakelin, *Collieries of Wales: Engineering and Architecture* (Abersystwyth: RCAHMW, n.d.).

James, John H., *A History and Survey of the Cathedral Church Llandaff* (Cardiff: Western Mail Ltd, 1898; second and revised edn, Cardiff: Wm. Lewis, 1929).

Johnstone, Neil, 'An Investigation into the Location of the Royal Courts of Thirteenth-Century Gwynedd', in N. Edwards (ed.), *Landscape and Settlement in Medieval Wales* (Oxford: Oxbow Books, 1997).

Jones, Anthony, *Welsh Chapels* (Cardiff: NMW, 1984; rev., 1996).

Jones, Glanville R. J., 'The Dark Ages', in D. H. Owen, *Settlement and Society in Wales* (Carduff: UWP, 1989).

Jones, Gwyn and Thomas Jones (trans.), *The Mabinogion* (London: Everyman edn, 1949).

Jones, S. R., and J. T. Smith, 'The Houses of Breconshire', parts I to VI, *Brycheiniog*, 9 (1963)–16 (1972).

Kenyon, John R., *The Medieval Castles of Wales* (Cardiff: UWP, 2010).

Kenyon, John R., and Richard Avent (eds), *Castles in Wales and the Marches: Essays in Honour of D. J. Cathcart King* (Cardiff: UWP, 1987).

Kenyon, John R., and Diane M. Williams (eds), *Cardiff: Architecture and Archaeology in the Medieval Diocese of Llandaff* (Leeds: British Archaeological Association and Maney Publishing, 2006).

Knight, Jeremy, *South Wales from the Romans to the Normans: Christianity, Literacy and Lordship* (Stroud: Amberley, 2013).

Laing, Lloyd, *The Archaeology of Celtic Britain and Ireland, c. AD 400–1200* (Cambridge: Cambridge University Press, 2006).

Lilley, Keith D., 'The Landscapes of Edward's New Towns: Their Planning and Design', in D. Williams and J. R. Kenyon, *The Impact of the Edwardian Castles in Wales* (Oxford: Oxbow Books, 2010).

Lloyd, Thomas, *The Lost Houses of Wales* (London: SAVE Britain's Heritage, 1986).

Longley, David, 'The Royal Courts of the Welsh Princes of Gwynedd, AD 400–1283', in N. Edwards (ed.), *Landscape and Settlement in Medieval Wales* (Oxford: Oxbow Books, 1997).

Lord, Peter, *The Visual Culture of Wales: Industrial Society* (Cardiff: UWP, 1998).

Lord, Peter, *The Visual Culture of Wales: Medieval Vision* (Cardiff: UWP, 2003).

Lynch, Francis, Stephen Aldhouse-Green and Jeffrey L. Davies, *Prehistoric Wales* (Stroud: Sutton Publishing, 2000).

Lynch, Francis, and Christpher Musson, 'A prehistoric and early medieval complex at Llandegai, near Bangor', *Arch. Camb.*, 150 (2001), 17–143.

Malkin, Benjamin Heath, *The Scenery, Antiquities and Biography of South Wales* (London: T. N. Longman, 1804; reprinted akefield: S.R. Publishing, 1970).

Morris, Bernard, *The Houses of Singleton: A Swansea Landscape and its History* (Swansea: West Glamorgan County Archive Service, 1995).

Murphy, Kenneth, 'The Castle and Borough of Wiston, Pembrokeshire', *Arch. Camb.*, 144, (1995), 1–102.

Nash, Gerallt D. (ed.), *Saving St Teilo's: Bringing a Medieval Church to Life* (Cardiff: NMW, 2009).

Owen, D. Huw (ed.), *Settlement and Society in Wales* (Cardiff: UWP, 1989).

Palmer, Marilyn, Michael Nevell, Michael and Mark Sissons, *Industrial Archaeology: A Handbook* (York: Council for British Archaeology, 2012).

Peate, Iorwerth C., *The Welsh House: A Study in Folk Culture*, third edn (Liverpool: The Brython Press, 1946).

Perry, Victoria, *Built for a Better Future: The Brynmawr Rubber Factory* (London: White Cockade, 1994).

Petts, David, *The Early Medieval Church in Wales* (Stroud: The History Press, 2009).

Powers, Alan, *Modern: The Modern Movement in Britain* (London: Merrell Publishers, 2005).

RCAMHW, *The Cathedral Church of St John the Evangelist, Brecon* (Brecon: Friends of Brecon Cathedral, 1994).

RCAHMW, *Glamorgan: Volume III, Part 1a: The Early Castles* (London: HMSO, 1991).

RCAHMW, *Glamorgan: Volume III, Part 2: Medieval Non-defensive Secular Monuments* (Cardiff: HMSO, 1982).

RCAHMW, *Glamorgan: Volume IV, Part 2: The Greater Houses* (Cardiff: HMSO, 1981).

Redknap, Mark, *The Celtic Christians: Treasures of Late Celtic Wales* (Cardiff: NMW, 1991).

Redknap, Mark, *Vikings in Wales: An Archaeological Quest* (Cardiff: NMW, 2000).

Rees, William, *An Historical Atlas of Wales, from Early to Modern Times* (Cardiff: City of Cardiff, 1951).

Renn, D. F., 'The Round Keeps of the Brecon Region', *Arch. Camb.*, 110 (1961), 129–43.

Renn, Derek, *Caerphilly Castle* (Cardiff: Cadw, 1997).

Richter, Michael, *Giraldus Cambrensis: The Growth of the Welsh Nation* (Aberystwyth: NLW, 1972).

Robinson, David, *Heritage in Wales: A Guide to the Ancient and Historic Sites in the Care of Cadw: Welsh Historic Monuments* (London: Macdonald Queen Anne Press, 1989).

Robinson, David (ed.), *The Cistercian Abbeys of Great Britain* (London: Batsford, 1998).

Rowlands, M. L. J., 'Monnow Bridge and Gate, Monmouth', *Arch. Camb.*, 142 (1993), (243–87).

Salter, Mike, *The Old Parish Churches of … Gwent Glamorgan and Gower* (1991); *Mid-Wales* (1991); *North Wales* (1993); *South-West Wales* (1994) (Malvern: Folly Publications).

Seaborne, Malcolm, *Schools in Wales 1500–1900: A Social and Architectural History* (Denbigh: Gee & Sons, 1992).

Smith, Peter, *Houses of the Welsh Countryside* (Aberystwyth: RCAHMW, 1978; rev. 1988).

Soulsby, Ian, *The Towns of Medieval Wales* (Chichester: Phillimore, 1983).

Spurgeon, C. J., 'Mottes and castle-ringworks in Wales', in Kenyon and Avent, *Castles in Wales and the Marches* (1987).

Suggett, Richard, *Houses and History in the March of Wales: Radnorshire 1400–1800* (Aberystwyth: RCAHMW, 2005).

Suggett, Richard, and Margaret Dunn, *Discovering the Historic Houses of Snowdonia* (Aberystwyth: RCAHMW, 2014).

Suggett, Richard, and Greg Stevenson, *Introducing Houses of the Welsh Countryside* (Talybont: Y Lolfa, 2010).

Taylor, A. J., *The King's Works in Wales* (London: HMSO, 1974), reprinted from H. M. Colvin, *The History of the King's Works* (London: HMSO, 1963).

Thomas, Charles, *Celtic Britain* (London: Thames & Hudson, 1986).

Thompson, M. W., 'The abandonment of the castle in Wales and the Marches', in Kenyon and Avent, *Castles in Wales and the Marches* (1987).

Thompson , M. W., *The Decline of the Castle* (Cambridge: Cambridge University Press, 1987).

Thompson, Noel, and C. Williams, *Robert Owen and His Legacy* (Cardiff: UWP, 2011).

Thorpe, Lewis, *Gerald of Wales: The Journey Through Wales and The Description of Wales* (Penguin, London, 1978).

Thurlby, Malcolm, *Romanesque Architecture and Sculpture in Wales* (Little Logaston, 2006).

Turner, Rick, and Johnson, Andy (eds), *Chepstow Castle, Its History and Buildings* (Logaston, 2006).

Wakelin, Peter, and Ralph A. Griffiths (eds), *Hidden Histories: Discovering the Heritage of Wales* (Aberystwyth: RCAHMW, 2008).

Watkin, David, *English Architecture: A Concise History* (Oxford: Oxford University Press, 1979).

Williams, D. M., and J. R. Kenyon (eds), *The Impact of the Edwardian Castles in Wales* (Oxford: Oxford University Press, 2010).

William, Eurwyn, *The Historical Farm Buildings of Wales* (Edinburgh: John Donald, 1986).

William, Eurwyn, *Home-made Homes: Dwellings of the Rural Poor in Wales*, second edn (Cardiff: NMW, 1993).

William, Eurwyn, *The Welsh Cottage, 1750–1900* (Aberystwyth: RCAHMW, 2010).

William, Eurwyn, *Welsh Long-houses: Four Centuries of Farming at Cilewent* (Cardiff: NMW, 1992).

Williams, Glanmor (ed.), *Swansea – An Illustrated History* (Swansea: Christopher Davies, 1990).

Wood, Margaret, *The English Mediaeval House* (London, 1965; reprinted Bracken Books, 1983).

Wooding, Jonathan M., and Nigel Yates, *A Guide to the Churches and Chapels of Wales* (Cardiff: UWP, 2011).

Williams, Moelwyn, *The South Wales Landscape* (London: Hodder & Stoughton, 1975).

Index of Architects, Artists and Engineers

Note: Only buildings mentioned in the text are included in this list. Generally, where only one date is shown it refers to the completion of the building. An asterisk before the name of a building indicates that the attribution is not certain. (D) after the name indicates that the building has been demolished.

Index of Places

Note: Only places and buildings mentioned in the text are included in this index. Place-names beginning with Ll are listed after place-names beginning with L.